Sable & Rosenfeld

ELEGANT ENTERTAINING COOKBOOK

Myra Sable

Sable & Rosenfeld

ELEGANT ENTERTAINING COOKBOOK

BANTAM BOOKS
TORONTO · NEW YORK · LONDON · SYDNEY · AUCKLAND

SABLE & ROSENFELD ELEGANT ENTERTAINING COOKBOOK
A Bantam Book / August 1986

This book was published simultaneously in hardcover and trade paperback.

All rights reserved.
Copyright © 1986 by Sable and Rosenfeld Foods Ltd.
Book design by Barbara N. Cohen.
Illustrations by Paula Munck.
Cover photograph copyright © 1986 by Robert Wigington.
This book may not be reproduced in whole or in part, by
mimeograph or any other means, without permission.
For information address: Bantam Books, Inc.

Library of Congress Cataloging-in-Publication Data

Sable, Myra.
　　Sable & Rosenfeld elegant entertaining cookbook.

　　Includes index.
　　1. Condiments.　2. Cookery.　I. Sable & Rosenfeld.　II. Title.　III. Title:
Sable and Rosenfeld, elegant entertaining cookbook.
TX819.A1S23　1986　642'.4　85-48277

ISBN 0-553-05178-4
ISBN 0-553-34284-3 (pbk.)

Published simultaneously in the United States and Canada

Bantam Books are published by Bantam Books, Inc. Its trademark, consisting of
the words "Bantam Books" and the portrayal of a rooster, is Registered in U.S.
Patent and Trademark Office and in other countries. Marca Registrada. Bantam
Books, Inc., 666 Fifth Avenue, New York, New York 10103.

PRINTED IN THE UNITED STATES OF AMERICA

DW　0　9　8　7　6　5　4　3　2　1

Beatrice Davidson; Colleen Mathew;
Ethel Teitlebaum; Maralyn Glick;
Agnes Bevc; Lillian Kaplun;
Marilyn Hamel; Bob Riggs; Roni Shier;
Susan Davidson; Theresa Rubens;
Simon Kattar; Jean Michel Centeno
and James Molloy; Canyon Ranch Spa;
Jamie Kennedy; Michael Stadtlander;
Hazel Mah

Gary Ikona; Peter Demarco and
Gary Perpich

Joe Hatt-Cook

Herb Kolm

KAY SPICER
Barb Hollend
Jerry Anthony

Michael de Haas

Joanna Sable; Milton Sable; Kelly Sable;
Harris Davidson; Matthew Davidson

Jeanne F. Bernkopf

Richard Weiner
Joan Carris

Beverley Slopen

Joe Hatt-Cook Ltd.

Paula Munck

Donna Gordon; Joanna Sable; Bea Goldberg;
Larry Rich; Steven Fields

Leonard Sadkin
Henry Goldman

Dedicated to Roger

Contents

CONTENTS

Sable & Rosenfeld
ELEGANT
ENTERTAINING
COOKBOOK

Introduction

The beginnings of this cookbook go back to 1971 when my friend and former partner, Carol Rosenfeld, and I decided to turn our mutual love of cooking into a business. We both had recipes for special sauces, mustards, and preserves which we had discovered could be used in a variety of ways to make relatively simple foods a new and exciting experience. Things like Carol's Sweet Russian Mustard—handed on to her by her grandmother; my own Poached Pears in Cointreau with a twist of lemon; my crunchy antipasto, which I use for everything from a taco dip to a pasta sauce or tangy soup base.

With about half a dozen of these selections, we opened a specialty food boutique in Toronto's most elegant woman's store.

That is what really led to this book. Customers frequently had questions on how to use a sauce or condiment, and I found myself discussing menus, giving serving tips, and scribbling out recipes for them.

Often, when they got home with their jar of sauce or marinade, they would have forgotten what to do with it and I would get frantic phone calls for help. It was not unusual to find myself constructing an entire dinner menu for someone who had bought a jar of pears in Cointreau and needed an appetizer, a main course, and a vegetable to serve around it. Usually the occasion was for the same evening and the party for anywhere from eight people up.

All the recipes are special, festive, and easy. By easy I mean simple to prepare and uncomplicated to serve. I hate to break up a lively conversation in order to push guests to the table merely because the first course is ready. There is no dish in this book which will not taste just fine at room temperature if necessary.

Since the way food looks on the plate is important, I have tried to offer suggestions for serving and garnishing that are imaginative yet simple.

None of the recipes depends on Sable & Rosenfeld products, but it was my love for condiments that led me to turn a hobby for preserving into a business, and it continues to reflect my approach to food. Relishes, chutneys, mustards, and other accompaniments can dress up an otherwise ordinary meal. Plain roast chicken will become festive if you serve it with sweet plum chutney, hot curried fruits, gingered pears, and a Dijon mustard—especially if you put them in beautiful silver jam pots arranged on a tray decorated with a sprig of spring lilac or pine cones and winter berries. A simple rare roast beef sandwich becomes elegant when the bread is covered with a tangy liptauer cheese spread and the beef is topped with chili sauce and garnished with crunchy mustard beans. And for the diet conscious, condiments and accompaniments offer the option of diversity without fattening sauces.

I first began preserving antipasto, jams, sauces and relishes when I was home with three small children and studying to be a concert pianist at the same time. It was my form of relaxation in the evenings. Friends would gather in my kitchen at the end of August to eat the first batch of chili sauce straight from the pot with French bread and wine. And when the fields of corn had formed their ears, my friends arrived expecting bowls of my hot corn chowder.

As it turned out, music became my hobby and canning launched a career in food. Fortunately, food and guests remain special sources of pleasure for me, and I hope this book will offer you and your guests equal satisfaction.

THE PARTY BEGINS

You're On!
The Opening Act!

Don't panic, don't get stage fright! When the doorbell rings and the first guests arrive, there you will be, dressed for the part, and ready to entertain. It's as exciting as an opening night and you are the producer, the director. In charge of everything from the lights to the music to the selection of the all-star cast of tastes and textures you have selected to produce a memorable evening.

Whatever kind of entertainment you want to create—small and intimate like a little revue, a formal sitdown meal with several courses and a caterer, a picnic, a wedding, a themed evening to celebrate an event, or a holiday party with all the traditional trappings—the most important part is the preproduction. Survey your resources and see what will work best in your urban apartment or suburban villa. Is your freezer full of ready to heat and serve goodies or will you start from scratch? What's plentiful in the supermarket and how much time can you devote to getting it ready? Plan, plan, plan! Make notes and consult them and adjust them as you go along. Write them down or hold them in your head if you can.

So let's start planning. Here come the opening numbers.

APPETIZER BUFFET PARTY

An all hors d'oeuvre menu makes for a marvelous evening of mixing and munching among your guests.

Offer a full bar for this kind of party as most people will want to choose their own drinks. But do have lots of white wine cooling and red wine breathing.

MARINATED SALMON MONTMORENCY
with thinly sliced and buttered pumpernickel bread

LEMON PEPPER BOURSIN ROLL
with basket of breadsticks

RED CAVIAR CREAM
and
DIPSIDOODLE CRAB DIP
served with a tray of crudités,
including tiny, cold new potatoes

SWEDISH MEATBALLS
and
SAUSAGE ROLL-UPS
with pots of hot mustard

TINY MUSHROOM CAPS STUFFED WITH PECANS AND CREAM

ARTICHOKE BOTTOMS WITH PARMESAN CHEESE

ELEGANT ESCARGOT CROUSTADES

MARINATED SALMON MONTMORENCY

This makes the perfect centerpiece.

You have never seen such a gorgeous dish. Red or very pink salmon with bright yellow lemon, red cherries, and orange carrots. The big challenge is to slice your salmon paper thin.

Serve with bowls of green olives and thinly sliced and buttered black Russian bread, along with chilled aquavit.

¼ cup	coarse salt	50 ml
2 tbs	sugar	25 ml
1 tsp	freshly ground pepper	5 ml
3 lb	fresh salmon fillets, sliced into thinnest possible diagonal slices	1.5 kg
5	onions, thinly sliced	5
7	carrots, thinly sliced	7
4	lemons, thinly sliced	4
12	brandied cherries	12
1¼ cups	lemon juice	300 ml
½ cup	dry white wine	125 ml
½ cup	white vinegar	125 ml
2 tbs	olive oil	25 ml

1. Combine salt, sugar, and pepper. Sprinkle on both sides of salmon.
2. Combine sliced onions, carrots, and lemons.
3. Make a "bed" by spreading ⅓ of the onion mixture on bottom of 9″ × 13″ (23 × 33 cm) baking dish. Cover with a layer of salmon, taking care not to overlap salmon slices.
4. Cover salmon with a second layer (⅓) of onion mixture. Add a second layer of salmon.
5. Sprinkle cherries around salmon. Top with remaining onion mixture.
6. Pat down so top is even.
7. Combine lemon juice, wine, and vinegar. Pour carefully over salmon.
8. Cover and refrigerate 2 to 3 days.
9. Remove onion mixture and cherries; reserve for garnish.
10. Thinly slice salmon and arrange on a chilled platter. Brush slices with olive oil.
11. Garnish with reserved vegetables and cherries.

Makes 12 servings.

*At cocktail parties, smaller flower arrangements are lost in "the crowd."
Go for large-scale impact on a hall table or dining room sideboard.*

LEMON PEPPER BOURSIN ROLL

*Creamy, peppery spread. Serve on warm crackers or place it on a big lettuce
leaf surrounded by homemade melba toast. Or dot each individual serving with
a small square of smoked salmon.*

1	(8 oz/250 g) pkg cream cheese	1
1	clove garlic, minced	1
1 tsp	chopped fresh chives	5 ml
1 tsp	chopped fresh basil	5 ml
1 tsp	caraway seed	5 ml
1 tsp	dill weed	5 ml
	lemon pepper	

1. In a small bowl beat cheese. Add garlic, chives, basil, caraway seed, and
   dill. Stir well to blend.
2. Form cheese into a ball and roll in lemon pepper. Wrap in waxed paper
   and chill.

Makes 16 servings.

THE CHAMPAGNE WALTZ:

*With champagne, I can never imagine doing any dance except a waltz,
but there are lots of other things to do with it and all as easy as
one-two-slide, one-two-slide.*

*I like to make my own version of Kir. That is lacing the bubbly with
a teaspoon or two of exotic eau de vie or liqueurs. Framboise (raspberry), Mirabelle (small yellow plums), Poire William (pear liqueur).*

*The eaux de vie were invented by a convent of quiet little French
nuns, but they pack a punch that would rock a pontiff. Be careful!
Just enough to make guests wonder what kind of champagne you've
discovered.*

RED CAVIAR CREAM

A delightfully deep pink party piece. I serve this with tiny roasted new potatoes still warm from the pan.

½ cup	heavy or whipping cream	125 ml
¼ cup	salmon caviar	50 ml
2 tbs	finely chopped green onion	25 ml
1	hard-cooked egg, sieved	1

1. In a mixer, whip cream until soft peaks form.
2. In a bowl, combine whipped cream, caviar, onion, and egg; mix well.
3. Spoon into a small dish or crock. Cover and chill.
   Serve with potatoes or with crackers or toast.

Makes 1 cup (250 ml).

RED CAVIAR DIP

¼ cup	salmon caviar	50 ml
4 oz	cream cheese, softened	125 g
¼ cup	2% yogurt	50 ml
1 tsp	lemon juice	5 ml

1. In a bowl, combine caviar and cream cheese; mix well.
2. Fold in yogurt and lemon juice.
3. Spoon into a small dish or crock, cover, and chill.
   Serve as a dip for raw vegetables.

Makes 1½ cups (375 ml).

DIPSIDOODLE CRAB DIP

Thick and satisfying. Serve with sticks: celery sticks, carrot sticks, endive scoops.

1 cup	sour cream	250 ml
¼ cup	mayonnaise	50 ml
2 cups	cooked crabmeat	500 ml
1 tbs	capers	15 ml
1 tbs	chopped onion	15 ml
1 tbs	lemon juice	15 ml
¼ tsp	salt	1 ml
¼ tsp	freshly ground black pepper	1 ml

1. In a blender or food processor combine sour cream, mayonnaise, crabmeat, capers, onion, lemon juice, salt, and pepper. Process 2 minutes until smooth.
2. Transfer to a small dish or crock. Cover and refrigerate to chill thoroughly before serving.

Makes 2 cups (500 ml).

SWEDISH MEATBALLS

I usually serve these on toothpicks. They look great with their little feathers of dill.

2	eggs, lightly beaten	2
1 cup	milk	250 ml
½ cup	dry breadcrumbs	125 ml
3 tbs	butter	45 ml
½ cup	finely chopped onion	125 ml
1 lb	medium ground beef	500 g
¼ lb	ground pork	125 g
1 tsp	salt	5 ml
¾ tsp	dried dill	4 ml
¼ tsp	allspice	1 ml
pinch	nutmeg	pinch
pinch	ground cardamom	pinch
3 tbs	all-purpose flour	45 ml
⅛ tsp	freshly ground black pepper	0.5 ml
1 cup	beef stock	250 ml
½ cup	cream	125 ml
	fresh dill sprigs	

1. In a large bowl combine eggs, milk, and breadcrumbs.
2. In a skillet heat 1 tbs (15 ml) butter; add onions, sauté 5 minutes until softened.
3. Add sautéed onions to crumb mixture along with ground beef, pork, salt, ¼ tsp (1 ml) dill, allspice, nutmeg, and cardamom; mix well.
4. Cover and chill 1 hour.
5. Preheat oven to 325°F (160°C).
6. Shape meat mixture into balls, each about 1 inch (2.5 cm) in diameter. Heat remaining butter and sauté the meatballs, half of them at a time, until brown. Transfer to an 8 cup (2 l) casserole.
7. Remove skillet from heat; remove all but 2 tbs (25 ml) drippings from pan. To drippings in skillet add flour, salt, and pepper. Stir to make a smooth paste.

8. Gradually stir in beef stock; bring to a boil, reduce heat, stirring constantly about 3 minutes until smooth.
9. Stir in cream and remaining dill; pour sauce over meatballs.
10. Cover and bake for 30 minutes until bubbling.
  Garnish with fresh dill sprigs.

Makes 6 servings.

SAUSAGE ROLL-UPS

Pretty pink pastry delivered by the substitution of tomato juice for water. These add a touch of glamour to your buffet or cocktail party.

2 cups	all-purpose flour	500 ml
4 tsp	baking powder	20 ml
½ tsp	salt	2 ml
½ cup	cold sweet butter	125 ml
⅔ cup	tomato juice	150 ml
2 tbs	Dijon mustard	25 ml
48	cooked party sausages, 1 inch (2.5 cm) long	48
2 tbs	heavy or whipping cream	25 ml

1. Preheat oven to 400°F (200°C).
2. In a small bowl, combine flour, baking powder, and salt.
3. With a pastry blender or 2 knives, cut in butter until mixture is crumbly.
4. Stir in juice and mix well until dough forms a ball.
5. On a lightly floured board roll out dough to about ⅛ inch (3 mm) thick. Cut into rectangles large enough to wrap around sausages. Spread each one thinly with mustard.
6. Wrap squares around sausages. Place seam side down on greased baking sheet. Brush with cream.
7. Bake for 10 to 12 minutes or until golden brown. Serve hot.

Makes 48 tiny roll-ups.

TINY MUSHROOM CAPS STUFFED WITH PECANS AND CREAM

For handing around at cocktail parties, where my rule is finger food only, I serve these at room temperature nested on a bed of shredded lettuce. They can be readied for cooking well in advance and stored in the refrigerator until it's time to cook them.

30	medium mushrooms	30
1 cup	pecans, finely chopped	250 ml
¼ cup	chopped fresh parsley	50 ml
¼ cup	soft sweet butter	50 ml
1	clove garlic, finely chopped	1
½ tsp	salt	2 ml
¼ tsp	dried thyme	1 ml
¼ tsp	freshly ground black pepper	1 ml
¼ cup	heavy or whipping cream	50 ml
	sliced pimento	
	shredded lettuce	

1. Preheat oven to 350°F (180°C).
2. Remove mushroom stems, finely chop them, and set aside. Wipe caps with damp cloth and arrange in a shallow baking dish, hollow side up.
3. In a bowl combine 1 cup (250 ml) chopped mushroom stems with pecans and parsley. Stir in butter, garlic, salt, thyme, and pepper. Heap mixture into mushroom caps.
4. Drizzle cream over each mushroom cap and bake for 20 minutes until heated through and beginning to brown.

Makes 30 appetizers.

ARTICHOKE BOTTOMS WITH PARMESAN CHEESE

The tinier the better for these. They make a luxurious addition to any buffet party.

12	cooked *small* artichoke bottoms	12
2 tbs	olive oil	25 ml
2 tbs	soft sweet butter	25 ml
⅔ cup	freshly grated Parmesan cheese	150 ml
1 tbs	chopped fresh parsley	15 ml

1. Preheat oven to 450°F (220°C).
2. In a shallow baking dish, combine olive oil and 1 tbs (15 ml) butter.
3. Arrange artichoke bottoms in a single layer, cut side up. Dot with remaining butter.

4. Sprinkle with cheese.
5. Bake for 12 minutes until cheese turns golden brown.
6. Place on paper towel for 1 minute to drain. Sprinkle with parsley. Serve hot.

Makes 4 servings.

ELEGANT ESCARGOT CROUSTADES

These are little bread cups, toasted and then stuffed with something extremely rich and satisfying. While they can be handed around at cocktail parties, I find myself turning to this recipe when I am planning a very special sitdown meal in the European fashion with many small courses served with special wines. One escargot per guest is really all you need, especially if it is a formal meal.

6 slices	white bread, crusts trimmed	6 slices
1 tbs	melted sweet butter	15 ml
12	medium escargots, rinsed and patted dry	12
½ cup	dry white wine	125 ml
½ cup	rich chicken broth	125 ml
¼ cup	finely chopped shallots	50 ml
½ tsp	dried thyme	2 ml
1	bay leaf	1
1 cup	heavy or whipping cream	250 ml
2	cloves garlic, minced	2
	salt and freshly ground black pepper to taste	
¼ cup	sweet butter	50 ml
2 tbs	finely chopped fresh parsley	25 ml

1. Preheat oven to 400°F (200°C).
2. With a rolling pin, roll each slice of bread very thin. Cut 2 rounds 2 inches (5 cm) in diameter from each slice. Fit each round gently into a well-buttered 1¼ inch (3 cm) muffin tin.
3. Brush tops of rounds with melted butter and bake them for 10 minutes, or until edges are golden brown. Remove from tins and cool.
4. In a medium skillet combine escargots, wine, chicken stock, shallots, thyme, and bay leaf. Bring to a boil and reduce liquid to ¼ cup (50 ml).
5. Stir in cream, garlic, salt, and pepper. Reduce liquid to ⅓ cup (75 ml).
6. Remove bay leaf. Stir in butter.
7. Fill each croustade with 1 escargot and some of the sauce. Sprinkle each with minced parsley.

Makes 12 hors d'oeuvres.

THE PERFECT BAR

This is a checklist to put inside the door of your liquor cabinet. There may be other more exotic drinks to add, but these are the basics.

Ice bucket and tongs
Large glass jug
Small glass jug
Small serving tray
Corkscrew
Two decanters
Bar towels
Funnel or wine strainer
Stir spoon for Martinis
Napkins
Coasters

Assorted glasswear

Large highball glasses
Large old-fashioned glasses
Large wineglasses
  White wine
  Red wine
  Champagne
Snifters (not too balloon)
Water glasses
Liqueur glasses

Except for liqueurs, all sizes are 40 oz.

2 bottles of Scotch	1 Dark rum	1 Cognac
2 Vodka	1 Dry vermouth	1 Cointreau
1 Bourbon	1 Campari	1 Frangelica
1 Rye	1 Grand Marnier	2 White wine
1 Gin	1 Crème de Menthe	1 Red wine
1 Tequila	1 Armagnac	1 Lillet
1 White rum	1 Tia Maria	1 Champagne

Mixers

Soda water	Mineral water	Tabasco
Tonic water	Diet soda	Salt, pepper,
Seltzer	Tomato juice	horseradish
Coca-Cola	Worcestershire	Olives, lemons, limes
Gingerale	sauce	Lots of ice

Remember, when using a caterer, never surrender your individuality. State clearly what you want, otherwise what you will end up with is a smoothly running, fashionable party that is a statement of the caterer and not your own.

For cocktail parties, be specific and hold yourself to the times given, six to eight or seven to nine. Encourage people to be on time, as it is unfair for the kitchen to have to come up with ten rounds of hors d'oeuvres for late arrivals when they were only scheduled to produce them for two hours. Although most caterers always bring extra, don't strain them by deciding to invite the neighbors at the last minute.

CHINESE LANTERN BUFFET PARTY

More and more hosts and hostesses are finding out how easy Chinese cooking can be. So with thoughts of the Orient, here are a few wonderfully easy Chinese appetizers, as colorful and varied as characters in a Chinese opera.

CHINESE ASPARAGUS SALAD

GINGER STRING BEAN SALAD

HOT SZECHUAN CUCUMBER STICKS

RAINBOW CHOPPED IN CRYSTAL FOLD

MANDARIN HONEY GARLIC RIBS AND WINGS

DEEP-FRIED WONTONS

IMPERIAL ROLLS

PUNGENT PEKING CHICKEN BITES

CHUN KING CHINESE PORK SLICES

SHRIMP TOASTS

ROAST DUCK WITH HOISIN SAUCE IN CHINESE PANCAKES,
and lots of Chinese mustard, plum sauce, and hot pepper sauce

ALMOND WAFER ROLLS

LEMON CLOUDS IN MERINGUE BASKETS

BASKETS OF MANDARIN ORANGES

BOWLS OF LICHEE NUTS

BASKETS OF POMEGRANATES

This can be a spring, summer, or fall party. In fact, any time of the year. It is rather fun to hold it during warm weather when you can festoon the patio or the garden or the balcony of your apartment with colorful Chinese lanterns, fluttering prayer and good luck ribbons.

You'll also want to shop in Chinatown beforehand to make sure you've got all the ingredients you need and to pick up fresh Lichee nuts. I have provided a shopping list of special Chinese ingredients to cover all the recipes included in this book. You'll find it under Woking and Talking (page 190).

CHINESE ASPARAGUS SALAD

Make this just before the party as it does not improve with age. You can add a border of thinly sliced radishes and a good dab of Russian mustard. Sprinkle with sesame seeds for that added Oriental look and flavor.

2 lb	fresh asparagus, each stalk ½ inch (1 cm) thick	1 kg
1 tbs	soy sauce	15 ml
1 tbs	sesame oil	15 ml
1 tsp	sugar	5 ml
½ tsp	salt	2 ml
4 drops	hot pepper sauce	4 drops
¼ cup	toasted sesame seeds	50 ml

1. Snap tough root end off asparagus. Slice stalks into 1½ inch (1.75 cm) lengths to make 3 cups (750 ml) asparagus pieces.
2. In 2 quarts (2 l) of rapidly boiling, salted water, blanch asparagus for 1 minute. Drain immediately, running cold water over asparagus to stop cooking and set color. Spread on a double thickness of paper towel and pat dry.
3. In a glass bowl, combine soy sauce, sesame oil, sugar, salt, and hot pepper sauce. Mix until sugar is completely dissolved.
4. Add asparagus. Toss to coat each asparagus piece with dressing.
5. Chill 1 to 2 hours. Sprinkle with toasted sesame seeds before serving.

Makes 4 servings.

GINGER STRING BEAN SALAD

Lots of toasted almonds and the wonderful Oriental taste of fresh ginger make this a hot and delicious salad. Shop diligently for thin young beans.

You'll want to use the dressing with other crisp vegetables such as broccoli and spinach, cauliflower, and even red cabbage.

⅓ cup	slivered almonds	75 ml
1 lb	fresh green beans	500 g
1 tbs	finely chopped, fresh ginger root	15 ml

1. Toast almonds on baking sheet in medium oven until golden. Let cool.
2. Trim beans and cut into pieces about 2 inches (5 cm) long. Blanch beans in boiling water about 4 minutes until tender but still crisp. Drain and rinse with cold water to stop cooking. Place in bowl.
3. Add ginger root and almonds; toss to mix.

ORIENTAL DRESSING:

2 tsp	dry mustard	10 ml
1 tsp	cold water	5 ml
4 tsp	white vinegar	20 ml
1 tbs	sesame oil	15 ml
1 tbs	light soy sauce	15 ml
1 tsp	sugar	5 ml
1 tsp	salt	5 ml

1. In a small mixing bowl place mustard powder and gradually stir in water to make a smooth paste. Add vinegar, sesame oil, soy sauce, sugar, and salt; mix well.
2. Pour over bean mixture and toss until thoroughly coated. Serve at room temperature.

Makes 3 to 4 servings.

HOT SZECHUAN CUCUMBER STICKS

A recipe from my friend Hazel Mah, who owns The Cuisine Imperiale in Toronto.

1	English cucumber	1
½ cup	white vinegar	125 ml
½ cup	granulated sugar	125 ml
¼ cup	Hot Chili Oil	50 ml
dash	hot pepper sauce	dash
¼ tsp	shredded fresh ginger root	1 ml

1. Cut cucumber into 2 inch (5 cm) sticks. Place in a bowl, cover with lightly salted ice water. Let stand ½ hour. Drain and rinse.
2. In a bowl combine vinegar, sugar, chili oil, hot pepper sauce, and ginger root. Pour over cucumber sticks; marinate in the refrigerator for ½ hour only.
3. Remove from marinade and serve.

Makes 6 servings.

HOT CHILI OIL

½ cup	sesame oil	125 ml
2	dried whole chilies, crushed	2

1. In a glass bowl combine sesame oil and crushed chilies; stir well. Allow to stand at room temperature for 24 hours.
2. Line a sieve with cheesecloth or all-purpose cloth. Strain oil into a glass container.
3. Cover and store at room temperature.

Makes ½ cup (125 ml).

RAINBOW CHOPPED IN CRYSTAL FOLD

Doesn't that sound unbelievable? The crystal fold is a lettuce leaf, the rainbows are the chopped vegetables, but still it remains totally Land of Oz.

When you serve these, make sure you put them on plates as they are inclined to drip.

4 cups	peanut oil	1 l
about 1 cup	rice vermicelli	about 250 ml
½ lb	pork loin, chopped fine	250 g
2	pieces (2 inch/5 cm) Chinese sausages, chopped fine	2
3	green onions, finely chopped	3
1	medium carrot, finely chopped	1
1	stalk celery, finely chopped	1
2 tsp	oyster sauce*	10 ml
1 tsp	soy sauce	5 ml
¼ tsp	salt	1 ml
½ tsp	cornstarch	2 ml
1 tbs	cold water	15 ml
	lettuce leaves	

*Oyster sauce is available in Oriental markets.

1. In a large skillet or wok, heat oil until very hot. Add vermicelli; cook about 3 seconds until it puffs up and floats on the surface. Remove and drain on paper towel.
2. Add pork to oil and cook for about 1 minute. With slotted spoon remove the pork. Pour out oil, leaving just a coating on the bottom of pan.
3. Add sausage, onions, carrot, and celery. Stir in pork, oyster sauce, soy sauce, and salt. Cook and stir for 2 to 3 minutes.
4. Dissolve cornstarch in cold water. Stir into hot mixture and cook for an additional 30 seconds, until thickened.
5. Spoon mixture onto lettuce leaves. Fold the leaves over and eat with fingers like a taco.

Makes 4 servings.

Whenever possible, use fresh flowers from your garden or wild flowers from the country. They won't last as long as commercial flowers, but they always create a warmer atmosphere.

MANDARIN HONEY GARLIC RIBS AND WINGS

Divinely sweet and sticky, all because I discovered the magic "sticky" ingredient!: consommé. It really does preserve the moistness and give the consistency I love.

2 tbs	molasses	25 ml
¼ cup	honey	50 ml
2 tbs	soy sauce	25 ml
4	cloves garlic, minced	4
1 tbs	hoisin sauce*	15 ml
1	can (10 oz/284 ml) beef consommé	1
1½ lb	chicken wings, tips removed	750 g
1½ lb	pork side ribs, cut in rib-size portions	750 g

1. Preheat oven to 375°F (190°C).
2. In a small bowl combine molasses, honey, soy sauce, garlic, hoisin sauce, and consommé; stir well.
3. In a shallow baking dish arrange wings and ribs. Pour sauce over, cover and marinate 1 hour in refrigerator.
4. Bake, uncovered, for 40 to 45 minutes until meat is tender and sauce is sticky.

Makes 10 to 12 servings.

*Hoisin sauce is available in Oriental markets.

DEEP-FRIED WONTONS

Perfect finger food. Ideal to serve with cocktails. Put out a few bowls of Chinese mustard and your own plum sauce and you'll make your guests very happy.
When you shop for Chinese ingredients, ask for the thin wonton wrappers.

1 tsp	cornstarch	5 ml
1 tsp	sake or dry sherry	5 ml
½ lb	ground pork	250 g
½ lb	raw shrimp, shelled, deveined, coarsely chopped	250 g
2	large dried Chinese mushrooms, finely chopped	2
4	green onions, finely chopped	4
¼ cup	water chestnuts or bamboo shoots, finely chopped	50 ml
¼ cup	rich chicken stock	50 ml
1 tsp	salt	5 ml
½ tsp	granulated sugar	2 ml
¼ tsp	grated fresh ginger root	1 ml
24	wonton wrappers	24
	peanut oil for frying	

1. In a medium bowl, combine cornstarch and sake; mix well. Add pork and shrimp. Stir well to coat.
2. In a large skillet, heat oil. Add shrimp and pork mixture, stir-fry about 5 minutes, or until pork is no longer pink. Cool mixture.
3. Soak mushrooms in cold water to cover for 3 minutes, drain. Stir into pork mixture. Add onion, water chestnuts, stock, salt, sugar, and ginger root mix well.
4. Place a spoonful of shrimp filling on each wonton wrapper. Moisten wrapper edges with water. Fold in triangle around filling. Bring two corners of folded edge together and pinch.
5. Heat peanut oil in wok or deep skillet to 375°F (190°C). Deep-fry wontons a few at a time 1 to 2 minutes until very pale golden. Drain on paper towel. Cool.
6. Fry second time to deep gold. Drain on paper towel.

Makes 24 wontons.

Anything today can be rented, but try and use some of your own things to give a more homey, natural look. Use your own glassware and fine crystal for small parties, but for larger ones, the risk of breakage and the time involved in washing up make it too complicated.

SWEET AND TANGY WONTON DIPPING SAUCE

1 cup	freshly squeezed orange juice	250 ml
½ cup	brown sugar	125 ml
⅓ cup	cider vinegar	75 ml
¼ cup	ketchup	50 ml
2 tbs	light soy sauce	25 ml
2 tbs	cornstarch	25 ml
1 tbs	tomato paste	15 ml
2 tsp	Worcestershire sauce	10 ml
¼ tsp	hot pepper sauce	1 ml

1. In a saucepan, combine orange juice, brown sugar, vinegar, ketchup, soy sauce, cornstarch, tomato paste, Worcestershire sauce, and hot pepper sauce; mix well.
2. Bring to a boil; stir constantly about 3 minutes until thick and clear.
3. Cool.
4. Best when fresh.

Makes 2 cups (500 ml).

IMPERIAL ROLLS WITH HOT CHINESE MUSTARD

Don't hesitate to try these. Wrappers are available at Chinese food stores.

¾ lb	ground pork shoulder	375 g
¼ cup	chopped dried black mushrooms	50 ml
¼ cup	arrowroot noodles, cut in 2 inch (5 cm) pieces	50 ml
2 tbs	lukewarm water	25 ml
3	small carrots, shredded	3
2 cups	shredded cabbage	500 ml
1	medium onion, finely chopped	1
1	clove garlic, finely chopped	1
1	egg, slightly beaten	1
1 tbs	soy sauce	15 ml
½ tsp	ground ginger	2 ml
25	frozen spring roll shells (10 inches/25 cm diameter) vegetable oil to deep-fry (4 inches/10 cm deep)	25

1. In a skillet, cook ground pork, stirring, until browned.
2. In a small bowl soak mushrooms in hot water to cover for 10 minutes; drain.
3. In a separate bowl soak noodles in lukewarm water about 10 minutes until liquid is absorbed.
4. In a large bowl combine mushrooms, noodles, carrots, cabbage, onion, garlic, pork, egg, soy sauce, and ginger. Mix well.
5. Place 2 tbs (25 ml) of mixture on each shell. Fold in sides and roll up.
6. Deep-fry at 375°F (190°C) once, 3 minutes; remove and place on paper towel. Deep-fry a second time about 4 minutes, until outside is golden brown. Drain on paper towel.
   Serve hot.

Makes 25 rolls.

HOT CHINESE MUSTARD

½ cup	dry mustard	125 ml
¼ cup	rice vinegar	50 ml
¼ cup	water	50 ml
pinch	salt	pinch
pinch	granulated sugar	pinch

1. In a small saucepan combine mustard, vinegar, water, salt, and sugar. Bring to a boil, reduce heat; simmer, stirring, about 2 minutes, until thickened.
2. Pour into a container; cover and store in refrigerator. Keeps for up to 2 months.

Makes 1 cup (250 ml).

PUNGENT PEKING CHICKEN BITES

These delightful morsels travel well, and I often take a jar of the dipping sauce and a plastic bag full of "bites" to my cottage. They reheat beautifully.

2 lb	skinless, boneless chicken breasts	1 kg
2	eggs, beaten	2
½ cup	all-purpose flour	125 ml
¼ cup	beer or water	50 ml
1 tsp	salt	5 ml
	vegetable oil for deep frying (2 inches/5 cm deep)	

1. Cut chicken breasts into 1 inch (2.5 cm) cubes.
2. In a small bowl combine eggs, flour, beer or water, and salt; blend well.
3. In a deep skillet or deep-fryer heat oil to 375°F (190°C). Dip chicken in batter; slip into hot oil; deep-fry, turning once, about 5 to 6 minutes until coating is golden brown.
4. Drain on paper towel and keep warm. Serve with Dipping Sauce.

DIPPING SAUCE:

1	can (14 oz/398 ml) unsweetened crushed pineapple	1
1	clove garlic, finely chopped	1
½ cup	lightly packed brown sugar	125 ml
¼ cup	vinegar	50 ml
3 tbs	cornstarch	45 ml
1½ tbs	soy sauce	20 ml
½ tsp	grated fresh ginger root	2 ml

1. In a saucepan, combine pineapple, garlic, sugar, vinegar, cornstarch, soy sauce, and ginger; mix well.
2. Cook, stirring, about 10 minutes until sauce thickens. Serve warm or cold.

Makes 6 to 8 servings.

CHUN KING CHINESE PORK SLICES

You can use this also as a divine luncheon dish to serve with Chinese asparagus salad.

Make it ahead of time so you can slice it and serve it cold with hot sweet Russian or Chinese mustard.

¼ cup	red currant jelly or jam	50 ml
¼ cup	sherry	50 ml
2 tbs	soy sauce	25 ml
1	clove garlic, finely chopped	1
1 tsp	five-spice powder*	5 ml
2	pork tenderloins (1 lb/500 g each)	2

1. In a large bowl, combine jelly or jam, sherry, soy sauce, garlic, and five-spice powder.
2. Add tenderloins, turning to coat.
3. Cover and marinate in refrigerator overnight, turning once or twice.
4. Preheat oven to 325°F (160°C).
5. Remove meat from marinade and place in a shallow casserole. Brush with marinade.
6. Cover and bake, basting frequently, for 1 to 1¼ hours, until meat is tender and no longer pink. Uncover during last 30 minutes.
   To serve, cut meat into thin slices.

Makes 4 to 6 servings.

For a casual summer buffet, fill a large glass water pitcher with as many cosmos as you can fit in it. Let the cosmos fall and bend as they will over the lip of the vase. Remember to fill the vase completely so the water line can't be seen. This magnifies the stems and makes the arrangement clean and complete.

---

*Five-spice powder is available at Oriental markets.

SHRIMP TOASTS

These are perfect finger foods. I started making them for friends, and soon I had to keep the recipe handy as people fell in love with them. It is now one of my most treasured recipes.

They can be prepared in advance and popped into the cooking oil right from the freezer.

1 lb	shrimp, shelled and deveined	500 g
4	water chestnuts, finely chopped	4
1	green onion, finely chopped	1
1 tbs	finely chopped fresh ginger root	15 ml
1 tsp	sesame oil	5 ml
1 tsp	sake or dry sherry	5 ml
1 tsp	salt	5 ml
1	egg white, beaten until foamy	1
1 tbs	cornstarch	15 ml
¼ cup	cold water	50 ml
12	slices sandwich bread, crusts trimmed	12
	vegetable oil for deep frying	

1. In a food processor or blender, combine shrimp, water chestnuts, green onion, ginger, and sesame oil. Add sake or sherry and salt. Process with 4 to 5 on/off motions until finely chopped. Add egg white and blend.
2. Dissolve cornstarch in water and blend into shrimp mixture.
3. Spread shrimp mixture on bread slices. Cut each slice of bread into four triangles.
4. Freeze or refrigerate until just before serving.
5. In a deep fryer or deep skillet, heat oil to 375°F (190°C). Slip bread triangles into oil, shrimp side down. Cook 1 to 2 minutes and turn. Cook 1 minute more, until bread is golden.
6. Remove from oil, drain on paper towel.
Serve immediately.

Makes 48 squares.

ROAST DUCK WITH HOISIN SAUCE IN CHINESE PANCAKES

You need no longer dine in Chinese restaurants to have Golden Peking Duck. The little pancakes are like pita bread. Stuffed with the sliced duck and its wonderful sauces, they make a munchie to drool over. Try it and see.

4–5 lb	duck	2–3 kg
	juice of ½ lemon	
½ tsp	ground ginger	2 ml
½ tsp	white pepper	2 ml
¼ tsp	cinnamon	1 ml
¼ tsp	nutmeg	1 ml
¼ tsp	salt	1 ml
pinch	ground cloves	pinch
½ cup	hoisin sauce*	125 ml
2 tbs	light soy sauce	25 ml
1 cup	shredded green onion	250 ml

1. Preheat oven to 425°F (220°C).
2. Clean duck and remove excess fat; discard neck and giblets. Pierce skin well.
3. Squeeze lemon juice inside cavity and over skin of duck.
4. Combine ginger, pepper, cinnamon, nutmeg, salt, and cloves. Sprinkle half of seasoning mixture inside duck and the remainder on the skin.
5. Place duck breast side up on a roasting rack in a shallow roasting pan and sear in oven for 30 minutes.
6. Reduce temperature to 350°F (180°C). Pierce skin again and roast for 50 to 60 minutes, or until juices run clear when duck is pierced. During last 30 minutes, baste duck with a combination of 1 tbs (15 ml) hoisin sauce and the soy sauce.
7. Let duck rest 15 minutes. Cut into very thin slices.

To serve, place some of remaining hoisin sauce, shredded green onion, and duck inside a Chinese Pancake and roll up.

Makes 16 servings.

*Hoisin sauce is available in Oriental markets.

CHINESE PANCAKES

2 cups	all-purpose flour	500 ml
¾ cup	boiling water	175 ml
2 tsp	sesame oil	10 ml

1. Place flour in a large bowl. Pour boiling water over flour and stir with a wooden spoon until it clumps together.
2. Knead on a floured work surface until dough is soft and smooth, about 5 minutes. Form dough into ball, cover with an inverted bowl, and let stand for 30 to 60 minutes.
3. With your hands, roll dough into a cylinder, then cut it into 16 equal pieces. Again using the lightly floured work surface, flatten balls of dough with a rolling pin into 3 inch (7.5 cm) rounds.
4. Brush half the rounds with sesame oil, making sure to coat the edges. Place unbrushed rounds on oiled ones and use rolling pin to flatten them into 8 thin pancakes, about 8 inches (20 cm) in diameter.
5. Heat a heavy, ungreased, small skillet. Cook pancakes, 1 at a time, over medium heat 1 to 2 minutes until small bubbles appear on surface. Turn and cook on other side until a few golden spots appear.
6. Remove from skillet and gently pull apart into 2 pancakes. Pile pancakes on a plate and cover with plastic wrap so they won't dry out.
7. To reheat, wrap in foil, and heat in a 350°F (180°C) oven for 10 minutes. Or steam, unwrapped, in steamer for 5 minutes. Or place in microwave covered with plastic wrap or waxed paper at medium for 3 to 4 minutes, or until warm.

Makes 16 pancakes.

THE FISHERMAN'S WHARF

A good prowl around the local seafood stores can stimulate your imagination and eventually your guests' appetites.

I love finding a dozen or so perfectly fresh, giant saltwater shrimps, fresh oysters, or some gorgeously pink smoked salmon, baby clams, or even, when your luck's in, fresh cod roe. All of them are extremely stimulating to the dedicated party planner.

There is something about the strongly defined yet subtle flavors of these foods that make them ideal for appetizers, especially when you have done your magic and given them a magic all their own.

SCALLOP SEVICHE

You won't believe how beautiful this looks—and how beautiful it tastes. It is a delicate white and green, and so pretty I used it to set the color scheme for a wedding.
Try it out for your elegant cocktail party.

1 lb	fresh bay scallops	500 g
½ cup	fresh lime juice (2 limes)	125 ml
1	large green pepper, finely chopped	1
2	green onions, finely chopped	2
2 tbs	chopped fresh parsley	25 ml
2 tbs	vegetable oil	25 ml
1 tbs	prepared horseradish	15 ml
¼ tsp	hot pepper sauce	1 ml
½ tsp	salt	2 ml
¼ tsp	freshly ground black pepper	1 ml
	shredded lettuce (optional)	
1	avocado, peeled and cut into wedges	1
1	lime, cut in thin slices	1

1. In a small bowl combine scallops and lime juice.
2. Marinate in refrigerator, turning often, for 2 hours (longer if you prefer a more cooked taste). Drain, leaving a little lime juice.
3. Add green peppers, green onions, 1 tbs (15 ml) parsley, oil, horseradish, and hot pepper sauce. Toss well and chill at least 2 hours, or until ready to serve.
4. Season with salt and pepper.
5. Place on a bed of shredded lettuce, if desired, and garnish with avocado, lime slices, and remaining parsley.

Makes 6 servings.

MARINATED SOLE FINGERS

Sole is such a delicate fish, you either do very little with it, like Sole Bonne Femme, or do everything with it, using the delicate texture and taste to act as a vehicle for other taste sensations.

These Marinated Sole Fingers taste divine dipped in my version of Tartar or Creole Sauce. Serve hot from the stove or, if you have a skillet you particularly love, spear them with toothpicks and hand them around still sizzling in the pan.

1 lb	sole fillets, cut in finger length pieces, about 1 × 2 inches (2.5 × 5 cm)	500 g
¼ cup	olive oil	50 ml
2 tbs	lemon juice	25 ml
1 tbs	chopped parsley	15 ml
1	clove garlic, finely chopped	1
1 tsp	dried rosemary leaves	5 ml
1 tsp	dry mustard	5 ml
½ tsp	salt	2 ml
¼ tsp	freshly ground black pepper	1 ml
1	can (50 g) anchovy fillets, drained and finely chopped	1
½ cup	all-purpose flour	125 ml
2	eggs, lightly beaten	2
1 cup	vegetable oil	250 ml
	lemon wedges	
	Tartar Sauce or Creole Sauce	

1. Place the fish pieces in a shallow dish.
2. Combine olive oil, lemon juice, parsley, garlic, rosemary, mustard, salt, pepper, and chopped anchovies. Spoon over sole pieces; cover and marinate in refrigerator at least 1 hour, overnight if possible.
3. Remove fish from marinade. Roll each piece in flour and dip in beaten eggs. Refrigerate until just before cooking.
4. In a small skillet or saucepan, heat oil for deep frying (see page 23). With tongs add fish pieces a few pieces at a time. Deep-fry 3 to 4 minutes, until fish is golden brown and flakes easily with a fork.
5. Remove with slotted spoon, drain on paper towel, serve immediately with Tartar Sauce or Creole Sauce and lemon wedges.

Makes 4 servings.

TARTAR SAUCE

1 cup	mayonnaise (recipe p. 227)	250 ml
¼ cup	finely chopped onion	50 ml
2 tbs	sweet relish	25 ml
1 tbs	chopped pimento	15 ml
1 tbs	lemon juice	15 ml
1 tsp	Dijon mustard with basil	5 ml
½ tsp	salt	2 ml
¼ tsp	freshly ground black pepper	1 ml

1. In a bowl, combine mayonnaise, onion, sweet relish, pimento, lemon juice, mustard, salt, and pepper; stir well.
2. Store in the refrigerator in a plastic or glass-covered container.

Makes 1½ cups (375 ml).

CREOLE SAUCE

The right accompaniment for Marinated Sole Fingers or any other fish fingers. It is also good poured over an omelette.

1 tbs	sweet butter	15 ml
1	medium clove garlic, finely chopped	1
1	medium onion, coarsely chopped	1
1	medium green pepper, coarsely chopped	1
¼ cup	chopped mushrooms	50 ml
6	pitted green olives, chopped	6
1 cup	rich beef stock	250 ml
½ cup	dry white wine	125 ml
1	can (5½ oz/156 ml) tomato paste	1
1 tsp	chili powder	5 ml
1 tsp	Worcestershire sauce	5 ml
½ tsp	salt	2 ml
¼ tsp	freshly ground black pepper	1 ml

1. In a large skillet heat butter. Add garlic, onion, green pepper, mushrooms, and olives. Sauté 5 minutes until onions are soft.
2. Stir in stock, wine, tomato paste, chili powder, Worcestershire sauce, salt, and pepper. Bring to a boil, reduce heat and simmer, uncovered, stirring occasionally, 30 minutes, until sauce is thick.
3. Store in covered container in refrigerator.

Makes 2 cups (500 ml).

RED CAVIAR MOUSSE

This is "Old Russia" from the time of the Tsars.
Serve it with vodka that has spent the night in the freezer.
The horseradish gives this a nice nip. It can be served as a cocktail nibbler
with toasts or as the opening act of a larger, more sophisticated dinner.

6 oz	red caviar	170 g
¼ cup	chopped fresh parsley	50 ml
2 tbs	prepared horseradish	25 ml
1 tbs	grated onion	15 ml
1 tsp	grated lemon rind	5 ml
2 cups	sour cream	500 ml
1	envelope unflavored gelatin	1
¼ cup	cold water	50 ml
½ cup	heavy or whipping cream	125 ml
	freshly ground black pepper	

1. In a large bowl combine caviar, parsley, horseradish, onion, and lemon rind. Stir in sour cream.
2. In a small saucepan, sprinkle gelatin over cold water; let stand to soften. Place over low heat, stirring until gelatin is completely dissolved. Stir gelatin into sour cream mixture.
3. Whip cream and fold it in. Add pepper to taste.
4. Pour into mold and chill at least 4 hours, until set. Unmold on serving plate.

Makes 8 servings.

GARLICKY-SPICY-CRAB-DIP

This is a pretty pink color that speaks of spring and demands mounds of baby
mushrooms, thin young zucchini, and tender green onions.

2 cups	cooked crabmeat	500 ml
1 cup	mayonnaise	250 ml
5	water chestnuts	5
3	cloves garlic	3
1 tsp	tomato chili sauce	5 ml
1 tsp	Worcestershire sauce	5 ml
½ tsp	salt	2 ml
¼ tsp	hot pepper sauce	1 ml
¼ tsp	freshly ground black pepper	1 ml
2	green onions, finely chopped	2

1. In a blender or food processor combine crabmeat, mayonnaise, water chestnuts, garlic, chili sauce, Worcestershire sauce, salt, hot pepper sauce, and black pepper.
2. Process with on/off motion for 1 to 2 minutes, until smooth.
3. Transfer to a small bowl and fold in green onions.
4. Cover and refrigerate 1 hour to chill thoroughly before serving.

Makes 2 cups (500 ml).

HOT CRABMEAT DIP

This one's for winter, although you can serve it any time of year, especially if you are doing an Indian party. The rich curry flavor starts people thinking of elephants and the Taj Mahal.

But I think of this in connection with skiing: of dipping breadsticks or toast into the golden goodness while waiting for the aches to start and the dinner to cook.

1	pkg (8 oz/250 g) cream cheese	1
1 cup	cooked crabmeat	250 ml
1	medium onion, finely chopped	1
1 tsp	lemon juice	5 ml
1 tsp	Worcestershire sauce	5 ml
1 tsp	curry powder	5 ml
½ tsp	salt	2 ml
¼ tsp	freshly ground black pepper	1 ml
	toast triangles	

1. In a small saucepan combine cream cheese, crabmeat, lemon juice, Worcestershire sauce, curry powder, salt, and pepper.
2. Heat, stirring to break up crabmeat, and mix thoroughly, about 3 to 4 minutes, until bubbling.
   Serve with toast triangles for dipping.

Makes 2 cups (500 ml).

LOBSTER SOUFFLÉ LOG

This is beautiful for pre-Christmas cocktail parties, all red and green, covered with mayonnaise and decorated with chopped parsley, limes, and lobster claws.

½ cup	cake or pastry flour	125 ml
pinch	cayenne pepper	pinch
4	eggs, separated	4
½ tsp	salt	2 ml
¼ tsp	cream of tartar	1 ml
1 tbs	chopped fresh dill, or 1 tsp (5 ml) dried dill	15 ml

1. Preheat oven to 400°F (200°C).
2. Lightly grease a 15″ × 10″ (38 × 25 cm) jelly roll pan and line pan with greased waxed paper.
3. Sift flour once before measuring. In a bowl combine flour and cayenne; mix well.
4. In a mixing bowl beat together egg whites, salt, and cream of tartar about 4 minutes until stiff.
5. In separate bowl, beat together yolks and dill about 5 minutes, until thick and lemon-colored.
6. Fold yolks into whites until partially combined; then fold in flour mixture.
7. Pour into prepared pan. Bake for 8 minutes, until set.
8. Turn out onto a clean, dry tea towel, remove waxed paper, and trim off crisp edges.

LOBSTER FILLING:

1 cup	cooked lobster	250 ml
¼ cup	finely chopped celery	50 ml
¼ cup	mayonnaise (recipe p. 227)	50 ml
1 tbs	freshly minced parsley	15 ml
1 tbs	lemon juice	15 ml
1 tsp	grated lemon rind	5 ml
½ tsp	dried chervil	2 ml
½ tsp	salt	2 ml
pinch	cayenne	pinch
pinch	white pepper	pinch
5	drained gherkins	5
2 tbs	mayonnaise	25 ml
	lime slices	
	fresh parsley sprigs	

1. In a blender or food processor, combine lobster, celery, mayonnaise, parsley, lemon juice, lemon rind, chervil, salt, cayenne, and white pepper. Process about 3 minutes using an on/off motion, until a smooth paste forms.

2. Spread salad over roll. Place a row of gherkins along one narrow end and roll up, jelly roll fashion. Chill 1 hour.

Frost with mayonnaise and garnish with lime slices and parsley sprigs. Serve at room temperature.

Makes 20 slices.

SALMON MOUSSE IN ARTICHOKE BOTTOMS

Great fork and knife starter for an elegant sit-down dinner, with its watercress garnish and Sauce Rémoulade.

I often make extra Salmon Mousse and mold it into individual fish shapes. Buy tail pieces for this. They are perfectly delicious and quite economical.

1 lb	piece fresh salmon	500 g
¼ cup	finely chopped celery leaves	50 ml
1½ tsp	finely chopped onion	7 ml
¾ tsp	salt	4 ml
⅛ tsp	freshly ground black pepper	0.5 ml
1	small bay leaf, crumbled	1
¼ cup	soft sweet butter	50 ml
1 tbs	egg white	15 ml
2 tsp	lemon juice	10 ml
½ tsp	salt	2 ml
¼ tsp	cayenne pepper	1 ml
pinch	white pepper	pinch
pinch	dried leaf tarragon	pinch
1	envelope unflavored gelatin	1
¼ cup	cold water	50 ml
¼ cup	mayonnaise (recipe p. 227)	50 ml
¼ cup	heavy or whipping cream	50 ml
8	cooked large artichoke bottoms	8
	Sauce Rémoulade	
	caviar lettuce	

1. On a large piece of aluminum foil place salmon. Measure thickness of fish for calculation of cooking time. Sprinkle with celery, onion, salt, pepper, and bay leaf. Wrap salmon in foil.
2. Place in large saucepan of boiling water to cover. Boil 10 minutes per inch (2.5 cm) thickness. Remove immediately. Cool.
3. Remove all skin and bones from salmon. Place in blender or food processor. Add butter and egg white and process 1 minute, until smooth and fluffy. Blend in lemon juice, salt, cayenne, white pepper, and tarragon.
4. Soak gelatin in cold water 5 minutes. Place over low heat, stir about 2 minutes, until gelatin dissolves. Cool, but do not chill.

5. Beat gelatin into mayonnaise and then beat into salmon mixture. Whip cream and fold in.
6. Pipe through pastry tube or spoon onto artichoke bottoms, piling it up well. Chill 1 hour before serving.

Top with a dab of Sauce Rémoulade and caviar. Serve on leaf of lettuce.

Makes 8 servings.

SAUCE RÉMOULADE

Capers, sweet pickle, Dijon mustard, all whipped into the creamy mayonnaise, make this pretty close to the ultimate in elegant, luxurious sauces. It lifts such party specialties as fried fish fingers, shrimps, scallops, and cold lobster to new heights of delight.

1 cup	mayonnaise (recipe p. 227)	250 ml
1	green onion, finely chopped	1
1 tbs	sweet pickle relish	15 ml
1 tbs	drained capers, finely chopped	15 ml
1 tbs	chopped fresh chervil, or 1 tsp (5 ml) dried	15 ml
1 tbs	chopped fresh parsley, or 1 tsp (5 ml) dried	15 ml
1 tsp	garlic parsley mustard*	5 ml

1. In a bowl, combine mayonnaise, onion, relish, capers, chervil, parsley, and mustard; mix well.
2. Spoon into small dish. Store, covered, in refrigerator.

Makes about 1¼ cups (300 ml).

Your home team just won the World Series. It's time to celebrate. Dozens of pennants everywhere: in vases and urns, hanging on strings from the ceiling, and all around the front door. Long curly ribbons in your team's colors. Fill large bowls with baseballs and more ribbon. Don't be afraid to overdo it. This is a celebration.

---

*Available in specialty food shops.

SCAMPI ALLEGRO (GARLIC SHRIMPS)

These can be prepared the night before a party and popped under the broiler at the crucial moment. They make a great beginning for an Italian supper. Your guests can nibble on the scampi while you prepare your favorite pasta.

2 lb	large raw shrimps	1 kg
3	large cloves garlic, chopped	3
¼ cup	vegetable oil	50 ml
¼ cup	melted sweet butter	50 ml
2 tbs	chopped fresh parsley	25 ml
2 tbs	lemon juice	25 ml
½ tsp	salt	2 ml
¼ tsp	freshly ground black pepper	1 ml

1. Shell and devein shrimps, leaving tails on. With a knife, split lengthwise, if desired.
2. Combine garlic, oil, butter, parsley, lemon juice, salt, and pepper.
3. Place shrimps in a single layer on a foil-lined jelly roll pan. Pour garlic mixture over shrimps. Cover and marinate, in refrigerator, overnight.
4. Broil in same pan, 3 inches (7 cm) from heat, 2 minutes per side, until shrimps are pink. Remove to a warm platter.
5. Spoon marinade remaining in pan over top. Serve immediately.

Makes 4 servings.

SMOKED MACKEREL DIP

You can serve this with crisp vegetable sticks or stuffed into chilled artichoke hearts. You can also do a number of cunning variations, such as using well-drained smoked oysters, smoked salmon, or smoked trout. Takes only moments to put together when friends drop in.

4 oz	cream cheese	125 g
4 oz	skinless, boneless smoked mackerel	125 g
¼ cup	sour cream	50 ml
4	green onions, white part only	4
1 tbs	prepared horseradish	15 ml
1 tbs	mayonnaise (recipe p. 227)	15 ml
2 tsp	chopped fresh dill	10 ml
1 tsp	salt	5 ml

1. In a blender or food processor, combine cream cheese, mackerel, sour cream, onions, horseradish, mayonnaise, dill, and salt. Process 1 to 2 minutes until smooth.
2. Spoon into a crock and refrigerate.

Makes 1 cup (250 ml), 16 servings.

VARIATIONS:
Smoked Trout Dip: Use smoked trout in place of smoked mackerel.
Smoked Salmon Dip: Use smoked salmon in place of smoked mackerel.
Smoked Oyster Dip: Use 1 can (3.6 oz/104 g) smoked oysters, well drained, in place of smoked mackerel.

HOT ANCHOVY DIP

If you enjoy Caesar Salad, you'll love this zesty little dip. It needs plenty to cling to, so serve it with a combo of Brussels sprouts, broccoli, and cauliflower florettes that have been blanched for just three minutes.

¼ cup	salted butter	50 ml
¼ cup	olive oil	50 ml
6	cloves garlic, minced	6
½ cup	finely chopped anchovies	125 ml

1. In top of double boiler over hot (not boiling) water, melt butter with olive oil and garlic.
2. Remove double boiler from heat, but keep mixture over hot water.
3. Add anchovies; stir well.
4. Set aside for 10 minutes for flavors to blend.

Makes 1 cup (250 ml).

THE DELICATE COOKERY OF JAPAN

Here is an introduction to sashimi for you. Raw fish. Yes, raw fish, and if you have ever tried raw oysters or raw beef, then give this a whirl too.

Sashimi is particularly tasty and well worth steeling your stomach for the first mouthful.

Try always to use ocean fish for your sashimi, tuna being my first choice.

Serve grated radish and grated carrots on each dish, and for those who like it hot, an extra dab of wasabi.

Toro, the fattier and light pink tuna, is the one sashimi-lovers prize, but the dish can work with the Maguro tuna, which is much leaner.

SASHIMI

1 lb	fresh tuna	500 g
1 cup	grated raw carrot	250 ml
1 cup	grated giant white radish	250 ml
1 tbs	wasabi*	15 ml
2 tsp	water	10 ml
½ cup	Japanese soy sauce	125 ml

1. Partially freeze tuna to make it easier to slice. With a sharp knife slice tuna into very thin slices. Cover and refrigerate.
2. Divide carrot and radish evenly and arrange on 4 chilled salad plates. Lay slices of tuna on top.
3. In a small dish, mix wasabi and water to make a paste; spoon a dollop onto each plate.
4. Pour soy sauce into 4 small bowls. Serve beside salad plates for dipping tuna.
   Other fish such as sea bass, striped bass, or red snapper may be used.

Makes 4 servings.

*Wasabi is available at Oriental markets.

A CHOICE OF CHEESE

The original hors d'oeuvre or simple snack was a collection of cheeses, crackers, and bread. But there are many more interesting things you can do with cheese, such as frying it, marinating it, rolling it with fruit.

CHEESE STRAWS

Buttery, cheesey. You can make up vast quantities of these when you are in the mood, store them in something like a coffee tin, and serve them as the occasion arises.

3 cups	all-purpose flour	750 ml
1 tsp	salt	5 ml
1 cup	cold lard	250 ml
1 cup	grated aged Cheddar cheese	250 ml
6 tbs	cold water	90 ml
2 tbs	soft sweet butter	25 ml

1. In a large bowl combine flour and salt. With a pastry blender or two knives cut in lard until mixture is crumbly and resembles small peas. Stir in cheese.
2. Sprinkle water over crumbly mixture and mix with hands until it forms a ball of dough. Chill.
3. Preheat oven to 350°F (180°C).
4. Turn dough out onto a floured board and roll out. Spread with 1 tbs (15 ml) butter, fold over twice. Roll out again, spread with remaining butter, and fold again.

5. Roll out to ¼ inch (5 mm) thickness. Cut into 1″ × 4″ (2.5 × 10 cm) sticks. Twist if desired and place on an ungreased baking sheet.
6. Bake for 15 minutes, or until golden brown.

Makes 2 dozen straws.

VARIATION:
Seasoned Cheese Straws: Lightly brush cheese straws with milk and sprinkle with seasonings—dried herbs and spices such as basil, thyme, tarragon, curry, chili powder, ground cumin. Bake as directed above.

DEEP-FRIED CAMEMBERT AND BRIE

Camembert and Brie, those best known of French cheeses, benefit from deep frying in an amazing way.
The cheese wedges can be breaded and stored in the fridge in advance and slipped into the deep fryer minutes before you want to serve them.
I sometimes serve this combination as a late night snack with pots of jam and Irish coffee loaded with whipped cream. And sometimes I team these with tomato coulis and a green salad for a quick, light meal.

1 lb	Camembert or Brie	500 g
2	eggs, lightly beaten	2
2 tbs	water	25 ml
1 cup	fine breadcrumbs	250 ml
	vegetable oil for deep frying	

1. With a sharp knife cut cheese into 12 equal wedges; chill 15 minutes.
2. In a bowl, combine eggs and water, mix well. Dip cheese wedges in egg mixture, let excess drain off, then roll in breadcrumbs. Repeat this process once more, and chill 1 hour until firm.
3. In a deep fryer or large skillet, heat oil to 375°F (190°C). Fry cheese wedges, a few at a time, 2 minutes, or until golden.
4. Drain on paper towel. Transfer to a warm platter and serve with Tomato Coulis or with Chutney or Raspberry Jam (page 349).

Makes 12 appetizer servings.

TOMATO COULIS

½ cup	chopped smoked ham	125 ml
2 tbs	sweet butter	25 ml
2 tbs	olive oil	25 ml
1	carrot, finely chopped	1
1	medium onion, finely chopped	1
1	clove garlic, finely chopped	1
2 lb	tomatoes, peeled and finely chopped	1 kg
1 cup	rich beef stock	250 ml
½ tsp	dried thyme	2 ml
½ tsp	dried basil	2 ml
½ tsp	brown sugar	2 ml
½ tsp	salt	2 ml
pinch	white pepper	pinch
1	bay leaf	1

1. Preheat oven to 350°F (180°C).
2. In a large skillet combine ham, butter, and oil; heat and cook for 4 minutes.
3. Add carrot, onion, and garlic. Sauté 5 minutes, until onion is soft.
4. Stir in tomatoes and stock; bring to a boil.
5. Stir in thyme, basil, sugar, salt, pepper, and bay leaf. Transfer to a casserole.
6. Bake for 1 hour and 30 minutes, until thick.
7. Cool. Remove bay leaf and discard.
8. Transfer sauce to container of blender or food processor, process 1 to 2 minutes until smooth.
   Store in refrigerator up to 1 week.

Makes 2½ cups (625 ml).

MARINATED CHÈVRE (GOAT CHEESE)

This goat cheese will keep refrigerated for up to a week.
  It can be used as a first course with your favorite green salad, or you can let your guests slice off chunks to put on top of melba toast or crackers.

1	clove garlic	1
1	green onion, cut in four	1
8	green peppercorns	8
1 tsp	dried basil	5 ml
1 tsp	dried thyme	5 ml
½ tsp	dried oregano	2 ml
1½ cups	olive oil	375 ml
8 oz	goat cheese	250 g

1. In food processor, with machine running, drop garlic and onion through feed tube and chop coarsely. Add peppercorns, basil, thyme, and oregano. Process with 3 to 4 on/off motions. Add oil and process just to blend.
2. To make by hand, mince garlic and onion, mix with peppercorns, basil, thyme, and oregano. Stir in olive oil.
3. Cut cheese into four pieces and place in a jar or bowl. Add marinade. Coat cheese well. Marinate 2 to 3 days in refrigerator, or overnight at room temperature.

Makes 16 servings.

CHEESE WAFERS

Thin, crispy, nippy cheese bites that are great for a nibble or to serve with an asparagus salad for a first course.

2 cups	grated sharp Cheddar cheese	500 ml
¼ cup	soft sweet butter	50 ml
½ cup	all-purpose flour	125 ml
1½ tsp	Worcestershire sauce	7 ml
1 tsp	salt	5 ml
¼ tsp	cayenne pepper	1 ml

1. In a bowl, combine cheese and butter; blend well. Stir in flour, Worcestershire sauce, salt, and cayenne pepper.
2. Shape into a long roll, 1 inch (2.5 cm) round. Chill well for at least 3 hours, until firm.
3. Preheat oven to 450°F (230°C).
4. Cut roll into thin slices and arrange on ungreased baking sheets.
5. Bake for 5 minutes, until lightly browned.

Makes 4 dozen wafers.

ROQUEFORT BUTTER

This little butter combines a number of tastes that complement the unique continental accent of this gorgeous French cheese.

Use it as a spread by itself, on crackers or little rounds of toast, or as the basis for your most exotic pickle or favorite fruit. Use it on steaks and hamburgers to lift them beyond the barbecue to the realm of Cordon Bleu.

½ cup	soft sweet butter	125 ml
¼ cup	crumbled Roquefort or blue cheese	50 ml
¼ cup	snipped chives	50 ml
1 tbs	fresh lemon juice	15 ml
¼ tsp	Worcestershire sauce	1 ml
1 tsp	Cognac	5 ml

1. In a small bowl with a wooden spoon or with an electric mixer at medium speed, beat butter until light and fluffy. Gradually beat in cheese, chives, lemon juice, Worcestershire sauce, and Cognac.
2. Transfer to a small crock or bowl. Serve immediately or cover and store in refrigerator up to 1 week.

Before serving, let stand at room temperature about 10 minutes until slightly softened.

Makes ¾ cup (175 ml).

BURGUNDY BUTTER

A wonderful purple surprise. I use the leftover wine from a party to make this and use the result to stuff tiny cocktail mushrooms or as a spread for a toasted hamburger bun just before the burger is settled onto it.

1 cup	red Burgundy wine	250 ml
1	clove garlic, finely chopped	1
1	small onion, finely chopped	1
⅓ cup	soft sweet butter	75 ml
1 tsp	finely chopped fresh parsley	5 ml
¼ tsp	freshly ground black pepper	1 ml

1. In a small saucepan, combine Burgundy, garlic, and onion. Heat to boiling and reduce to ½ its volume. Cool.
2. In a bowl, cream together butter and Burgundy mixture. Stir in parsley and pepper. Cover and store in refrigerator up to 1 week.

Makes ½ cup (125 ml).

BRIE BUTTER

A perfect spread for rare roast beef on rounds of Russian rye or for stuffing into halves of fresh apricots caught at the peak of ripeness.

| 1 cup | soft sweet butter | 250 ml |
| ½ lb | Brie | 250 g |

1. In a processor whip butter until fluffy.
2. Peel outside crust from Brie, break cheese into pieces, and gradually whip into butter until smooth.
   Use to spread on crackers or on bread for sandwiches.

Makes 2½ cups (625 ml).

LIPTAUER CHEESE

A delicious spread with plenty of Mediterranean tastes to carry your guests away on wings of praise. I think it is the chopped anchovy fillets that do it.

1	pkg (8 oz/250 g) cream cheese	1
1 cup	salted butter	250 ml
1 tbs	chopped onions	15 ml
1 tbs	drained capers	15 ml
1	can (1.75 oz/50 g) anchovy fillets, drained and chopped	1
1 tsp	white pepper	5 ml
1 tsp	prepared mustard	5 ml
1 tsp	caraway seed	5 ml
	pumpernickel bread	

1. In a blender or food processor combine cream cheese and butter. Process 1 to 2 minutes, until smooth. Add onions, capers and anchovies, process 10 seconds.
2. Transfer to a small bowl. Stir in white pepper, mustard, and caraway seed.
3. Press into a crock, cover, and store in refrigerator until serving time. Serve with pumpernickel bread.

Makes 16 to 20 appetizer servings.

THE ELEGANT TUREEN

Drama at Every Dip

Soup served from a large, elegant tureen gets a dinner or lunch off to a wonderfully intriguing start.

When the lid comes off the tureen and the steam rises and fills the nostrils with rich and rare scents of vegetables, meats, and herbs, all kinds of memories are stimulated.

Or if you are serving a cold soup, the action of pouring into the bowl, garnishing with chives or chopped nuts or a sprig of dill, and, as I will often do, adding a shot of gin or rum or sherry, is bound to stimulate eager concentration on the part of your guests, whether around the table or at the buffet.

Even at the most elegant dinners the hostess should serve the soup. The movement of the ladle, the pouring, the garnishing, is so lovely it should be made the most of.

If you are interested in antiques, spend a rainy day visiting the little antique stores in your town, where you can usually find one or two soup tureens for sale. If cooking and entertaining is your pleasure, even three or five tureens that take your fancy are not too many.

THE CREAM SOUPS

With the advent of the blender and now the food processor, whipping up a vegetable purée—the basis for so many cream soups—takes only moments. So here is a whole collection of cream soups—ready for your machine.

CREAMED SPINACH SOUP

An elegant and tempting light green soup alive with the subtle taste of spinach.

⅓ cup	sweet butter	75 ml
1 lb	fresh spinach, coarsely chopped	500 g
¼ cup	all-purpose flour	50 ml
1 tsp	salt	5 ml
½ tsp	freshly ground black pepper	2 ml
pinch	nutmeg	pinch
3 cups	milk	750 ml
⅓ cup	heavy or whipping cream	75 ml
1	hard-cooked egg, finely chopped or sieved	1

1. In a large saucepan, heat ¼ cup (50 ml) butter; add spinach, and sauté about 7 minutes, until limp.
2. Transfer to a food processor or blender; process 1 to 2 minutes until puréed and smooth; set aside.
3. In the same saucepan, melt remaining butter. Stir in flour, salt, pepper, and nutmeg until blended. Gradually add milk, whisking constantly until mixture is smooth. Bring to a boil and cook, whisking, until mixture is thickened.

4. Whisk in puréed spinach and heavy cream. Cook about 2 minutes longer to heat through.
5. Ladle into hot soup bowls. Garnish with chopped or sieved egg.

Makes 6 to 8 servings.

> *Fill a deep, round bowl or soup tureen with bright yellow tulips. Surround the bowl with green apples, yellow pears, and dark blue grapes.*

CREAMED ONION SOUP

Everyone expects onion soup to have a cheese surface even if it's creamed. I always grate a little old Cheddar over it and pop it under the grill just to start it melting. That's how it comes to the table, and that's why the guests give it rave reviews.

⅓ cup	sweet butter	75 ml
4	medium onions, coarsely chopped	4
¼ cup	all-purpose flour	50 ml
1 tsp	salt	5 ml
½ tsp	white pepper	2 ml
3 cups	milk	750 ml
⅓ cup	heavy or whipping cream	75 ml
¼ cup	freshly grated, aged Cheddar cheese	50 ml

1. In a large saucepan, heat ¼ cup (50 ml) butter; add onion and sauté 10 minutes, until softened but not brown.
2. Transfer to a food processor or blender; process 1 to 2 minutes until puréed and smooth; set aside.
3. In the same saucepan, melt remaining butter; stir in flour, salt, and pepper until blended. Gradually add milk, whisking constantly until mixture is smooth. Bring to a boil and cook, whisking, until mixture is thickened.
4. Whisk in puréed onion and heavy cream. Cook about 2 minutes longer to heat through.
5. Ladle into hot soup bowls. Sprinkle cheese over surface of each bowl of soup and put under grill to start cheese melting.

Makes 6 to 8 servings.

CREAM OF MUSHROOM SOUP WITH BRANDY

If you live below the Mason-Dixon line, your appreciation for the joys of arriving home late on a cold winter night and heating up a mug of cream of mushroom soup is probably limited.

On the other hand, if you ski, you'll know what I mean, especially when you consider the possibilities of a shot of Cognac in the mug. This soup is so light and delicious and warming and comforting.

2 tbs	sweet butter	25 ml
3 cups	thinly sliced mushrooms	750 ml
¼ cup	finely chopped Spanish onion	50 ml
2	cloves garlic, finely chopped	2
3 cups	chicken stock	750 ml
¼ cup	soft sweet butter	50 ml
¼ cup	all-purpose flour	50 ml
2½ cups	milk	625 ml
½ tsp	salt	5 ml
¼ tsp	white pepper	1 ml
¼ tsp	ground nutmeg	1 ml
2 tbs	brandy or Cognac	25 ml

1. In a large saucepan heat butter. Add mushrooms, onion, and garlic; sauté 5 minutes, until softened.
2. Add chicken stock. Bring to boil; reduce heat and simmer 15 minutes.
3. Combine butter and flour; blend to form a paste. Stir into soup, 1 tbs (15 ml) at a time, continuing to cook until soup is smooth and thickened.
4. Stir in milk, salt, pepper, and nutmeg. Heat to simmering.
5. Stir in brandy and serve.

Makes 4 to 6 servings.

CHICKEN STOCK

Wherever chicken stock is suggested in these recipes, you might want to try a homemade variety.

4 lb	whole chicken	2 kg
2	medium onions, coarsely chopped	2
2	medium carrots, thickly sliced	2
2	stalks celery with leaves, coarsely chopped	2
1	medium parsnip, thickly sliced	1
1 tbs	chopped fresh dill, or 1 tsp (5 ml) dried dill	15 ml
1 tbs	chopped fresh parsley	15 ml
6	peppercorns	6
1 tbs	salt	15 ml
12 cups	water	3 l
2	washed egg shells	2

1. In a stock pot or large kettle, combine chicken, onions, carrots, celery, parsnip, dill, parsley, peppercorns, and salt. Add cold water.
2. Slowly bring to a boil. Remove from heat and skim until top of stock is clear. Bring to a boil again, reduce heat, half-cover pot, and simmer for 1¼ hours, until chicken is tender.
3. Remove chicken; strip meat from bones, and reserve meat for another use. Return bones to pot, add egg shells, and simmer 1 hour more.
4. Line a sieve with a double layer of cheesecloth. Pour stock through lined sieve into a container.
5. Cover and store in refrigerator for up to 1 week, or in the freezer for up to 2 months. (Defat stock by removing congealed fat from top before using.)

To make rich stock, boil the strained stock, uncovered, to reduce it by ⅓.

Makes 8 to 10 cups (1 to 1.5 l).

> *Hollow out six pumpkin shells and use them as vases for a Halloween party. Use a plastic container as a liner and fill them with bittersweet and orange and yellow gerbera daisies.*

SMOOTH PUMPKIN SOUP WITH DARK RUM AND WALNUTS

I have a garden full of pumpkins and squash, so I have plenty on hand year-round in my freezer. One of my favorite ways to serve them is in this creamy, delicious, slightly tipsy soup, and my favorite time of year is just before Halloween, when the frost is on the pumpkin.

¼ cup	finely chopped walnuts	50 ml
⅓ cup	sweet butter	75 ml
¼ cup	all-purpose flour	50 ml
1 tsp	salt	5 ml
½ tsp	white pepper	2 ml
pinch	cinnamon	pinch
3 cups	milk	750 ml
2 cups	mashed or puréed cooked pumpkin or squash	500 ml
⅓ cup	heavy or whipping cream	75 ml
2 tbs	dark rum	25 ml

1. Place walnuts on a baking sheet. Toast in a 350°F (180°C) oven for about 10 minutes.
2. In a large saucepan, melt butter; stir in flour, salt, pepper, and cinnamon until blended. Gradually add milk, whisking constantly until mixture is smooth.
3. Bring to a boil and cook, whisking, until mixture is thickened.
4. Whisk in pumpkin and cream. Cook about 2 minutes longer to heat through. Stir in rum.
5. Ladle into hot soup bowls. Garnish with toasted chopped walnuts.

Makes 6 to 8 servings.

WILD MUSHROOM SOUP

When you serve this to guests it's always a good idea to talk knowledgeably about the lesser-known mushrooms, such as chanterelles and shitake. Sometimes a departure into the more exotic mushrooms requires a little reassurance. But get them to taste it, and you've got a hit on your hands.

¾ lb	shitake mushrooms or chanterelles*	375 g
2 tbs	sweet butter	25 ml
1	shallot, finely chopped	1
4 cups	chicken stock	1 l
¼ tsp	salt	1 ml
⅛ tsp	pepper	0.5 ml
	grated rind of 1 lemon	
¼ cup	sour cream	50 ml
	snipped chives	

1. Trim mushrooms and wipe with a damp cloth.
2. In a medium saucepan heat butter. Add mushrooms; sauté 3 to 4 minutes, until limp.
3. Add shallot; sauté 3 to 4 minutes, until soft.
4. Stir in chicken stock, salt, pepper, and lemon rind. Bring to a boil, reduce heat. Cover and simmer 10 minutes.
5. With a slotted spoon remove mushrooms from stock. Add to a food processor, process 30 to 60 seconds, until finely chopped. Return to saucepan. Heat to simmering.
6. Remove from heat and stir in sour cream. Serve garnished with snipped chives.

Makes 4 servings.

*If preferred, 2 oz (60 g) dried mushrooms may be used. Soak dried mushrooms in water to cover for 30 minutes; discard soaking liquid, and follow recipe above.

SEA SHANTY MUSHROOM SOUP

This one is indeed something for sailors to sing about, and a great simple soup to serve to your favorite yachtsmen and women. The clam juice adds the redolence of the sea.
  Serve with a dollop of sour cream in the center to give it a natural nip.

¼ cup	sweet butter	50 ml
1½ lbs	mushrooms, finely chopped	750 g
4	shallots, finely chopped	4
2 cups	clam juice	500 ml
½ tsp	pepper	2 ml
1 cup	light or table cream	250 ml

1. In a large saucepan heat butter, add mushrooms and shallots; sauté 15 minutes.
2. Stir in clam juice, bring mixture to a boil, reduce heat, and simmer 20 minutes. Add pepper.
3. Transfer to a blender or food processor and purée with the on/off motion about 2 minutes, until smooth.
4. Return to saucepan. Stir in cream. Heat just to warm through.
5. Pour into individual serving bowls and serve warm.

Makes 8 servings.

CURRIED CARROT AND LEEK SOUP

This can be served hot or cold, and it is equally delicious and mysterious either way. It's the combination of carrots and leeks abetted by the curry that does it.
Serve with bowls of garlicky croutons, and consider it as a soup course for an elegant Indian dinner.

¼ cup	sweet butter	50 ml
2	medium leeks, white part only, finely chopped	2
6	medium carrots, peeled and sliced	6
2 tsp	curry powder, or more to taste	10 ml
½ tsp	ground cumin	2 ml
¼ tsp	ground nutmeg	1 ml
2½ cups	chicken stock	625 ml
⅓ cup	fresh orange juice	75 ml
1 cup	heavy or whipping cream	250 ml
½ tsp	salt	2 ml
	white pepper	
	Garlic Croutons	

1. In a large saucepan, heat butter; add leeks and carrots; sauté about 5 minutes, until leeks are soft but not brown.
2. Stir in curry powder, cumin, and nutmeg.
3. Add chicken stock and orange juice. Bring to a boil, reduce heat, cover, and simmer 25 to 30 minutes, or until vegetables are tender.
4. Cool slightly, and in batches purée in blender or food processor.
5. Return to saucepan; stir in cream, salt, and pepper, to taste.
   Serve hot or cold. Garnish with Garlic Croutons.

Makes 4 cups (1 l).

Garlic Croutons

1. Preheat oven to 350°F (180°C).
2. Butter ½ inch (1 cm) thick slices French or Italian bread with garlic butter and cut into cubes.
3. Heat a skillet over medium heat and add bread cubes. Toss until butter melts and is absorbed by the bread.
4. Spread on baking sheet and bake about 7 to 8 minutes, turning once or twice, until crisp and golden.
5. Cool completely and store in airtight containers.

Creamed Crab Soup

This is a quick and delicious soup that everyone will think you worked over for hours. To add to the illusion I always serve it from one of those antique soup tureens I mentioned at the start of this section.

Always remember to warm your tureen before pouring the soup in. It protects your tureen from mishaps and helps keep the soup hot.

2 tbs	sweet butter	25 ml
1	large onion, finely chopped	1
1	clove garlic, finely chopped	1
¾ lb	crabmeat	375 g
½ tsp	salt	2 ml
¼ tsp	white pepper	1 ml
2 cups	milk	500 ml
1 cup	heavy or whipping cream	250 ml
2 tbs	Irish Mist or Drambuie	25 ml
2 tsp	lemon juice	10 ml
⅛ tsp	cayenne pepper	0.5 ml
1 tbs	chopped fresh parsley	15 ml

1. In a medium saucepan, heat butter. Add onion and garlic; sauté, about 10 minutes, until softened.
2. Stir in crabmeat, salt, and pepper; cook 1 minute.
3. Stir in milk. Bring to just below simmering, cover, and heat for 15 minutes. *Do not boil.*
4. Stir in cream, Irish Mist, lemon juice, and cayenne. Heat to just below simmering, 3 minutes longer.
5. Pour into warm soup tureen or individual soup bowls. Garnish with parsley.

Makes 4 servings.

AN ELEGANT AUTUMN LUNCHEON

SMOOTH PUMPKIN SOUP
with Dark Rum and Walnuts

HOT CHÈVRE AND LAMB SALAD

SPICY ORANGE FRUIT
and Nut Bran Loaf or Muffins

SMALL POTS OF APPLE BUTTER

ASSORTED SMALL SQUARES AND BARS

TEA   COFFEE

The wines for this are essentially light in nature, preferably red. A Beaujolais or Beaujolais Villages from France would be suitable. An Italian Barbera and a Valdepenas from Spain. From California, a Barbera, or again, a Beaujolais from Canada.

No wines are recommended with the dessert.

MINESTRONE AND OTHER
HEARTY VEGETABLE SOUPS

The French are famous for their bisques, purées, and cream soups, but the Italians are known for their wonderful minestrones and hearty soups.

I am starting this short section off with three Italian entries that may sound familiar, but which are definitely different from their parents.

MINESTRONE ALLA GENOESE

From the great northern Italian seaport of Genoa comes this meal-in-a-pot soup. Serve it to your guests late at night or in combination with a simple salad and plenty of Italian bread. It's packed with macaroni, beans, spinach, and other veggies and looks really Picassoesque in a bowl.

Pass the pepper mill when you serve.

2 tbs	olive oil	25 ml
4	medium carrots, grated	4
4	medium potatoes, diced	4
2	medium onions, coarsely chopped	2
2	leeks, thinly sliced	2
2 cups	shredded raw spinach	500 ml
6 cups	beef stock	1.5 l
1	can (19 oz/540 ml) Italian plum tomatoes	1
3 cups	cooked kidney beans	750 ml
1–2 tsp	salt	5–10 ml
¼ tsp	freshly ground black pepper	1 ml
¼ cup	chopped fresh parsley	50 ml
½ tsp	dried basil leaves	2 ml
½ tsp	dried oregano leaves	2 ml
2	cloves garlic, finely chopped	2
4	slices bacon, chopped	4
1½ cups	macaroni	375 ml
	grated Parmesan cheese	

1. In a large soup kettle, heat oil. Add carrots, potatoes, onions, leeks, and spinach; cook over medium heat 5 minutes, until onions are limp.
2. Stir in stock, tomatoes, beans, salt, and pepper. Bring to a boil, reduce heat, cover, and simmer 1 hour, until potatoes are tender.
3. In a blender or food processor, combine parsley, basil, oregano, garlic, and bacon. Purée about 1 minute, until a paste forms. Stir into soup.
4. Add macaroni. Bring to a boil, reduce heat, cover, and simmer 15 minutes, or until macaroni is tender.

Serve with grated Parmesan cheese.

Makes 12 servings, about 20 cups (5 l).

MEATBALL SOUP

If you are off on another ski weekend, this is the soup to serve your guests. If you want to make it even more nourishing, add some of your favorite pasta to it. I serve it with my nippy Liptauer Cheese and lots of warm bread.

1½ lb	lean ground beef	750 g
½ cup	fine dry breadcrumbs	125 ml
1 tbs	chopped fresh parsley	15 ml
1 tsp	salt	5 ml
¼ tsp	freshly ground black pepper	1 ml
1	egg	1
1 tbs	vegetable oil	15 ml
3 tbs	sweet butter	45 ml
2	medium onions, coarsely chopped	2
2	medium carrots, thinly sliced	2
¼ cup	finely chopped celery	50 ml
1	can (14 oz/398 ml) tomatoes	1
2 cups	rich beef stock	500 ml
¼ tsp	dried oregano leaves	1 ml
¼ tsp	dried basil leaves	1 ml
1	bay leaf	1
	chopped fresh parsley, optional	
	freshly grated Parmesan cheese	

1. In a large bowl, combine beef, breadcrumbs, parsley, salt, and pepper. Stir in egg; mix thoroughly. Using hands, shape into small meatballs ½ inch (1 cm) in diameter.
2. In a large skillet, heat oil and 1 tbs (15 ml) butter. Add meatballs; cook, turning, about 10 minutes, until brown. Drain on paper towel.
3. In a large saucepan, heat remaining 2 tbs (25 ml) butter. Add onions, carrots, and celery; sauté 5 minutes, until onions are softened.
4. Stir in tomatoes, stock, oregano, basil, bay leaf, and meatballs. Bring to a boil, cover, and simmer 20 minutes, until carrots are tender. Remove bay leaf.

Serve in warm bowls. Garnish with additional chopped parsley, if desired, and Parmesan cheese.

Makes 6 servings.

MILANESE BEAN AND VEGETABLE SOUP

Well worth the effort of soaking dried beans and softening them up for guests.
   These bean-based soups are part of the history of soups, soups made when there was little else but a ham bone, a handful or two of dried beans, and a lot of imagination with which to work. Of course, a lot more goes into this one from Italy's industrial north.

1 cup	dry white pea beans	250 ml
	water	
3	slices bacon, chopped	3
2 tbs	olive oil	25 ml
2	medium onions, thinly sliced	2
1	large carrot, diced	1
2	medium potatoes, diced	2
2	medium zucchini, diced	2
¼ cup	red wine	50 ml
3	large tomatoes, coarsely chopped	3
2 cups	shredded cabbage	500 ml
2	cloves garlic, finely chopped	2
2 tsp	salt	10 ml
¾ tsp	freshly ground black pepper	3 ml
1½ tsp	chopped fresh basil, or ½ tsp (2 ml) dried	7 ml
¼ cup	long grain rice	50 ml
2 tbs	finely chopped fresh parsley	25 ml
½ cup	grated Parmesan cheese	125 ml

1. Wash beans and place in a large saucepan. Cover with water and bring to boil. Remove from heat and set aside 1 hour to soak. Drain off water.
2. Add 10 cups (2.5 l) fresh water to beans. Bring to a boil, reduce heat, cover, and simmer 50 to 60 minutes, until beans are tender.
3. While beans are cooking, prepare vegetables. In a large skillet, cook bacon. Add olive oil and onions; sauté 5 minutes, until onions are softened.
4. Add carrot, potatoes, and zucchini. Sauté 5 minutes, until tender crisp. Stir into cooked beans.
5. Add wine to skillet, cook, scraping up any bits to deglaze skillet. Add this liquid to soup.
6. Stir in tomatoes, cabbage, garlic, salt, pepper, and basil. Bring to a boil, reduce heat, cover, and simmer, stirring occasionally, for 1 hour.
7. Stir in rice and parsley. Cover and simmer 20 minutes longer, until rice is tender.
8. Just before serving, stir in cheese.

Makes 12 servings, about 20 cups (5 l).

VERY VEGETABLE SOUP

If you don't want to spend the time making Milanese Bean Soup, here's one at the opposite end of the preparation time scale. It's the fastest vegetable soup recipe I've used, and yet it has a great look and a taste that says you slaved over it.

5	carrots, finely chopped	5
4	stalks celery with leaves, finely chopped	4
2	onions, finely chopped	2
2	cobs fresh sweet corn, kernels removed	2
4 cups	chicken stock	1 l
1	can (28 oz/796 ml) Italian tomatoes	1
1 tsp	salt	5 ml
½ tsp	freshly ground black pepper	2 ml
½ tsp	dried oregano	2 ml

1. In a large saucepan, combine carrots, celery, onion, corn, stock, tomatoes, salt, pepper, and oregano.
2. Bring to a boil, reduce heat, and simmer, stirring occasionally to break up tomatoes, for 45 minutes, until vegetables are tender.
3. Ladle into warm soup bowls and serve.

Makes 4 to 6 servings.

FRESH TOMATO SOUP

*There is something radiant about field-ripened summer tomatoes.
Here is a soup for those of you who know what I'm talking about.*

5	large fresh tomatoes, peeled, seeded, and finely chopped	5
1	stalk celery, finely chopped	1
2	fresh basil leaves	2
1	medium onion, finely chopped	1
	juice of ½ lemon	
2 cups	chicken stock	500 ml
1	bay leaf	1
1 tbs	tomato paste	15 ml
2 tsp	granulated sugar	10 ml
½ tsp	salt	2 ml
¼ tsp	freshly ground black pepper	1 ml
⅛ tsp	ground ginger	0.5 ml
pinch	allspice	pinch
dash	Worcestershire sauce	dash
	grated rind of ½ lemon	
	whipped cream	
	fresh dill	

1. In a large pot, combine tomatoes, celery, basil, onion, lemon juice, chicken stock, and bay leaf. Bring mixture to a boil, reduce heat, and simmer ½ hour, until slightly thickened. Remove bay leaf.
2. Transfer to a blender or food processor and with an on/off motion purée about 4 minutes, until smooth.
3. Return purée to pot and stir in tomato paste, sugar, salt, pepper, ginger, allspice, Worcestershire sauce, and lemon rind. Bring to a boil and serve hot, or remove from heat, chill, and serve cold.
4. Spoon into individual soup bowls, garnish with unsweetened whipped cream, and top with fresh snips of dill.

Makes 4 to 6 servings.

POTATO CHOWDER

This is a perfect winter soup to serve after a morning on the ski slopes, when everyone comes in rosy-cheeked and ravenous. It's loaded with bacon, onions, and potatoes.

4	slices bacon, coarsely chopped	4
2	onions, coarsely chopped	2
6	medium potatoes, cut into ¼ inch (5 mm) cubes	6
3 cups	chicken stock	750 ml
¼ cup	all-purpose flour	50 ml
1 tsp	salt	5 ml
½ tsp	freshly ground black pepper	2 ml
2 cups	milk	500 ml
1 cup	light or table cream	250 ml

1. In a large saucepan, combine bacon and onion. Cook, stirring until fat renders from bacon.
2. Add potatoes and chicken stock. Bring to a boil, reduce heat, and simmer 20 minutes, or until tender but not mushy.
3. Combine flour, salt, pepper, and ½ cup (125 ml) milk; stir until smooth. Gradually pour into potato mixture, stirring until mixture begins to thicken.
4. Stir in remaining milk and cream. Heat to warm through but do not boil. Soup freezes well before or after the addition of the milk and cream.

Makes 8 cups (2 l).

NEW ENGLAND CLAM CHOWDER

This is the soup I always made when we summered in Maine. It, along with a couple of pans of corn muffins, made up my Labor Day Soup Party—held when I've packed most things away pending the closing of the summer cottage.

This recipe is for six, but I always make enough for twenty-four. If there is any left over, it freezes well.

5 dozen	small hard-shelled clams (steamers)	5 dozen
4	slices bacon, coarsely chopped	4
2	stalks celery, coarsely chopped	2
1	clove garlic, finely chopped	1
1	large onion, coarsely chopped	1
4	medium potatoes, diced	4
1 tsp	salt	5 ml
½ tsp	freshly ground black pepper	2 ml
½ tsp	dried thyme leaves	2 ml
2 cups	milk	500 ml
1 tbs	sweet butter	15 ml
1 cup	light or table cream	250 ml
2 tbs	soft sweet butter	25 ml
2 tbs	all-purpose flour	25 ml

1. Scrub clams thoroughly. Place clams in a large kettle, and cover with cold water. Bring to a boil, reduce heat, cover, and simmer 10 minutes, until clams open. *Discard any clams that do not open.*
2. Strain broth through cheesecloth and reserve. Remove clams from their shell, chop, and set aside.
3. In a large saucepan, cook bacon for 2 to 3 minutes. Add celery, garlic, and onion and cook about 5 minutes, until softened. Add potatoes and cook all vegetables together 5 minutes longer.
4. Add 3 cups (750 ml) of the reserved clam broth, salt, pepper, and thyme. Bring to a boil, reduce heat, cover, and simmer 20 minutes. Stir in milk and reserved chopped clams. Heat thoroughly.
3. To thicken soup, combine soft butter and flour, stir well to form a paste. Stir in paste 1 tbs (15 ml) at a time and continue to cook until soup is smooth and thickened. Stir in cream. Heat just to simmering.

Makes 6 servings.

BEEF CONSOMMÉ BORDEAUX

This rich beef consommé is like the Vin du Pays: deep, dark, and spicy. The spice comes from the cinnamon, which is unusual in a soup and particularly interesting. Float the egg whites on the top of each bowl and garnish with chopped chives.

4 cups	clear beef stock or consommé	1 l
1	cinnamon stick, 1 inch (2.5 cm) long	1
1 cup	dry red wine	250 ml
1 cup	boiling water	250 ml
2	eggs, separated	2
½ tsp	salt	2 ml
¼ tsp	freshly ground black pepper	1 ml
pinch	cayenne	pinch
	chopped chives	

1. In a large saucepan, heat broth; add cinnamon stick. Bring to a boil, reduce heat, and simmer 5 minutes.
2. Stir in red wine and boiling water; simmer 5 minutes longer.
3. In a bowl lightly beat egg yolks.
4. Beat egg whites until stiff.
5. Remove cinnamon stick and pour yolks slowly into broth, stirring constantly. Season with salt, pepper, and cayenne.
6. Ladle immediately into warmed bouillon cups. Float a dollop of beaten egg white on each serving, and sprinkle with chopped chives.

Makes 6 servings.

There is a special way to shuck corn which I've developed over the years: Pinch the leaves and the cornsilk firmly together and pull down to the stem. But don't try to take too much at once or you won't get a nice clean strip. And try not to let your guests become too competitive over the number of ears they shuck. Quality, not quantity, is what you are after. Of course, you could establish a prize for the cleanest twenty ears.

Friends who have watched my rather slow process of removing kernels from the cobs with a small, hard-edged knife, have searched the world of kitchen technology for a better way. I have a drawer full of these devices— everything from a tiny, complicated lathe to what looks like a simple paint scraper. None do the job as well as a knife, but then maybe that's because I'm used to it.

MY OWN SPECIAL CORN CHOWDER

This recipe started with our driving to and from the summer cottage with an eye on the fields of farmers' corn. When the corn was as high as an elephant's eye, it would go on sale by the roadside, and I always purchased far too much. So I made corn chowder with the excess. At first I had to recruit friends to help me shuck the corn. Now they phone up to ask when I'm making it and can they help.

6	cobs corn (about 2 cups/500 ml kernels)	6
¼ lb	slab bacon, chopped	125 g
1 tbs	sweet butter	15 ml
2	stalks celery, finely chopped	2
1	medium onion, finely chopped	1
1	medium potato, peeled and diced	1
4 cups	chicken stock	1 l
¼ cup	all-purpose flour	50 ml
¼ tsp	white pepper	1 ml
2 cups	milk	500 ml
1 cup	heavy or whipping cream	250 ml

1. With a sharp knife, cut kernels from corn cobs; set them aside.
2. In a large saucepan, heat bacon and butter. Cook, stirring about 4 minutes, until fat renders from bacon.
3. Add celery, onion, and potato. Sauté about 7 minutes, until potato is tender.
4. Stir in corn kernels. Stir and cook 2 minutes longer.
5. Add stock, bring to a boil, reduce heat, and simmer for about 40 minutes.
6. Combine flour, pepper, and ½ cup (125 ml) milk; stir until smooth. Gradually pour into corn mixture, stirring until mixture begins to thicken. Stir in remaining milk and cream.
7. Heat to warm through, but do not boil.
Soup freezes well before or after the addition of the milk and cream.

Makes 12 cups (3 l).

CORN HARVEST BARBECUE

You can have a corn harvest party with just vast quantities of Corn Chowder for everyone. But the time of year and the ripe corn call out for a barbecue, and that's what I'm proposing.

BITE-SIZE EMPANADAS

MY OWN SPECIAL CORN CHOWDER

CHEESE STRAWS

BARBECUED LEMON MUSTARD CHICKEN
CRISP POTATO PANCAKES
SOUR CREAM AND APPLESAUCE

CLAY POTS OF CURRY RELISH
and
SUMMER FRUIT
CHILI SAUCE

CRISP BRANDY CONES
filled with Pralines 'n' Cream

THE COOL, PASTEL SOUPS
OF SUMMER

I don't know why I associate cold soups with summer. I've certainly served vichyssoise and gazpacho in the dead of winter. Perhaps it's their colors that make them look like summer dresses.

If you live in a climate that has the four seasons, it's natural to think hot soup in winter, cool in summer, but don't make that an unbendable rule.

WEST INDIES AVOCADO SOUP

No cooking. Quick and easy. Doesn't that say summer?

I'll wager none of your guests will figure out the combination of ingredients that give this soup its mysterious appeal.

Decorate each bowl with a thin slice of lime.

1	ripe avocado	1
2 cups	chicken stock	500 ml
1 cup	light or table cream	250 ml
2 tbs	white rum	25 ml
½ tsp	curry powder	2 ml
½ tsp	salt	2 ml
	juice of 1 lime	
pinch	white pepper	pinch

1. Peel avocado; cut into pieces.

2. In a blender or food processor, combine avocado, stock, cream, rum, curry powder, salt, lime juice, and white pepper. Process 1 to 2 minutes, until smooth and creamy.
3. Chill 1 hour before serving.

Makes 4 servings.

GAZPACHO

I serve this Spanish classic in a tall glass with a dash of vodka for zip. It's sort of my own version of the Bloody Mary.

If the group you've got coming is a little standoffish, consider retaining the dash of vodka when you serve this in a bowl.

5	medium ripe tomatoes, peeled, seeded, and coarsely chopped	5
3	cloves garlic	3
3	slices bread, crusts removed and cubed	3
1	cucumber, peeled, seeded, and coarsely chopped	1
1	green pepper, seeded and coarsely chopped	1
2 cups	tomato juice	500 ml
2 cups	water	500 ml
¼ cup	olive oil	50 ml
¼ cup	red wine vinegar	50 ml
1 tsp	salt	5 ml
	freshly ground black pepper	
few dashes	hot pepper sauce	few dashes
	diced cucumber and green pepper	

1. In a food processor, in batches, combine tomatoes, garlic, bread, cucumber, green pepper, tomato juice, water, olive oil, and vinegar. Process until puréed. Season with salt, pepper, and hot pepper sauce.
2. Pour into refrigerator container, cover, and chill at least 1 hour until serving time.
3. Garnish with diced cucumber and green pepper.

Makes 9 cups (2.25 l).

Nasturtium flowers and one or two of their round peppery leaves make a beautiful garnish for any summer dish.

CRÈME BORDELAISE (FRESH PEA SOUP)

A smooth, aristocratic, pale green soup with a worldwide reputation as one of the great French discoveries. Serve it cold, in chilled bowls, or if you want a hot soup, just heat it up.

7 cups	shelled green peas	1.75 l
3 cups	chicken stock	750 ml
1 tsp	granulated sugar	5 ml
1 tbs	sweet butter	15 ml
4	green onions, finely chopped	4
2 tbs	chopped fresh mint	25 ml
2 tbs	all-purpose flour	25 ml
2 cups	milk or cream	500 ml
	salt and freshly ground black pepper, to taste	
	lime slices or fresh mint leaves	

1. In a large saucepan or pot, combine peas, stock, and sugar. Cover and bring to a boil; cook 20 minutes, until peas are tender.
2. Transfer to a blender or food processor and with an on/off motion, purée 1 minute, until smooth.
3. In a saucepan melt butter, add onion and mint, and sauté 2 minutes, until limp.
4. Add flour; mix well, until a thick paste forms. Gradually stir in milk until mixture is smooth and creamy.
5. Combine milk mixture and green pea purée. Season to taste with salt and pepper. Chill 2 hours.

When cold, pour into individual soup bowls and garnish with a thin lime slice or a small sprig of fresh mint.

Makes 6 servings.

ZESTY SUMMERTIME SOUP

Sort of a sophisticated Gazpacho. The buttermilk tends to tone it down to an inviting pink.

4	green onions, cut into pieces	4
1	green pepper, seeded and coarsely chopped	1
1	small cucumber, peeled, seeded, and cut into chunks	1
1 cup	tomato juice	250 ml
2 cups	buttermilk	500 ml
½ tsp	Worcestershire sauce	2 ml
few dashes	hot pepper sauce	few dashes

1. In blender or food processor, combine onions, half the pepper, cucumber, and tomato juice; process 1 to 2 minutes, until smooth and puréed. Pour into a refrigerator container.
2. Stir in buttermilk, Worcestershire, and hot pepper sauce.
3. Chill at least 2 hours, or until serving, and serve in chilled soup bowls. Garnish with remaining green pepper, diced.

Makes 5 cups (1.25 l).

WATERCRESS VICHYSSOISE

I often wonder, when I start going through my recipes, why leeks don't turn up more often. I think it may be that they are difficult to clean because of the tightly packed stems. However, in this soup and the next, they are well worth the effort.

¼ cup	sweet butter	50 ml
4	leeks, white part only, finely chopped	4
1	medium onion, finely chopped	1
5	medium potatoes, peeled and thickly sliced	5
4 cups	chicken stock	1 l
1 tsp	salt	5 ml
1	bunch watercress, stems removed and leaves chopped	1
1 cup	heavy or whipping cream	250 ml
	salt and white pepper to taste	
	fresh dill sprigs	

1. In a large saucepan, heat butter, add leeks and onions. Sauté 5 minutes, until softened.
2. Add potatoes, chicken stock, and salt. Bring to a boil, reduce heat, cover, and simmer 15 to 20 minutes, or until potatoes are tender.
3. Add watercress, simmer 7 minutes, until watercress is limp. Cool slightly.
4. In batches, process in blender or food processor, about 3 minutes, until smooth.
5. Stir in heavy cream and chill 2 hours, until serving. Taste and season with salt and white pepper.
Serve in chilled soup bowls. Garnish with fresh dill sprigs.

Makes 8 cups (2 l).

Cleaning Leeks

Cut off the excess and damaged leaves. Cut a right-angle cross in the top and well down into the white portion of the vegetable. Let cold water run into the stalk and then soak for a few minutes. This will wash out all the miniscule bits of sand.

PEAR AND LEEK SOUP

My friend Margo Lane has everything. Beauty, brains, sophistication, and a glamorous career as one of Toronto's top TV producers.

One thing she doesn't have anymore, though, is her recipe for Pear and Leek Soup. I finally got it from her when I told her it would appear in print. Now she will have to come up with something new for her elegant dinner parties.

⅓ cup	sweet butter	75 ml
3 cups	sliced leeks, 4 to 5	750 ml
4	pears, peeled, cored and coarsely chopped	4
6 cups	chicken stock	1.5 l
1 tsp	ground savory	5 ml
¼ tsp	white pepper	1 ml
1 tbs	lemon juice	15 ml
1	pear, peeled, cored, and sliced	1
	blue cheese	

1. In a large saucepan heat butter. Add leeks; sauté 10 minutes, until softened.
2. Add chopped pears, chicken stock, savory, and pepper. Bring to a boil, reduce heat, and simmer 20 minutes, until pears are softened. Stir in lemon juice.
3. In batches, purée in blender or food processor, until smooth.

Soup may be served hot or cold. If serving hot, return to saucepan and heat through. If serving cold, pour into large bowl and chill.

Garnish with pear slices and crumbled blue cheese.

Makes 8 servings.

COLD CUCUMBER SOUP EMPRESS

Refreshing and quick, with no cooking involved.
  Serve chilled with bowls of toasted almonds to nibble on and a sprinkling of chopped chives or dill as a garnish.

1	cucumber, peeled, seeded, and finely chopped	1
1	cucumber, unpeeled, seeded, and finely chopped	1
4 cups	buttermilk	1 l
1 cup	sour cream	250 ml
¼ cup	chopped fresh parsley	50 ml
¼ cup	chopped fresh dill	50 ml
1 tsp	salt	5 ml
few dashes	hot pepper sauce	few dashes
	chopped chives	

1. In a bowl combine cucumber, buttermilk, sour cream, parsley, dill, salt, and hot pepper sauce. Chill at least 2 hours.
2. Taste and adjust seasonings. Garnish each serving with chives.

Makes 7 cups (1.75 l).

CHILLED ZUCCHINI SOUP

My friends call this my summertime soup, and it must be served well chilled. I use my most colorful bowls as backgrounds for the pale green soup and float snipped chives on the top.

⅓ cup	sweet butter	75 ml
1 lb	zucchini (4 medium), thickly sliced	500 g
1	medium onion, coarsely chopped	1
1	clove garlic, coarsely chopped	1
1–2 tsp	curry powder	5–10 ml
1 tsp	ground cumin	5 ml
½ tsp	salt	2 ml
2 cups	chicken stock	500 ml
3 cups	buttermilk	750 ml
	paprika	

1. In a large saucepan heat butter. Add zucchini, onion, and garlic; sauté for 15 minutes.
2. Stir in curry powder, cumin, and salt. Cook 5 minutes longer, or until zucchini is softened. Stir in chicken stock.
3. In a food processor or blender, in batches, purée mixture until smooth.
4. Pour into a large bowl. Stir in buttermilk. Chill.
   Serve in chilled bowls or mugs. Garnish with sprinkling of paprika.

Makes 6 servings.

SALAD DAYS

FESTIVE LUNCHEONS

Misted leaves of lettuce, blushing radishes, glistening cucumbers, gold and white spears of endive. These fresh and delicate gems have an attraction all their own, and most good cooks know how to handle them.

Keep it simple, keep it fresh. Most of my salad recipes are geared to more than a supporting role, either as a main course for lunch or an individual course. So let's start with a biggie.

CAPONATA

This is a difficult dish to categorize. It can be a lunch or an exciting first course for a big dinner when served with Garlic Bread, or a tempting bowl of mystery for an hors d'oeuvre buffet.

4 lb	eggplant, peeled and cut into ½ inch (1 cm) cubes	2 kg
2 tbs	salt	25 ml
1 cup	olive oil	250 ml
4	stalks celery, coarsely chopped	4
3	medium onions, coarsely chopped	3
2	cloves garlic, finely chopped	2
2	cans (28 oz/796 ml each) Italian plum tomatoes	2
⅔ cup	balsamic vinegar	150 ml
2 tbs	granulated sugar	25 ml
2 tbs	tomato paste	25 ml
10	pitted green olives, thinly sliced	10
¼ cup	drained capers	50 ml
1	can (1.75 oz/50 g) anchovy fillets, drained	1
½ tsp	freshly ground black pepper	2 ml

1. In a bowl, sprinkle eggplant cubes with 1 tbs (15 ml) salt and set aside for 30 minutes. Drain and pat dry with paper towel.
2. In a large saucepan or Dutch oven, heat ½ cup (125 ml) olive oil. Add celery; cook, stirring 10 minutes, until limp.
3. Add onions and garlic; cook 10 minutes, or until onions are softened.
4. With slotted spoon, remove vegetables from skillet; place in a bowl and set aside. Add remaining oil to skillet. Add eggplant cubes and cook, stirring, 10 minutes, or until lightly browned.
5. Return celery mixture to skillet. Stir in tomatoes, vinegar, sugar, tomato paste, olives, and capers.
6. With a fork, mash anchovies and stir into saucepan. Stir in remaining salt and pepper. Bring mixture to a boil, reduce heat, and simmer, stirring frequently for 20 minutes, until thickened but still chunky.
7. Refrigerate and serve cold.

Makes 20 servings.

DILLY SEAFOOD SPINACH FETTUCINE

The green of the spinach fettucine and the fresh touch of dill give this salad a look and a taste that make luncheon guests ask for seconds. Make a little extra because it is that appetizing.

Serve for a leisurely summer lunch with many glasses of cool, white wine.

½ lb	peeled small raw shrimp	250 g
¼ lb	bay scallops	125 g
1 lb	fresh spinach fettucine	500 g
few drops	olive oil	few drops
3	fresh ripe tomatoes, peeled, seeded, and coarsely chopped	3
3	green onions, chopped	3
½ tsp	salt	2 ml
½ tsp	freshly ground black pepper	2 ml
	juice of ½ lemon	
⅓ cup	vegetable oil	75 ml
2 tbs	finely chopped fresh parsley	25 ml
2 tbs	finely chopped fresh dill	25 ml
2	cloves garlic, finely chopped	2

1. In a pot of salted boiling water, cook shrimp and scallops for about 3 minutes, until shrimp are pink. Remove and drain. Plunge into cold water to stop the cooking.
2. In a large pot of salted boiling water, cook fettucine about 10 minutes, until al dente. Drain well. Add olive oil and toss through pasta to prevent from sticking.

3. In a large bowl, combine shrimp, scallops, pasta, tomatoes, onions, salt, pepper, lemon juice, oil, parsley, dill, and garlic. Toss together.
4. Refrigerate about 2 hours to chill thoroughly.

Makes 4 servings.

PASTA SALAD PRIMAVERA

This pasta is bright, colorful, and alive with fresh garden flavors.
I serve it all summer long with slivers of prosciutto ham, a pepper mill, and a large chunk of Parmesan for those who want to grate extra on this delicious dish.
For a special touch, serve with Garlic Bread hot from the oven.

2 tbs	sweet butter	25 ml
2	shallots, minced	2
¼ cup	fresh green peas	50 ml
1	medium zucchini, cut in julienne strips	1
2	medium carrots, cut in julienne strips	2
1	large tomato, seeds and liquid removed, diced	1
¼ cup	dry white wine	50 ml
½ lb	spaghettini noodles	250 g

1. In a small skillet heat butter; add shallots, sauté over low heat for 2 minutes. Add peas, zucchini, carrots, tomatoes, and wine. Cook 5 minutes.
2. In a large pot of salted boiling water, cook noodles for 6 minutes, or until al dente. Drain thoroughly.
3. In a large salad bowl, combine noodles and vegetable mixture.

DRESSING:

¼ cup	mayonnaise	50 ml
¼ cup	olive oil	50 ml
¼ cup	chopped fresh parsley	50 ml
1	clove garlic, finely chopped	1
1 tsp	white wine	5 ml
1 tsp	dried oregano	5 ml
1 tsp	dried basil	5 ml
½ tsp	salt	2 ml
¼ tsp	freshly ground black pepper	1 ml
	juice and rind of 1 lemon	

GARNISH:

2 tbs	grated Parmesan cheese	25 ml
2	slices prosciutto ham, sliced thinly	2

1. In a blender or food processor, combine mayonnaise, olive oil, parsley, garlic, wine, oregano, basil, salt, pepper, lemon juice and rind. Process 1 minute, until mixture forms a smooth sauce.
2. Pour dressing over noodle-vegetable mixture; toss gently. Refrigerate.

At serving time sprinkle generously with Parmesan cheese and garnish with prosciutto ham.

Makes 4 servings.

For a springtime patio lunch, fill a six-inch rose bowl with Grape Hyacinth and place it on a round bed of Galax leaves in the center of a round table with a white linen tablecloth.

Tuck a single stem of the Grape Hyacinth between each silver napkin ring and a crisp white linen napkin.

SALMON SEVICHE IN TOMATO CUPS

Before you say, "Oh God, it's raw," remember that marinating is a very slow form of cooking. So think of this as you would smoked salmon.

I serve the Seviche in tomato cups and mixed with the chopped tomato innards. Then I garnish the serving plate with slices of avocado for an elegant and unusual spring lunch.

1 lb	salmon fillet, cut into 2 inch (5 cm) cubes	500 g
	juice of 2 limes	
6	green onions, chopped	6
2	ripe tomatoes, peeled, seeded, and chopped	2
⅓ cup	olive oil	75 ml
1 tsp	salt	5 ml
½ tsp	freshly ground black pepper	2 ml
½ tsp	ground oregano	2 ml

1. In a large bowl, combine salmon and lime juice. Let stand in refrigerator 1 hour.
2. Stir in onions, tomatoes, oil, salt, pepper, and oregano. Toss gently.

Makes 4 to 6 servings.

DILLED CHICKEN SALAD

This chicken salad is a bright and beautiful alternative to the mayonnaise variety that usually turns up at table. Garnish it with fresh cantaloupe slices and a handful of fresh mint leaves.

The dressing is what really helps make this dish. It can also do great things for fresh green vegetables cooked al dente: asparagus, young green beans, snow peas, or broccoli.

For a variation to this dilly dressing, substitute half a teaspoon of curry powder.

2 cups	cooked, diced chicken (4 large half-breasts)	500 ml
1 cup	broccoli florets	250 ml
2 cups	thinly sliced water chestnuts, *or* jicama, julienne sliced	500 ml
10	green onions, coarsely chopped (¾ cup/175 ml)	10
1 cup	halved seedless green grapes (about ¼ lb/125 g)	250 ml

1. In a large salad bowl, combine chicken, broccoli, water chestnuts, green onions, and grapes.

DRESSING:

1 cup	sour cream	250 ml
2 tbs	soy sauce	25 ml
1 tsp	sesame oil	5 ml
8–10 drops	hot pepper sauce	8–10 drops
	white pepper to taste	
2 tbs	chopped fresh dill, or 2 tsp (10 ml) dried dill	25 ml

GARNISH:

cantaloupe slices and fresh mint

1. In a small bowl, combine sour cream, soy sauce, sesame oil, hot pepper sauce, and pepper to taste. Stir in dill.
2. Pour over chicken mixture; toss gently to combine. Chill 1 hour before serving.
   Garnish with peeled cantaloupe slices and fresh mint.

Makes 6 servings.

CHINESE CHICKEN SALAD IN A LETTUCE LEAF

This is like an egg roll, but the roll is a romaine lettuce leaf, and that makes it crunchy.

You can substitute fresh shrimp for the chicken if you would rather have a seafood salad.

I also like to serve this as a first course with my Gingered Oriental Fish.

2	boneless and skinless chicken breasts, cooked and chopped	1 kg
1 lb	bean sprouts	500 g
1	head lettuce, shredded	1
3	large carrots, shredded	3

1. In a large salad bowl, combine chicken, sprouts, lettuce, and carrots.

DRESSING:

1	clove garlic, finely chopped	1
2 tbs	chopped fresh mint or 2 tsp (10 ml) dried	25 ml
	juice of 3 lemons	
⅓ cup	water	75 ml
2 tbs	sesame oil	25 ml
½ tsp	red pepper flakes	2 ml
1 tbs	granulated sugar	15 ml
10 to 12	romaine lettuce leaves	10 to 12

1. Combine garlic, mint, lemon juice, water, sesame oil, pepper flakes, and sugar. Pour over chicken mixture. Toss to mix thoroughly.
2. Wash romaine and pat dry. Spoon salad onto romaine leaves, roll up to serve.

Makes 10 to 12 servings.

FRIED CHICKEN SALAD WITH CASHEWS

In addition to being a festive lunch salad, this makes a wonderful light supper for after-theater parties, or even for summer dinner parties when you want something not too heavy because of the heat.

For that summer dinner, serve it with a cold soup beforehand and a fluffy lemony dessert to follow.

3	whole chicken breasts, boned, skinned, and cut into ½ inch (1 cm) strips	3
⅓ cup	milk	75 ml
	all-purpose flour, salt, and pepper to dredge	
¼ cup	sesame oil	50 ml
2 tbs	tarragon vinegar	25 ml
1 tsp	soy sauce	5 ml
1 tbs	Dijon mustard	15 ml
1	shallot, finely chopped	1
½ cup	thinly sliced button mushrooms	125 ml
1	head curly endive, washed and leaves torn apart	1
2 cups	cherry tomatoes	500 ml
1	purple onion, thinly sliced and separated into rings	1
½ cup	whole cashews	125 ml

1. Dip chicken strips in milk; dredge in flour mixture.
2. In a medium-size skillet, heat oil. Fry strips about 7 minutes, until golden brown; remove and drain on paper towel.
3. Add vinegar to skillet and scrape to deglaze.
4. Pour into a bowl, add soy sauce and mustard; mix well. Stir in shallots and mushrooms and toss to coat.
5. Divide endive and tomatoes evenly onto 6 plates.
6. To serve, pour mushroom mixture over lettuce and tomatoes. Garnish with fried chicken, onion rings, and cashews.

Makes 6 servings.

STEAK SALAD

Admonition! Start with fine beef steaks. Use any cut, but don't attempt to do this with leftover steak or roasts.

2 tbs	soy sauce	25 ml
1 tbs	vegetable oil	15 ml
1	clove garlic, finely chopped	1
¼ tsp	freshly ground black pepper	1 ml
1 lb	sirloin steak	500 g
2	large red potatoes boiled with skins on, coarsely chopped	2
1	medium red onion, cut in rings	1
1	red pepper, thinly sliced	1
½ cup	cooked peas	125 ml
¼ cup	chopped Italian parsley	50 ml
½ cup	Classic Dressing (recipe page 106)	125 ml

1. In a small bowl, combine soy sauce, oil, garlic, and pepper. Brush over both sides of steak; marinate overnight in refrigerator. Remove steak from marinade.
2. Grill, broil, or barbecue steak for 3 to 4 minutes on each side, until rare. Cut diagonally, across the grain, into thin slices.
3. In a large bowl, combine hot steak slices, potatoes, onion, pepper, peas, and parsley.
4. Pour dressing over top and toss well to coat.

Makes 6 to 8 servings.

HOT CHÈVRE AND LAMB SALAD

This is an elegant and delicious luncheon salad. If your greengrocer doesn't have the lettuce varieties I suggest, then substitute your own favorites.
The recipe itself came from Jamie Kennedy, one of the great chefs of Toronto. He created it with me when I needed an elegant luncheon for twelve.

¾ lb	boned and trimmed loin or leg of lamb	350 g

MARINADE:

1 cup	olive oil	250 ml
2	cloves garlic, finely chopped	2
	grated rind of ½ lemon	
2	sprigs fresh rosemary, or ½ tsp (2 ml) dried	2
½ tsp	salt	2 ml
	coarsely ground black pepper	
5 or 6	juniper berries, crushed	5 or 6

SALAD:

4	bunches mache (lamb's lettuce)	4
1	head bibb lettuce	1
1	radicchio	1
¼	head curly endive	¼
2 tbs	olive oil	25 ml
	juice of ½ lemon	
pinch	salt	pinch

DRESSING:

⅓ lb	goat cheese	170 g
½ cup	heavy or whipping cream	125 ml
	juice of ½ lemon	
	freshly ground black pepper	

Place lamb in a glass dish.

To make Marinade: Combine olive oil, garlic, lemon rind, rosemary, salt, pepper, and juniper berries. Pour over lamb. Cover and marinate overnight in refrigerator.

To make Salad: Prepare salad greens, tearing into pieces, dry well, and chill.

To make Dressing: Crumble cheese into a bowl; combine with cream, lemon juice, and pepper; mix well.

To assemble:

1. Combine salad greens. Sprinkle with oil, lemon juice, and salt; toss to coat greens. Portion salad onto 4 plates.
2. Remove lamb from marinade; pat dry. Strain marinade and reserve. Cut lamb across the grain in 12 slices and pound flat.
3. In a large skillet heat 2 tbs (25 ml) reserved marinade. Add lamb slices; sauté quickly, until lightly seared and slightly pink.
4. Place 3 slices on top of each salad. Top with dressing and season with freshly grated black pepper.
   Serve immediately.

Makes 4 servings.

COUSCOUS SALAD

Years ago, it seems, all my children wanted to visit North Africa and the fabled cities of their dreams. One did and brought back couscous (which of course was already available in the gourmet stores here). So here we go with the Couscous Salad Joanna evolved.

1 cup	boiling water	250 ml
1 cup	couscous	250 ml
6 tbs	olive oil	90 ml
3 tbs	lemon juice	45 ml
¼ tsp	salt	1 ml
⅛ tsp	white pepper	0.5 ml
3	tomatoes, peeled, seeded, and coarsely chopped	3
¼ cup	chopped fresh parsley	50 ml
¼ cup	chopped fresh mint	50 ml
2	green onions, thinly sliced	2
½	English cucumber, coarsely chopped	½
½ cup	pitted black olives, sliced	125 ml

1. In a large bowl pour boiling water over couscous; stir well. Let stand 5 minutes, until all water is absorbed.
2. Combine oil, lemon juice, salt, and pepper; mix well.
3. Stir couscous with a fork and blend in 1 tbs (15 ml) lemon juice and oil dressing.
4. Add tomatoes, parsley, mint, green onions, and cucumber. Pour on remaining dressing and toss to mix well. Chill for 1 hour. At serving time, stir in olives.

Makes 6 servings.

POSITIVE POWER SALAD

A few years back my husband gave me a week in a spa: Canyon Ranch in Arizona. I came back with muscles firmed up, and with this recipe.

I served this to a crowd of 3,000 people at a political luncheon, and was thanked royally for the change from the traditional.

Jicama is usually available in smart supermarkets, Mexican grocers, or Chinese fruit markets.

⅓ cup	sunflower seeds	75 ml
2 cups	coarsely chopped broccoli	500 ml
2 cups	thinly sliced mushrooms	500 ml
1½ cups	coarsely chopped cauliflower	375 ml
1½ cups	diced jicama	375 ml
1 cup	diced carrots	250 ml
½ cup	diced yellow squash	125 ml
½ cup	diced zucchini	125 ml
½ cup	alfalfa sprouts	125 ml
¼ cup	finely chopped green onion tops	50 ml
2	apples, diced	2
½ cup	raisins	125 ml
½ cup	coarsely chopped almonds	125 ml
1 cup	diced Mozzarella cheese	250 ml
¼ cup	Canyon Ranch Dressing	50 ml

1. In a pan, toast sunflower seeds in a 325°F (160°C) oven for 8 to 10 minutes, until lightly browned.
2. In a large salad bowl, combine broccoli, mushrooms, cauliflower, jicama, carrots, squash, zucchini, sprouts, green onions, apples, raisins, almonds, and cheese.
3. Pour dressing over top and toss thoroughly. Sprinkle sunflower seeds on top.

Makes 8 servings.

CANYON RANCH DRESSING

½ cup	red wine vinegar	125 ml
¼ cup	vegetable oil	50 ml
2	cloves garlic, finely chopped	2
1 tbs	Dijon mustard	15 ml
2 tsp	granulated sugar	10 ml
2 tsp	Worcestershire sauce	10 ml
1½ tsp	dried tarragon	7 ml
1 tsp	dried basil	5 ml
¾ tsp	dried oregano	4 ml
¾ tsp	salt	4 ml
	juice of ½ lemon	
1 cup	water	250 ml

1. In a blender or food processor, combine vinegar, oil, garlic, mustard, sugar, Worcestershire sauce, tarragon, basil, oregano, salt, and lemon juice. Process using an on/off motion for 1 minute, until well blended. Add water and mix well.
2. Refrigerate in a jar with a tight-fitting lid 24 hours to allow the flavor to develop before using. Will keep for up to 2 weeks. Shake before serving.

Makes 2 cups (500 ml).

INDONESIAN BROWN RICE SALAD WITH TAMARI SAUCE

A hearty and satisfying salad that can become a lunch if you add a soup to the menu. Gazpacho or Clear Tomato Soup goes best with this.
   The raisins and nuts give this salad an exotic taste.
   Serve with thick slices of whole wheat bread and plenty of whipped butter in individual pots.

1 cup	brown rice	250 ml
1¾ cup	boiling water	425 ml
½ cup	raisins	125 ml
2	green onions, chopped	2
¼ cup	toasted sesame seeds*	50 ml
1 cup	fresh bean sprouts	250 ml
1 cup	toasted cashews*	250 ml
1	large green pepper, coarsely chopped	1
1	stalk celery, sliced diagonally	1
2 tbs	chopped fresh parsley	25 ml
	lettuce	

1. In a large saucepan combine rice with water. Cook over medium heat 30 minutes. Drain and let cool.
2. In a bowl combine rice, raisins, onions, sesame seeds, bean sprouts, cashews, green pepper, celery, and parsley. Toss thoroughly.

*See toasting instructions, p. 120.

DRESSING:

¼ cup	fresh orange juice	50 ml
½ cup	vegetable oil	125 ml
1 tbs	sesame oil	15 ml
¼ cup	Tamari Sauce	50 ml
2 tbs	dry sherry	25 ml
	juice of 1 lime	
1	clove garlic, finely chopped	1
1 tsp	grated fresh ginger root	5 ml
	salt and freshly ground black pepper to taste	

1. Into a blender or food processor, measure orange juice, oils, Tamari Sauce, sherry, lime juice, garlic, and ginger root. Process until smooth. Season with salt and pepper to taste.
2. Pour over salad and toss. Chill about 2 hours. Serve on a bed of lettuce.

Makes 10 to 12 servings.

TAMARI SAUCE

⅓ cup	lard or shortening	75 ml
1	clove garlic, finely chopped	1
¼ cup	soy sauce	50 ml
2 tbs	tamarind pulp*	25 ml
1 tbs	water	15 ml
1 tsp	granulated sugar	5 ml

1. In a small saucepan melt lard. Add garlic and cook until browned.
2. Stir in soy sauce, tamarind pulp, water, and sugar. Cook over low heat for 5 minutes, until just thickened. Remove from heat; cool.

Makes about ⅔ cup (150 ml).

*Tamarind pulp is available at Chinese specialty stores.

HOT CHÈVRE SALAD WITH BACON

A splendid Toronto restaurant named Auberge Gavroche has served this goat cheese salad to me so many times I think they had the recipe written out in anticipation of my requesting it. It stands alone at lunch and is also an elegant and delicious dish to serve for a formal dinner party.

2 oz	slab bacon, diced	50 g
1	head leaf lettuce	1
1	head radicchio	1
1	bunch watercress	1
2	Belgian endives	2
2	ripe tomatoes	2
2 tbs	Raspberry Vinegar (recipe p. 149)	25 ml
⅓ cup	olive oil	75 ml
	salt, freshly ground black pepper, and chopped chives	
⅔ lb	goat cheese	170 g
18	thin slices French stick, about 2 inches (5 cm) in diameter	18
⅓ cup	heavy or whipping cream	75 ml

1. Preheat oven to 350°F (180°C).
2. In a skillet, sauté bacon until crisp. Drain bacon bits on paper towel and keep warm.
3. Wash and trim lettuce, radicchio, watercress, and endives. Cut tomatoes into thin wedges. Arrange all attractively on 6 plates.
4. Combine vinegar, oil, salt, pepper, and chives to taste, whisk together, and pour over salads.
5. Cut cheese in 18 slices and arrange on bread slices. Place on a baking sheet. Spoon 1 tsp (5 ml) heavy cream over each piece. Bake 5 to 7 minutes, until melted.
6. Place 3 cheese toasts on each salad. Sprinkle with bacon bits. Serve immediately.

Makes 6 servings.

SIDE SALADS

CHEESE SALAD WITH ENDIVE

There are only a few months of the year when Belgian endive is not available in North America.

This comes with its own vinaigrette and makes an excellent salad almost year round.

6	Belgian endives	6
¼ lb	Bel Paese* cheese, cubed (1 cup/250 ml)	125 g
⅓ cup	olive oil	75 ml
1 tbs	lemon juice	15 ml
1 tbs	red wine vinegar	15 ml
½ tsp	salt	2 ml
¼ tsp	freshly ground black pepper	1 ml
¼ tsp	dried oregano leaves	1 ml
	Italian parsley	

1. With a sharp knife slice endive crosswise into 1 inch (2.5 cm) pieces. In a bowl, combine endive and cheese.
2. Combine oil, lemon juice, vinegar, salt, pepper, and oregano; mix well. Pour over endive and cheese. Toss lightly. Divide evenly and spoon onto 4 salad plates.
   Garnish with sprigs of Italian parsley.

Makes 4 servings.

*Fontina cheese may be substituted for Bel Paese, if desired.

> *Bunches of fresh lilacs off the tree, in a stoneware washing pitcher, fill the room with a beautiful fragrance and remind us spring is here.*

SALAD ROMANO (OR LOCARNO?)

I pose the question because this salad owes its personality to Swiss cheese. You can substitute an Italian cheese, but I find the Gruyère a perfect salad ingredient.

This is a hearty year-round salad, and I find myself using it for parties in the snowy months, for the mushrooms, celery, and cheese give that nice stick-to-the-ribs consistency.

½ lb	Gruyère cheese, cut in julienne strips	250 g
2	stalks celery, thinly sliced	2
½ lb	fresh mushrooms, thinly sliced	250 g
¼ cup	chopped fresh parsley	50 ml
2 tbs	Tarragon Vinaigrette	25 ml

1. In a large salad bowl toss together cheese, celery, mushrooms, and parsley. Pour Tarragon Vinaigrette on top; toss well.
2. Let stand 15 minutes before serving; toss again.

Makes 6 servings.

TARRAGON VINAIGRETTE

One of the most prized and surprising tastes in the world comes from tarragon. It is used for many things, especially for tarragon chicken and for flavoring salad dressings. Here's the definitive vinaigrette to round out your year-round dressings.

½ cup	chopped fresh parsley	125 ml
½ cup	olive oil	125 ml
⅓ cup	wine vinegar	75 ml
¼ cup	chopped capers	50 ml
1 tbs	chopped fresh tarragon, or 1 tsp (5 ml) dried	15 ml
2 tsp	Dijon mustard	10 ml
2 tsp	salt	10 ml
1 tsp	freshly ground black pepper	5 ml
1	clove garlic, finely chopped	1
1 tsp	Worcestershire sauce	5 ml

1. In a jar with a tight-fitting lid, combine parsley, oil, vinegar, capers, tarragon, mustard, salt, pepper, garlic, and Worcestershire sauce. Secure lid; shake well.
2. Store in refrigerator up to 2 weeks. Shake well before using.

Makes 1 cup (250 ml).

MEDITERRANEAN MENU

SALAD ROMANO
with Tarragon Vinaigrette

POULET AUX DEUX MOUTARDES

GREEN RICE

CHILLED PRUNES IN MULLED WINE

FRENCH ORANGE CAKE

BEET MOLD

I tend to shy away from jellied molds, but this one is a beautiful color, and it unmolds perfectly every time.
Looks great as part of a buffet dinner.

1	envelope unflavored gelatin	1
¼ cup	cold water	50 ml
1 cup	boiling water	250 ml
⅔ cup	granulated sugar	150 ml
½ cup	lemon juice	125 ml
2 tbs	prepared horseradish	25 ml
1 tbs	vinegar	15 ml
½ tsp	salt	2 ml
¼ tsp	celery salt	1 ml
1 cup	finely chopped cabbage	250 ml
1 cup	finely chopped, cooked beets* (3 medium)	250 ml
1 cup	finely chopped celery	250 ml
3–4 drops	hot pepper sauce	3–4 drops
	shredded lettuce	

*To cook beets, trim, wash, and wrap each beet in foil. Bake in a 375°F (190°C) oven for 1 to 1½ hours, until tender. Cool and peel.

1. In a large bowl, soften gelatin in cold water. Add boiling water and stir until dissolved. Stir in sugar, lemon juice, horseradish, vinegar, salt, and celery salt. Chill until slightly thickened.
2. Fold in cabbage, beets, celery, and hot pepper sauce. Pour into 6 cup (1.5 l) mold; chill at least 4 hours, until firm.

To serve: Unmold onto serving plate. Garnish around mold with shredded lettuce.

Makes 8 servings.

BROCCOLI, BACON, AND MUSHROOM SALAD

This goes very well as a side salad with almost any kind of roast, or as a salad for a sandwich party. Imagine it with cold roast beef sandwiches on pumpernickel slathered with Sweet Russian Mustard.

3 cups	broccoli florets, steamed until tender crisp, cooled	750 ml
2 tbs	crumbled crisp bacon	25 ml
½ cup	thinly sliced mushrooms	125 ml

1. In a large bowl, combine broccoli, bacon, and mushrooms.

DRESSING:

½ cup	sour cream	125 ml
1 tsp	freshly ground black pepper	5 ml
1	clove garlic, finely chopped	1
½ tsp	Worcestershire sauce	2 ml
½ tsp	salt	2 ml

1. In a small bowl, combine sour cream, pepper, garlic, Worcestershire sauce, and salt; mix well.
2. Pour dressing over broccoli mixture; toss gently.
3. Refrigerate until serving time to chill thoroughly. Toss again before serving.

Makes 4 servings.

Use unusual branches in your large arrangements. They give motion, height, and excitement to any floral display.

CRUNCHY BROCCOLI SALAD

I find the wonderfully blue-green fresh broccoli in the market almost irresistible. Its wine, lemon, and sour cream dressing is light and delicate, making this a perfect salad to serve with a spicy main course.

2 lb	fresh broccoli, florets and stems, cut into bite-size pieces	1 kg
1	lemon	1
¾ tsp	freshly ground black pepper	3 ml

1. In a large pot of salted boiling water, cook broccoli 2 minutes, until tender but firm. Drain and rinse immediately with ice cold water. Drain and spread on paper towel to dry. Sprinkle with juice of 1 lemon and pepper. Place in a salad bowl.

DRESSING:

½ cup	dry white wine	125 ml
3	shallots, minced	3
1½ cups	mayonnaise (recipe p. 227)	375 ml
1 tbs	chopped chives or parsley	15 ml

1. In a small saucepan combine wine and shallots. Reduce until about 3 tbs (45 ml) remain.
2. In a small bowl combine mayonnaise, chives, and shallot mixture.
3. Pour over broccoli. Toss gently.
4. Refrigerate 2 hours before serving. Toss again and serve.

Makes 6 to 8 servings.

PEPPERBLAST COLESLAW

Joanna, the elder of my two daughters, achieved a Cordon Bleu diploma in London. This is her own coleslaw creation, which is very hot, very crunchy, and shocking to guests who aren't prepared.

4 cups	shredded white cabbage	1 l
4 cups	shredded purple cabbage	1 l
4	green onions, coarsely chopped	4
2	carrots, peeled and diced	2
1	yellow pepper, coarsely chopped	1
1	red pepper, coarsely chopped	1
1	green pepper, coarsely chopped	1
1	red chili pepper, seeded and thinly sliced	1
4 tbs	chopped fresh basil	50 ml

In a large bowl combine white and purple cabbage, onions, carrots, yellow, red, and green peppers, chili pepper, and basil; toss well.

DRESSING:

½ cup	sour cream	125 ml
½ cup	mayonnaise (recipe p. 227)	125 ml
1	clove garlic, finely chopped	1
½ tsp	chili powder	2 ml
pinch	cayenne pepper	pinch

1. In a bowl combine sour cream, mayonnaise, garlic, chili powder, and cayenne; mix well. Pour over vegetables and toss.
2. Chill 20 to 30 minutes or overnight before serving.

Makes 10 to 12 servings.

RED AND GREEN ROASTED PEPPERS AND OLIVES

This could be a salad, an antipasto or a pasta sauce. I placed it here because I first tasted it as a salad in a Greek household. Since then I have served it both hot and cold.

3	large red peppers	3
3	large green peppers	3
1 tsp	salt	5 ml
½ cup	olive oil	125 ml
1½ cups	pitted black olives	375 ml
2	cloves garlic, minced	2
6	anchovy fillets, minced	6

1. Preheat broiler.
2. Broil peppers as close to heat as possible, until skins turn black on all sides. Transfer to a bag and seal. Allow peppers to sweat for 30 minutes.
3. Pull off skins; cut peppers into narrow strips, discarding seeds and fibers. Sprinkle with salt.
4. In a skillet, heat oil. Add peppers and sauté for 2 minutes. Stir in olives, garlic, and anchovies; cook 2 minutes longer, until peppers are coated. Serve hot or cold.

Makes 6 to 12 servings as part of an antipasto tray.

CUCUMBER SPINACH RAITA

Keep this recipe in mind for any menu in which the main dishes are apt to be more than ordinarily spicy. Indian or Tex-Mex particularly. It is light and refreshing to the palate.

1	English cucumber	1
2	green onions, finely chopped	2
1 cup	packed fresh spinach leaves	250 ml
1 tsp	salt	5 ml
2	cloves garlic, finely chopped	2
2 tbs	chopped fresh parsley	25 ml
½ tsp	ground cumin	2 ml
⅛ tsp	freshly ground black pepper	0.5 ml
1 cup	plain yogurt	250 ml
	paprika	

1. Cut cucumbers lengthwise into halves; scoop out seeds.
2. In a blender or food processor with an on/off motion chop cucumbers, onions, and spinach. Transfer to a bowl, add salt, and let stand 10 minutes.
3. Add garlic, parsley, cumin, and pepper; toss with cucumber mixture.
4. Cover and refrigerate at least 1 hour. Drain thoroughly. Just before serving fold in yogurt.
Garnish with a sprinkling of paprika.

Makes 6 servings.

DILLY CUCUMBERS AND RED ONIONS

I make this salad frequently.

My family likes it best when I drain off the marinade and fold in the sour cream. Usually I don't do this unless I'm serving it with curry, but they'll eat it with anything.

| 1 | English cucumber, cut into ¼ inch (5 mm) slices | 1 |
| 1 | red onion, thinly sliced | 1 |

In a bowl, combine cucumber and onion.

MARINADE:

½ cup	white vinegar	125 ml
¼ cup	water	50 ml
¼ cup	granulated sugar	50 ml
2 tbs	vegetable oil	25 ml
1 tbs	chopped fresh dill, or 1 tsp (5 ml) dried dill weed	15 ml
1 tsp	salt	5 ml
¼ tsp	white pepper	1 ml

1. In a small bowl, combine vinegar, water, sugar, oil, dill, salt, and pepper. Pour over cucumber mixture; toss to coat thoroughly.
2. Chill for at least 2 hours, stirring occasionally.

Makes 4 to 6 servings.

VARIATION:

Creamed Dilly Cucumber and Onions: Thoroughly drain marinade from cucumber mixture, then fold in ½ cup (125 ml) sour cream or yogurt. To serve, sprinkle with chopped dill.

MARINATED GREEN BEAN SALAD

Use the tenderest, greenest, youngest beans you can find, and put them in the tomato sauce marinade for one or two days.

When they are ready, you have a salad that adds immeasurably to an antipasto buffet or as the first course of a pasta dinner.

| 1 lb | green beans, trimmed | 500 g |

In a saucepan of lightly salted boiling water, blanch beans for 2 minutes. With a slotted spoon, remove to a bowl of ice water and chill thoroughly.

MARINADE:

1 cup	Tomato Sauce (recipe p. 340)	250 ml
½ tsp	cinnamon	2 ml
¼ tsp	nutmeg	1 ml
pinch	ground allspice	pinch
pinch	ground cloves	pinch

1. In a bowl combine Tomato Sauce, cinnamon, nutmeg, allspice, and cloves; mix well.
2. Drain beans thoroughly. Pour the sauce over beans. Toss gently to coat.
3. Cover and refrigerate 1 to 2 hours before serving. Toss again and serve.

Makes 4 to 6 servings.

CAULIFLOWER SALAD (INSALAT RINFORZATA)

The olives and anchovies make this so Italian I had to give you its Roman name. It's another variation for your antipasto plate and a natural to serve with any pasta dinner or lunch.

1	head cauliflower, separated into florets	1
2	cans (1.75 oz/50 g each) anchovy fillets, drained and chopped	2
1 cup	sliced pimento-stuffed olives	250 ml
1 tbs	drained capers	15 ml
¾ cup	olive oil	175 ml
2 tbs	lemon juice	25 ml
¼ tsp	freshly ground black pepper	1 ml

1. In a large pot of salted boiling water, cook cauliflower florets about 6 minutes, until tender but firm. Drain and cool.
2. In a bowl, combine cauliflower, anchovies, olives, and capers; toss gently.
3. In a small bowl, combine oil, lemon juice, and pepper. Pour over cauliflower mixture; toss again.
4. Refrigerate 2 hours before serving.

Makes 4 to 6 servings.

TUSCAN BEAN SALAD

This salad owes what it has as much to the kind of bean used as it does to the inclusion of onions, parsley, olive oil, and spices.
Serve it to your guests with a lamb roast or a Chicken Saag.

1½ cups	dried white beans	375 ml
½ cup	olive oil	125 ml
2 cups	thinly sliced onions	500 ml
1½ tsp	salt	7 ml
½ tsp	freshly ground black pepper	2 ml
2 tbs	minced parsley	25 ml

1. Wash beans. Put in a saucepan, cover with cold water, and bring to a boil. Remove from heat; cover and let soak 1 hour. Drain.
2. Cover with fresh water and bring to boil. Reduce heat, cover, and simmer 1½ hours, or until tender. Drain.
3. In a skillet heat oil. Add onions, sauté about 10 minutes, until light brown. Remove from heat and combine with beans, salt, and pepper.
4. Transfer to glass bowl. Chill at least 2 hours, preferably overnight.
5. Sprinkle with parsley and serve cold.

Makes 6 to 8 servings.

CUCUMBER SALAD WITH SPICY DRESSING

The excitement of this recipe is in the dressing. The interesting combination of Oriental and North American spices gives these cucumbers a special kick.

2	medium cucumbers	2
2 tbs	white vinegar	25 ml
1 tbs	sugar	15 ml
2 tsp	sesame oil	10 ml
1 tsp	soy sauce	5 ml
1 tsp	salt	5 ml
½ tsp	hot pepper sauce	2 ml

1. Peel cucumbers and cut lengthwise in two. Scrape out seeds; cut crosswise into ¼ inch (5 mm) slices.
2. In a small bowl combine vinegar, sugar, sesame oil, soy sauce, salt, and hot pepper sauce. Add cucumber. Toss to coat each slice.
3. Chill before serving.

Makes 4 to 6 servings.

RED ONION SALAD

Guests who swear they can't stand onions start with a nibble and keep on taking more. The anchovies make it right for an Italian meal, and the olives give it an added zip.

Make lots. It also doubles as an antipasto.

4	large red onions, peeled and thinly sliced	4
2 tsp	salt	10 ml
⅓ cup	olive oil	75 ml
2 tbs	lemon juice	25 ml
8	anchovy fillets, coarsely chopped	8
¼ cup	sliced, pitted black olives	50 ml

1. In a large bowl combine onions and salt. Cover with ice water and a few ice cubes. Let stand 30 minutes.
2. Drain and dry onions on paper towel. Place in a salad bowl, sprinkle with olive oil and lemon juice. Stir in anchovies and olives.
3. Cover and refrigerate until serving time.

Makes 6 to 8 servings.

HOT AND SPICY POTATO SALAD

Like the nonmayonnaise chicken salad, this is a welcome change for guests. The dressing also is perfect with fresh green salads, like young beans when they first appear in the market, snappy and full of moisture.

12	small red potatoes with skins, cooked until just tender	12
2 lb	fresh green beans, stems removed, cut in half diagonally	1 kg
1	medium jicama or Chinese radish, julienne-cut	1
2 cups	ripe, pitted black olives, sliced	500 ml
12	green onions, finely chopped, or 1 large red onion separated into rings	12

1. Cut cooked potatoes in half.
2. In a steamer basket over boiling water steam green beans about 4 minutes, until tender crisp; then plunge them immediately into cold water and drain thoroughly.
3. In a large bowl, combine potatoes, beans, jicama, olives, and green onions. Chill about 2 hours.

DRESSING:

⅔ cup	olive oil	150 ml
⅓ cup	sherry	75 ml
¼ cup	cider vinegar	50 ml
½ cup	crumbled Gorgonzola or blue cheese	125 ml
½ tsp	Worcestershire sauce	2 ml
½ tsp	salt	2 ml
¼ tsp	coarsely ground black pepper	1 ml
1	can (1.75 oz/50 g) anchovy fillets with their oil drained	1

In a blender or food processor combine oil, sherry, vinegar, cheese, Worcestershire sauce, salt, pepper, and anchovy fillets. Process about 1 minute until smooth. Pour over chilled potato mixture. Toss gently to coat.

Makes 12 servings.

GARLIC BREAD

¼ lb	soft sweet butter	125 g
1	large clove garlic, minced	1
12	slices crusty French bread	12

1. Preheat oven to 350°F (180°C).
2. In a bowl, combine butter and garlic; beat with a fork. Spread on both sides of bread slices.
3. Stack slices and wrap with aluminum foil. Bake for 20 minutes, until piping hot.

Makes 12 servings.

FOUR MORE SPECIAL DRESSINGS

OUR OWN CAESAR SALAD DRESSING

Like Caesar's wife, your Caesar salad must be above reproach. It is a classic salad and too much of a departure from the recipe will turn it into something different. I have had Caesars with apples in them and raisins, too, but to me they were no longer Caesar salads. Just the dressing and the torn romaine lettuce—that's the classic.

2	anchovies, mashed	2
1	large clove garlic, finely chopped	1
¼ cup	imported olive oil	50 ml
1 tbs	white wine vinegar	15 ml
	juice of ½ lemon	
1	egg yolk	1
½ tsp	dry mustard	2 ml
½ tsp	Worcestershire sauce	2 ml
3 drops	hot pepper sauce	3 drops

In a jar with a tight-fitting lid, combine anchovies, garlic, oil, vinegar, lemon juice, yolk, mustard, Worcestershire sauce, and hot pepper sauce. Cover tightly; shake well.

Store in refrigerator for up to 1 week. Shake well before using.

Makes ½ cup (125 ml).

HEARTY TOMATO DRESSING

Don't shy away from this just because it calls for ketchup. When you taste it, you will find that it is a tomatoey, garlicky, totally satisfying vinaigrette. My family and friends ladle more on their salads every time I serve it, especially if the salad has lots of radish, tomato, and onion in it.

1 cup	olive oil	250 ml
½ cup	ketchup	125 ml
½ cup	malt vinegar	125 ml
½ cup	granulated sugar	125 ml
1½ tsp	salt	7 ml
1 tsp	grated onion	5 ml
1 tsp	Worcestershire sauce	5 ml
¼ tsp	ground cloves	1 ml
1	clove garlic, minced	1

1. In a blender or food processor combine oil, ketchup, vinegar, sugar, salt, onion, Worcestershire sauce, cloves, and garlic. Process until thick. (*Or,* combine in a bowl and beat with a rotary beater.)
2. Pour into a screw-top jar or bottle. Refrigerate for up to 2 weeks. Shake well before using.

Makes 2 cups (500 ml).

CLASSIC DRESSING

Ever since I got into the business of making and selling condiments, people have been after me for "The Perfect Salad Dressing." Well here it is!

You can vary it by changing some ingredients and adding others. For instance, Roquefort or anchovies (reduce the salt a little). Or use a straight wine vinegar and add snipped fresh herbs.

½ cup	light cream	125 ml
½ cup	vegetable oil	125 ml
¼ cup	olive oil	50 ml
¼ cup	tarragon or balsamic vinegar	50 ml
1	egg, beaten lightly	1
2 tsp	finely chopped garlic	10 ml
1½ tsp	salt	7 ml
1 tsp	freshly ground black pepper	5 ml
1 tsp	Dijon mustard	5 ml
1 tsp	fresh lemon juice	5 ml
½ tsp	dry mustard	2 ml
¼ tsp	sugar	1 ml

In a jar with a screw-top lid, combine cream, oils, vinegar, egg, garlic, salt, pepper, Dijon mustard, lemon juice, dry mustard, and sugar. Cover tightly; shake well and refrigerate for up to 2 weeks. Always shake before using.

Makes 2 cups (500 ml).

VARIATIONS:
Anchovy Dressing: Add 2 tbs (25 ml) finely chopped anchovies to Classic Dressing in place of salt.
Roquefort Dressing: Add 2 tbs (25 ml) crumbled Roquefort or blue cheese to Classic Dressing.
Herb Classic Dressing: Add 2 tbs (25 ml) fresh or 2 tsp (10 ml) dried chopped basil, dill, summer savory, parsley, alone or in combination.

LIME HONEY DRESSING FOR FRUIT SALADS

I serve this dressing in half a Spanish melon and spoon it onto the fruit salad with a white ceramic ladle.
A wedge of solid cheese such as Cheddar, and a hot blueberry muffin will round out a quick, light lunch.

1 cup	vegetable oil	250 ml
⅓ cup	lime juice	75 ml
⅓ cup	honey	75 ml
½ tsp	paprika	2 ml
½ tsp	salt	2 ml
½ tsp	prepared mustard	2 ml
	grated rind of 1 lime	
dash	hot pepper sauce	dash

In a blender or food processor combine oil, lime juice, honey, paprika, salt, mustard, lime rind, and hot pepper sauce. Blend until smooth. Pour into a screw-top jar or bottle. Refrigerate until needed. Serve on melons or mixture of fresh fruit.

Makes 1½ cups (325 ml).

THE MAIN EVENT

The Super Stars

It can be a sitdown, formal dinner with the elegance of the opera. It can be a buffet in the kitchen. It can be an outdoor barbecue with anything from Grilled Salmon to a Sloppy Joe. It can be your finest china and crystal or gaily painted pottery and beer steins. It can be a night at the symphony with beautifully blended and harmonized dishes or a pot luck dinner in the country that is like a farmers' fair. It can be anything your imagination runs to.

The thing to concentrate on is how you feel, what kind of dinner you want to put together, and then plan your dishes to carry the event.

How are you to dress your dishes? In a sizzling copper pan, direct from the heat? Floating on a platter of rich sauce and vegetables? In an elaborate casserole? It is so exciting, the possibilities so endless, that you almost don't know where to start.

I start by deciding on what the main dish will be.

I have thrown a party because I walked into a fish store and saw a deep sea bass that was so beautiful I had to share it. I have woken up on a winter morning with the snow coming down and the clouds lowering and felt an urge to have friends in for a dinner of roast lamb and fine red wine to accompany it. I have strolled into a supermarket in April and been overcome by the crispness of the salad fixings, the lushness of strawberries and rhubarb, and decided that it was time to build a salute to spring around a beautiful garlic chicken. Then I plan the presentation, the flower arrangements, the lighting— everything to add to the excitement of the event I have in mind.

TREASURES FROM LAKE, STREAM, AND SEA

My home town is on a lake. I often envy my friends who live on the Atlantic or Pacific coasts and have all that freshly caught seafood at their command.

On the other hand, you probably have good fresh fish stores dotted around your city. So if your nose is good and you know what to sniff for, you can achieve some really good fish dishes to dazzle your guests.

I find that fish dishes on their own are partyish, but if you want to do honor to old King Neptune with some special decorations, you can fill large shells with the salt and pepper.

Another trick is to use what I call beach flowers for your table: anemones or big African daisies. Use the anemones for the vibrant blues and purples and reds, the daisies for the pastels. Mixed together, they are striking.

You can drape your rooms with ropes and add bollards to the decor.

The seated dinner party is probably the most satisfying form of domestic entertainment. It appeals to all senses and produces that glowing spirit of good will which is the aim of social gatherings.

There is no substitute for linen napkins. When using a linen table-cloth, an underpad should also be used, not only to protect the table but also to muffle the sound of glasses and plates.

Candles are the most beautiful lighting you can use, but be sure that they supply adequate lighting. If the room is poorly lit, it gives an aura of gloom. Besides, people like to see what they are eating.

GINGERED FISH ORIENTALE

This fish looks just great intact on a platter. It can marinate all day if you wish and will improve with every passing moment. Once cooked, the meat drops away easily from the bones.

Serve it covered with lots of Stir-Fried Chinese Vegetables and a mass of soft Japanese noodles strewn with cilantro.

1	whole snapper (4–5 lbs/2–2.5 kg) with head, or any fresh fish	1
¼ cup	light soy sauce	50 ml
¼ cup	sesame oil	50 ml
¼ cup	dry sherry	50 ml
2 tbs	grated fresh ginger root	25 ml
⅛ tsp	crushed red pepper	0.5 ml
3	cloves garlic, finely chopped	3
4	green onion brushes*	4

1. In a large shallow baking dish, place fish. Combine soy sauce, sesame oil, sherry, ginger root, red pepper, and garlic. Pour over fish, cover tightly with foil, and marinate in refrigerator 4 hours, turning once.
2. Preheat oven to 350°F (180°C).
3. Bake fish in marinade (still covered) for 45 minutes, or until it flakes easily with a fork. Garnish with green onion brushes. Serve with Stir-Fried Chinese Vegetables (recipe p. 233).

Makes 6 to 8 servings.

*To make green onion brushes: Wash green onions. Trim off root end and enough green to leave a 4 inch (10 cm) piece. At about 1 inch (2.5 cm) from ends, cut lengthwise slits in both ends. Put green onions in ice water and place in refrigerator for 30 minutes to allow cut ends to spread.

SOLE WITH ALMONDS AND GRAPES

Sole cooks extremely quickly. As soon as it starts to cloud over, you know it will be done by the time you can get it away from the heat.

Here is a quick and easy recipe that's as colorful as a springtime garden, particularly if you use a few bouquets of tiny fresh flowers to decorate the platter.

1 lb	sole fillets	500 g
½ tsp	salt	2 ml
¼ tsp	freshly ground black pepper	1 ml
2 tbs	all-purpose flour	25 ml
2 tbs	vegetable oil	25 ml
¼ cup	sweet butter	50 ml
½ cup	slivered almonds	125 ml
½ cup	seedless green grapes, halved	125 ml
½ cup	dry white wine	125 ml
1 tsp	Worcestershire sauce	5 ml
	juice of ½ lemon	

1. Season fish with salt and pepper. Dredge with flour.
2. In a large skillet, heat oil and 2 tbs (25 ml) butter. Sauté fish 3 to 4 minutes each side, until fish flakes easily with a fork and is lightly browned. Remove to warm platter and keep warm.
3. Add remaining butter to pan, stir in almonds and grapes; toss to coat with butter. Stir in wine, Worcestershire sauce, and lemon juice. Check seasonings. Spoon sauce over fish and serve.

Makes 4 servings.

FILLET OF SOLE EAST INDIAN

When you look at the myriad recipes the East Indians have for fish, you begin to realize how much ocean surrounds the Subcontinent and how many rivers, besides the Ganges and the Shalimar, run through it.

This is a mild little dish with lots of personality, and can be served with Indian Rice and oodles of chutneys, fresh fruits, and chopped onions.

2 tbs	melted sweet butter	25 ml
1 tsp	curry powder	5 ml
½ tsp	ground cumin	2 ml
½ tsp	salt	2 ml
¼ tsp	freshly ground black pepper	1 ml
2	limes, rind and juice	2
½ cup	dry white wine	125 ml
1 lb	sole fillets	500 g

1. In a bowl combine melted butter, curry powder, cumin, salt, pepper, lime rind and juice. Dip sole fillets into butter mixture.
2. Place sole in a large skillet. Pour wine over sole. Bring to a boil, reduce heat, and poach gently for 5 minutes, or until fish flakes easily with a fork.
3. Place sole in a shallow baking dish in a single layer. Reserve poaching liquid; set aside.

SAUCE:

2 tbs	sweet butter	25 ml
20	medium mushrooms, thinly sliced	20
1	shallot, finely chopped	1
2 tbs	all-purpose flour	25 ml
¼ tsp	dry mustard	1 ml
¼ cup	milk	50 ml
¼ cup	light or table cream	50 ml

1. Preheat oven to 350°F (180°C).
2. In a saucepan melt butter; add mushrooms and shallots; sauté about 2 minutes.
3. Stir in flour and mustard. Whisk in milk, cream, and ½ cup (125 ml) poaching liquid. Cook, stirring, over medium heat about 5 minutes, until thickened.
4. Pour over sole. Bake for 20 minutes, until sauce is bubbly.
   Garnish with lime slices and chopped chives.

Makes 4 servings.

COLD SOLE WITH ORANGE, LIME, AND GREEN PEPPER RINGS

The orange, lime, and green pepper rings make this a most attractive summer dinner plate, and it is also a natural for a buffet menu, as the longer it sits the better it gets.
Serve with my Hot Cheese Straws.

¼ cup	sweet butter	50 ml
¾ cup	vegetable oil	175 ml
6	small fillets of sole	6
	flour for dredging	
1 tsp	salt	5 ml
	freshly ground black pepper	
1	medium onion, thinly sliced and separated into rings	1
1	clove garlic, finely chopped	1
1	medium green pepper, sliced into thin rings	1

1. In a large skillet over medium heat, heat butter and 2 tbs (25 ml) oil. Coat fish with flour and sauté in hot fat, turning until browned on both sides. Season with salt and pepper.
2. Arrange fillets on a platter. Garnish with onion rings, garlic, and green pepper rings.

DRESSING:

½ cup	orange juice	125 ml
	juice of 2 limes	
¼ tsp	hot pepper sauce	1 ml
½ tsp	salt	2 ml
¼ tsp	freshly ground black pepper	1 ml

GARNISH:

	orange slices	
	lime slices	
1 tbs	grated orange rind	15 ml

1. In a small bowl, combine orange juice, lime juice, hot pepper sauce, salt, and pepper. Pour over warm fish.
2. Cover and refrigerate 12 to 24 hours.
3. Garnish with orange and lime slices and orange rind at serving time.

Makes 6 servings.

BARBECUED SUMMER SCALLOPS TERIYAKI

I like to do this on the barbecue, so I tend to think of it as a summertime dish. The skewered scallops can sit in the marinade right up to the time you're ready, and then they only take four minutes on a hot barbecue.

Serve these with spaghettini tossed with the marinade and a crunchy cucumber vinaigrette salad. For a simple summertime dessert, I serve blueberries in sour cream sprinkled with demerara sugar.

The marinade is also great for doing salmon steaks.

28	sea scallops, 1½ lbs/750 g	28
1	large red onion, quartered	1
4	slices bacon, cut in ½ inch (1 cm) pieces	4
2	green or red peppers, cut in 1 inch (2.5 cm) pieces	2
1	medium zucchini, cut in ½ inch (1 cm) slices	1

On 4 skewers, loosely thread scallops alternately with onion, bacon, pepper, and zucchini. Place skewers on shallow pan (a jelly roll pan works well).

TERIYAKI MARINADE:

1 cup	soy sauce	250 ml
⅓ cup	dry sherry	75 ml
3 tbs	brown sugar	45 ml
2 tbs	vegetable oil	25 ml
2 tsp	grated fresh ginger root, or ½ tsp (2 ml) ground ginger	10 ml
2	cloves garlic, finely chopped	2
2 drops	hot pepper sauce (optional)	2 drops
	grated rind and juice of ½ lime cooked spaghetti for 4	

1. Combine soy sauce, sherry, brown sugar, vegetable oil, ginger root, garlic, hot pepper sauce, and lime rind and juice. Pour marinade over skewers, cover, and marinate in refrigerator 2 hours. Remove filled skewers and reserve marinade in a bowl.
2. Brush skewers with vegetable oil before cooking. Barbecue, broil, or grill 6 inches from heat for 4 minutes on each side.
3. Use ½ of marinade to brush over skewers while cooking. Heat remainder of marinade and pour over cooked spaghetti and toss.
4. Arrange pasta on warm platter with skewered scallops over it.

Makes 4 servings.

BASQUE FISH ETHEL

This is as much for looks as for taste because the head and tail remain on. But if that offends you, cut them off: the fish is still impressive.

1	whole fish, cleaned, head and tail on (1 lb/500 g)	1
6 tbs	vegetable oil	90 ml
1 tbs	coarse salt	15 ml
¼ cup	vinegar	50 ml
4	cloves garlic, finely chopped	4
6 drops	hot pepper sauce	6 drops

1. Coat fish with ¼ cup (50 ml) oil; sprinkle with salt. Let stand for 1 hour.
2. Preheat broiler. Place fish in baking dish on lowest position of broiler. Broil for 5 minutes on each side, until fish flakes with a fork and skin is crisp. Remove fish to warm platter and keep warm. Reserve juices.
3. In a small saucepan heat remaining oil; sauté garlic about 2 minutes, until softened. Stir in vinegar, hot pepper sauce, and reserved fish juices. Bring to a boil and cook about 4 minutes, until reduced by half. Spoon over broiled fish.

Makes 2 servings.

BAKED TROUT ON A BED OF MUSHROOMS

The garlicky crumble of bread cubes combined with fresh mushrooms make this the recipe I have given to all my fishing buddies over the years.

Serve with lots of sliced lemon, a chilled semi-dry white wine, a salad and crusty rolls, and you have a filling and delicious lake supper.

Try the same recipe with another freshwater fish.

4	cleaned whole trout, ½ to ¾ lb (250 to 375 g) each	4
1½ tsp	salt	7 ml
1 tsp	paprika	5 ml
¾ tsp	freshly ground pepper	4 ml
3	lemons	3
2 tbs	all-purpose flour	25 ml
6 tbs	sweet butter	90 ml
2 tbs	olive oil	25 ml
20	medium mushrooms, thinly sliced	20
8	green onions, sliced	8
2	cloves garlic, finely chopped	2
1 cup	coarse fresh breadcrumbs	250 ml

1. Leave head and tail on trout, if desired. Two larger trout may be used instead of 4 small ones.
2. Combine 1 tsp (5 ml) salt, paprika, and ½ tsp (2 ml) pepper. Sprinkle over trout. Squeeze juice of 1 lemon over trout; set aside to marinate for 15 minutes.
3. Preheat oven to 425°F (220°C).
4. Dredge trout with flour. In a large skillet heat 2 tbs (25 ml) butter and olive oil. Sauté each trout 5 minutes per side. Remove to warm platter. Set aside.
5. Add 1 tbs (15 ml) butter to skillet, add mushrooms; sauté 3 minutes. Sprinkle with remaining salt and pepper, and juice of 1 lemon.
6. On bottom of shallow casserole large enough to hold trout in a single layer, spread mushrooms. Place trout on top of mushrooms.
7. Add 1 tbs (15 ml) butter to skillet and sauté green onions, about 5 minutes until softened. Spread over trout.
8. Melt remaining butter in skillet; add garlic; cook 1 minute. Add breadcrumbs, toss all together about 5 minutes until bread cubes are golden brown. Spread over trout.
9. Bake for 10 minutes, until fish flakes easily with a fork.
10. Slice remaining lemon, serve with fish.

Makes 4 servings.

FRESH-CAUGHT COD WITH SAFFRON SAUCE

This can work with haddock, halibut, or, as called for here, that old North Atlantic standby, fresh-caught cod.

Use a big skillet and thrill to how saffron threads will color and flavor a dish in moments.

Serve hot with finely chopped onions, chopped and seeded tomatoes, a pepper mill, and your favorite rice, to absorb the wonderful sauce.

¼ cup	olive oil	50 ml
2 tbs	chopped fresh parsley	25 ml
2 tbs	lemon juice	25 ml
2 tsp	all-purpose flour	25 ml
1 tsp	salt	5 ml
½ tsp	saffron threads	2 ml
¼ tsp	freshly ground black pepper	1 ml
1	clove garlic, finely chopped	1
2 lb	cod fillets, (½ inch/1 cm thick)	1 kg
½ cup	hot water	125 ml
1	small onion, finely chopped	1
1	tomato, peeled, seeded, and coarsely chopped	1
	freshly ground black pepper	

1. In a large skillet off the heat combine oil, parsley, lemon juice, flour, salt, saffron, pepper, and garlic; mix well. Add cod fillets, turning over in the mixture to coat with the seasonings.
2. Place skillet over low heat, cover and cook about 5 minutes, until top surface of cod turns white.
3. Turn fillets over and pour hot water over top. Bring to a boil and cook 1 minute longer, until fish flakes easily with a fork.
4. Remove from heat and serve. Garnish with chopped onion, tomato, and pepper.

Makes 6 servings.

SOUR CREAM JUMBO SHRIMP CURRY

This dish can be assembled well in advance and heated just before you are ready to serve, or you can serve it cold. Absolutely delicious either way.

16	jumbo shrimp	16
2 tbs	sweet butter	25 ml
⅓ cup	finely chopped onion	75 ml
¼ cup	finely chopped green pepper	50 ml
1	clove garlic, finely chopped	1
10	medium mushrooms, thinly sliced	10
1 cup	sour cream	250 ml
1 tsp	curry powder	5 ml
½ tsp	Worcestershire sauce	2 ml
½ tsp	salt	2 ml
¼ tsp	dry mustard	1 ml
⅛ tsp	white pepper	0.5 ml
¼ cup	toasted slivered almonds*	50 ml

1. In a saucepan of lightly salted boiling water, cook shrimp about 3 minutes, until shell turns pink and shrimp curls. Drain and cool for a few moments until easy to handle. Peel off shell, leaving tail in place. Devein and place in a warm bowl and keep warm.
2. In a skillet heat butter, add onion, green pepper, and garlic; sauté about 5 minutes, until softened.
3. Add mushrooms and sauté 5 minutes longer. Blend in sour cream, curry powder, Worcestershire sauce, salt, mustard, and pepper.
4. Serve over warm shrimps. Garnish with toasted almonds.

Makes 4 servings.

*Place nuts on a baking sheet. Toast in a 350°F (180°C) oven for about 10 minutes.

DILLY SAUCE FOR FISH AND VEGETABLES

Serve as a dip for hot vegetables, boiled new potatoes, broccoli or snow peas. Use hot or cold over poached salmon.

1¼ cups	mayonnaise (recipe p. 227)	300 ml
¼ cup	heavy or whipping cream	50 ml
2 tbs	lemon juice	25 ml
½ tsp	Dijon mustard	2 ml
½ tsp	salt	2 ml
¼ tsp	freshly ground black pepper	1 ml
dash	hot pepper sauce	dash
2 tbs	chopped fresh dill	25 ml

In a blender or food processor combine mayonnaise, cream, lemon juice, mustard, salt, pepper, and hot pepper sauce. Process 30 seconds until smooth. Transfer to a small bowl. Stir in dill. Refrigerate until serving time. Keeps well for 5 days.

Makes 2 cups.

Juxtapose an entire flat straight from the grower of open tulips or paperwhite narcissus, still in the rough wooden flats they're grown in, onto a long formal dining table, set with your finest silver and crystal. The contrast is striking.

THE FAIR FOWL

Now for that most versatile of all dinner party foods, the bird we so often turn to for showing off our culinary talents.

CHICKEN WAIKIKI

It seems anything with pineapple in or on it gets a Hawaiian name, so here we go with a gorgeous dish that can be doubled or tripled easily for large occasions. You can make up pans to serve thirty or forty guests if you wish.

Serve huge platters of it with the green of the pepper chunks, the gold of the pineapple, and, if you want a touch more color, add halves of fresh apricots. Offer lots of fruit sauce, coconut rice, and green onion brushes (see p. 113).

4	pieces chicken, legs or breasts, about 2 lb/1 kg total	4
¼ cup	melted sweet butter	50 ml
1 tbs	soy sauce	15 ml
½ tsp	dry mustard	2 ml
¼ tsp	freshly ground black pepper	1 ml
1	1 inch (2.5 cm) piece ginger root, peeled and chopped	1

1. Preheat oven to 350°F (180°C).
2. With a sharp knife, disjoint or cut each piece of chicken in half. In a shallow baking dish arrange chicken.

3. Combine butter, soy sauce, mustard, pepper, and ginger root. Brush over chicken. Bake for 45 minutes. While chicken is baking, prepare sauce.

FRUIT SAUCE:

1	can (14 oz/398 ml) unsweetened pineapple chunks	1
1	can (10 oz/284 ml) mandarin orange sections	1
2 tbs	cornstarch	25 ml
¼ cup	cider vinegar	50 ml
¼ cup	brown sugar	50 ml
1	green pepper, cut in large chunks	1
½ cup	toasted salted peanuts (see p. 120)	125 ml

1. Drain pineapple and oranges, reserving their juice. Combine the juices and reserve ¾ cup (175 ml).
2. In a saucepan combine cornstarch and vinegar; mix well. Stir in reserved juice. Bring to a boil, reduce heat; cook, stirring, about 5 minutes, until thickened. Stir in drained pineapple, orange sections, and brown sugar.
3. Pour hot sauce over chicken and bake 10 minutes longer. Sprinkle with green pepper and peanuts. Bake 5 minutes longer, until chicken is tender.

Makes 4 servings.

SESAME BAKED CHICKEN

I have dined on this when my mother-in-law has served it in her elegant home. I have served it at my own buffet parties. I have made it up for literally hundreds of people traveling out of town on a theater party, and I've never had a piece left over, just well-picked bones.

You won't believe what buttermilk does for chicken when you let it soak up all that goodness overnight. The sesame seed coating mixture is also great for your veal chops and butterfly pork chops.

8	pieces chicken, legs or breasts, about 4 lbs/2 kg total	8
2½ cups	buttermilk	625 ml
¾ cup	sweet butter, melted	175 ml
2 tbs	lemon juice	25 ml
2	cloves garlic, finely chopped	2
1½ cups	fine dry breadcrumbs	375 ml
½ cup	sesame seeds	125 ml
½ tsp	salt	2 ml
¼ tsp	white pepper	1 ml
2 tbs	freshly grated Parmesan cheese	25 ml

1. In a shallow baking dish, arrange chicken pieces. Pour buttermilk over chicken. Cover and refrigerate overnight. Next morning, pour off buttermilk and pat chicken dry.
2. When ready to cook, preheat oven to 450°F (220°C).
3. In a shallow dish combine butter, lemon juice, and garlic. In another dish combine breadcrumbs, sesame seeds, salt, pepper, and Parmesan.
4. Dip chicken in butter mixture, then roll in breadcrumb mixture to coat each piece well. Arrange chicken in a single layer in baking pan. Drizzle any remaining butter over chicken.
5. Bake for 10 minutes. Reduce heat to 350°F (180°C) and continue to bake, basting occasionally with drippings, for 1 hour, until golden brown and tender.

Makes 8 servings.

Set up and have tablecloths ironed the day before.
Check fireplaces and lay fire days before.
Check over silver dishes, glassware, and linen you wish to use prior to the party to make sure all is polished or cleaned.

MINTED CHICKEN BREASTS

Looks great. Tastes even better. The scent of the mint is irresistible.
Why we mentally reserve mint for lamb only, I will never know. There are so many other eating joys we can achieve with this special herb.

6	half chicken breasts, 3 lb/1.5 kg total	6
⅓ cup	sweet butter	75 ml
2 tbs	vegetable oil	25 ml
1	lemon, grated rind and juice	1
1 tsp	salt	5 ml
¼ tsp	freshly ground black pepper	1 ml
	chicken stock	
2 tbs	all-purpose flour	25 ml
½ cup	light cream	125 ml
2 tbs	chopped fresh mint, or 2 tsp (10 ml) dried	25 ml
1 tbs	chopped parsley	15 ml
1 tsp	dried thyme leaves	5 ml
1 tsp	granulated sugar	5 ml
1 tsp	paprika	5 ml

1. In a large skillet, heat 2 tbs (25 ml) butter and oil. Add chicken breasts; cook, turning, 5 to 10 minutes, until golden brown.
2. Add lemon rind and juice, salt, and pepper. Reduce heat, cover, and simmer 30 minutes. Remove chicken breasts, place in a single layer on a baking pan.
3. Pour any remaining juice from skillet into a measuring cup. Skim off fat. Add enough chicken stock to make 1 cup (250 ml).
4. In the same skillet, combine remaining butter and flour; stir in chicken stock mixture and cream. Cook over medium heat, stirring, about 5 minutes, until thickened. Stir in mint, parsley, and thyme.
5. Just before serving, preheat oven to 500°F (260°C).
6. Sprinkle chicken with sugar and paprika. Place chicken in oven just long enough for surface to become brown and crisp.
7. Remove to serving platter. Pour hot sauce over top and serve.

Makes 6 servings.

SPANISH CHICKEN AND RICE CASSEROLE

This is a deliciously classic Spanish recipe for chicken.
  First, cut your chicken into small pieces. It cooks faster, is easier to serve, and looks much more attractive. The saffron rice which is put in the bottom of the pan will bubble up through the pieces of chicken.

6	pieces chicken, legs or breasts (3 lb/1.5 kg total)	6
¼ cup	vegetable oil	50 ml
2	medium onions, coarsely chopped	2
3	cloves garlic, finely chopped	3
2 cups	chicken stock	500 ml
1 tsp	salt	5 ml
½ tsp	freshly ground black pepper	2 ml
1 tsp	saffron threads	5 ml
1 cup	long grain rice	250 ml

1. With a sharp knife, disjoint or cut each piece of chicken in half. In a large skillet heat oil, add half the chicken; cook about 7 minutes, until lightly browned. Remove chicken from skillet and keep warm. Repeat with remaining chicken.
2. Add onions and garlic; sauté 10 minutes, until softened.
3. Stir in stock, salt, pepper, and saffron. Bring to a boil, reduce heat, and simmer 5 minutes.

4. Preheat oven to 350°F (180°C).
5. In the bottom of a 9 × 13 inch (23 × 33 cm) shallow pan or casserole spread rice. Pour stock mixture over rice. Lay chicken pieces on top, cover and bake for 1 hour, until chicken is tender.

Makes 6 servings.

HONEY ORANGE CHICKEN

When it comes to the table, this simple dish is met with oohs and ahs!

1	chicken, 2½–3 lb (1.25–1.5 kg)	1
2 tbs	vegetable oil	25 ml
2	medium onions, coarsely chopped	2
2 tsp	salt	10 ml
2 tsp	paprika	10 ml
½ tsp	freshly ground black pepper	2 ml
4	oranges, grated rind and juice	4
¼ cup	honey	50 ml
2 tbs	Grand Marnier	25 ml
1	piece (1 inch/2.5 cm) ginger root, peeled and finely chopped	1
¼ tsp	ground nutmeg	1 ml
1 tbs	cold water	15 ml
2 tsp	cornstarch	10 ml

1. Preheat oven to 350°F (180°C).
2. With a sharp knife disjoint and cut chicken into 8 pieces. In a large skillet, heat oil. Add chicken pieces, a few at a time. Cook, turning, about 10 minutes, until brown.
3. In a baking dish or casserole, arrange chicken. Spread onions over top. Sprinkle with salt, paprika, and pepper.
4. Pour oil out of skillet. Add orange rind and juice, honey, Grand Marnier, ginger root, and nutmeg and deglaze pan by scraping down brown bits. Simmer 5 minutes. Pour over chicken.
5. Cover chicken and bake for 50 to 60 minutes, until tender. Remove chicken and onions to warm serving platter and keep warm.
6. Pour pan juices into a small saucepan. Combine water and cornstarch; mix until smooth. Stir into juices. Bring to a boil; cook, stirring about 2 minutes, until thickened. Pour over chicken and serve.

Makes 4 servings.

BARBECUED LEMON MUSTARD CHICKEN

You have to start this one the night before, but the flavor achieved by marinating in the lemon mustard and garlic has to be tasted to be believed. And of course, the glaze applied during the cooking brings the chicken to the table looking like a perfect ceramic reproduction.

6	pieces chicken, legs or breasts, about 3 lbs/1.5 kg total	6

MARINADE:

6	lemons	6
½ cup	coarse grainy garlic mustard	125 ml
1–2 tbs	coarsely ground black pepper	15–25 ml
1 tbs	chopped fresh tarragon, or 1 tsp (5 ml) dried	15 ml
4	cloves garlic, finely chopped	4
1 tsp	salt	5 ml

GLAZE:

¼ cup	honey	50 ml
1 tbs	cornstarch	15 ml

1. Place chicken pieces in a single layer in shallow baking dish.
2. To make Marinade: With a vegetable peeler, remove rind from lemons in large strips.
3. Squeeze juice from lemons; combine juice and lemon rind, mustard, pepper, tarragon, garlic, and salt.
4. Pour over chicken; cover and marinate in refrigerator overnight. Refrigerate until cooking time.
5. Remove chicken pieces from marinade; reserving 1 cup (250 ml) marinade.
6. To make Glaze: In a small saucepan combine reserved marinade, honey, and cornstarch. Bring to a boil; reduce heat and simmer, stirring occasionally, about 4 minutes, until thickened.
7. To barbecue chicken, preheat barbecue to medium heat.* Barbecue 4 to 5 inches (10 to 12.5 cm) above hot coals, turning occasionally, about 35 minutes. Continue to cook, brushing with glaze and turning for 10 minutes longer, until chicken is tender and no longer pink.
8. Remove to warm platter. Pour any remaining glaze over chicken and serve.

Makes 6 servings.

*Chicken may be baked in a baking dish in a 350° F (180° C) oven for 1 hour, brushed with glaze during last 15 minutes.

CHINESE ROAST CHICKEN

The ginger, soy sauce, garlic, and wine make this a handsome and tasty bird of Chinese persuasion.
  Serve it with sweet-scented rice and a salad or a vegetable stir fry.

1	chicken, 2–3 lbs (1–1.5 kg)	1
½ cup	soy sauce	125 ml
¼ cup	sake or dry sherry	50 ml
2 tbs	brown sugar	25 ml
1	1 inch (2.5 cm) piece ginger root, peeled and finely chopped	1
2	cloves garlic, finely chopped	2
4	green onions, finely chopped	4

1. In a medium bowl place chicken. Combine soy sauce, sake, brown sugar, ginger root, garlic, and onions. Pour over chicken. Cover and refrigerate overnight.
2. Preheat oven to 325°F (160°C).
3. Place chicken on a rack in a roasting pan and bake in oven, basting frequently with marinade, for 1 hour, until tender and no longer pink.

Makes 4 servings.

CRISP BAKED ALMOND CHICKEN IN SOUR CREAM

I have made pans and pans of this for proms, sweet sixteen, and surprise parties, and it is always a hit. You can serve it for a picnic or a sitdown dinner party with the most impressive guests. It tastes as good as it looks.

4	pieces chicken, legs or breasts, 2–3 lb (1–1.5 kg) total	4
¼ cup	all-purpose flour	50 ml
⅓ cup	sweet butter, melted	75 ml
1 tsp	celery salt	5 ml
1 tsp	paprika	5 ml
1 tsp	salt	5 ml
½ tsp	curry powder	2 ml
½ tsp	dried oregano leaves	2 ml
½ tsp	freshly ground black pepper	2 ml
¾ cup	sliced almonds	175 ml
1 cup	sour cream	250 ml
3 tbs	fine dry breadcrumbs	45 ml
1 tbs	soft sweet butter	15 ml

1. Preheat oven to 350°F (180°C).
2. Dredge chicken with flour. Combine melted butter, celery salt, paprika, salt, curry powder, oregano, and pepper. Coat chicken with seasoned butter.
3. In a shallow baking dish, arrange chicken in a single layer. Sprinkle with almonds, cover, and bake in oven for 45 minutes. Uncover.
4. Pour pan drippings into a bowl. Skim off fat. Combine ¼ cup (50 ml) drippings and sour cream; mix well. Pour sour cream mixture over chicken.
5. Rub soft butter into breadcrumbs. Sprinkle over sour cream. Bake, un-covered, 10 minutes longer, until almonds and crumbs brown and chicken is tender.

Makes 4 servings.

QUICK-FIX CHICKEN WINGS

These are great to have up your sleeve when the going gets tough and the guests are on their way. Serve these wings with any one of a number of dipping sauces, from plum to wonton.

2 lbs	chicken wings, tips removed	1 kg
½ cup	brown sugar	125 ml
¼ cup	soy sauce	50 ml
2 tbs	white or cider vinegar	25 ml
1	clove garlic, finely chopped	1
1 tsp	chicken stock base, or 1 chicken bouillon cube, crumbled	5 ml
½ tsp	salt	2 ml
¼ tsp	freshly ground black pepper	1 ml

1. Preheat oven to 325°F (160°C).
2. Wash wings and pat dry. Arrange wings in a 9 × 13 inch (23 × 33 cm) baking dish.
3. In a small bowl combine sugar, soy sauce, vinegar, garlic, stock base, salt, and pepper. Pour over wings, cover, and bake, basting occasionally, for 1 hour, or until tender and glazed.
   Serve warm or cold.

Makes 5 to 6 servings.

SHOPPING LIST FOR MEXICAN COOKING

Jalapeño peppers   *Chili powder*
Sesame seeds   *Whole nutmeg*
Anise seeds   *Ground cinnamon*
Tortillas   *Cilantro*
Bitter chocolate

CHICKEN MOLÉ
with bowls of
Chopped Onions, Tomatoes
and Radishes

GINGER GREEN BEAN SALAD

FRAGRANT SWEET SCENTED RICE

SAFFRON BANANAS

HOT BUTTERED TORTILLAS

Chilled Pineapple Spears with Lichee Fruit

Baskets of Small Desserts: *Butter Tarts,*
Nanaimo Bars, Lemon Coconut Squares

CHICKEN MOLÉ POBLANO

A super dish for a supper party. My friend Marilyn Hamel served this in her L.A. home to me and about seventy-five other people. For the occasion, she decorated her home with Mexican shawls, some Mexican pottery, and put her gorgeous tropical flowers in large Mexican pots around the house, from garden to front hall to party rooms to bathrooms.

Deliciously raisiny and moist with ground almonds and chocolate, the sauce and the chicken can be preassembled a day ahead. When you're ready to use it, just pour the sauce over the chicken and heat until it is bubbly hot.

8	large chicken legs	8
4	cloves garlic, finely chopped	4
3	medium tomatoes, peeled, seeded, and finely chopped	3
3	jalapeño peppers, seeded and finely chopped*	3
2	medium onions, coarsely chopped	2
½ cup	raisins	125 ml
¼ cup	ground almonds	50 ml
2 tbs	chili powder	25 ml
2 tbs	sesame seeds	25 ml
1 tsp	anise seeds	5 ml
1 tsp	salt	5 ml
1 tsp	ground cinnamon	5 ml
½ tsp	ground cloves	2 ml
½ tsp	ground coriander	2 ml
¼ tsp	freshly ground black pepper	1 ml
1	tortilla, broken in small pieces	1
3½ cups	chicken stock	875 ml
1	square (1 oz/28 g) unsweetened chocolate	1
2 tbs	vegetable oil	25 ml

*When handling hot peppers, wear gloves, or be sure to wash hands thoroughly in cold water after handling. Avoid touching eyes or lips.

1. With a sharp knife, cut chicken legs at joint to make 8 thighs and 8 drumsticks.
2. In a blender or food processor, combine garlic, tomatoes, peppers, onions, raisins, almonds, chili powder, sesame and anise seeds, salt, cinnamon, cloves, coriander, pepper, and tortilla pieces. Process with on/off motion for 1 to 2 minutes, until a paste forms.
3. In a large saucepan combine paste and 3 cups (750 ml) chicken stock; stir well. Bring to a boil, reduce heat, and simmer 10 to 15 minutes, until smooth. Stir in chocolate until it melts. Set aside.
4. In a large skillet heat oil, add chicken thighs; cook, turning, about 10 minutes, until lightly brown. Remove and set aside. Repeat with drumsticks. When all chicken is browned, return thighs to skillet.
5. Pour remaining chicken stock over all pieces in skillet. Cover and simmer 30 minutes, or until chicken is tender and no longer pink.
6. Preheat oven to 325°F (160°C).
7. Remove chicken to a large casserole. Pour sauce over chicken. Bake for 25 to 35 minutes, or until heated through.
  Casserole can be refrigerated up to 2 days before baking.

Makes 8 servings.

CHICKEN DIABLE

Quick and easy, little or nothing to chop or mix. Just put it together and wait for the excellent results.
  Serve with rice and chutneys and a cucumber and yogurt salad.

4	pieces chicken, legs or breasts, about 2 lb/1 kg	4
¼ cup	sweet butter	50 ml
½ cup	honey	125 ml
¼ cup	Dijon mustard	50 ml
1 tbs	curry powder	15 ml
1 tsp	salt	5 ml

1. Preheat oven to 350°F (180°C).
2. In a shallow baking dish, arrange chicken pieces.
3. In a small saucepan, melt butter. Stir in honey, mustard, curry powder, and salt. Pour honey mixture over chicken, turning pieces so they are coated.
4. Cover and bake in oven for 45 minutes.
5. Uncover and bake, basting frequently with sauce, for 15 minutes longer, until chicken is tender and golden.

Makes 4 servings.

POULET AUX DEUX MOUTARDES

This is a quick, easy, and very impressive dish, as long as you have all the ingredients on hand.

Once you know you are going to be strapped for time, plan on something like this. It's a great way to be able to put in a full day and still be the complete host or hostess in the evening.

Serve with sauteed mushrooms and a salad.

4	pieces chicken, legs or breasts, about 2 lb/1 kg total	4
2 tbs	all-purpose flour	25 ml
1 tsp	salt	5 ml
½ tsp	white pepper	2 ml
2 tbs	sweet butter	25 ml
2 tbs	peanut oil	25 ml
4	shallots, chopped	4
	bouquet garni	
1 cup	chicken stock	250 ml
¼ cup	dry vermouth	50 ml
2 tbs ·	Dijon mustard with tarragon	25 ml
1 tsp	dry mustard	5 ml
½ cup	heavy or whipping cream	125 ml

1. Combine flour, ½ tsp (2 ml) salt, and ¼ tsp (1 ml) pepper. Dredge chicken with seasoned flour.
2. In a large skillet, heat butter and oil. Add chicken pieces; sauté, turning, about 10 minutes, until golden brown.
3. Add shallots, bouquet garni, stock, and vermouth. Scrape down pan. Bring to a boil, reduce heat, and simmer, covered, about 30 minutes, until tender. Remove bouquet garni and discard. Place chicken on warm serving platter and keep warm.
4. Whisk 2 mustards and cream into skillet. Simmer gently for 2 minutes. Season with remaining salt and pepper. Return chicken to sauce to heat thoroughly.

Makes 4 servings.

On a country picnic bring along an extra wine carafe. Spend the morning walking through the fields, picking wildflowers such as buttercups, Queen Anne's lace, lupins, and anything that catches your eye. Arrange them loosely in the carafe, and your picnic table becomes a pretty reminder of your carefree morning.

COQ AU VIN

A hearty dinner. Cook it ahead (all but the last hour) and let it cool overnight so you can remove the accumulated fat.

When you serve your guests, give everyone two mushrooms, two potatoes, and two onions. Then ladle on the richly scented chicken with the dark aroma of burgundy and spices.

8	pieces chicken, legs or breasts, 4–5 lb/2–2.5 kg total	8
½ cup	all-purpose flour	125 ml
8	slices bacon, or 6 oz/170 g salt pork, chopped	8
16	small white onions	16
16	small new potatoes, peeled	16
16	small mushrooms	16
4	cloves garlic, finely chopped	4
2 tbs	chopped fresh parsley	25 ml
1 tsp	dried thyme leaves	5 ml
1	bay leaf	1
½ tsp	salt	2 ml
¼ tsp	freshly ground black pepper	1 ml
¼ cup	brandy	50 ml
2 cups	dry red wine	500 ml
2 cups	chicken stock	500 ml

1. Preheat oven to 350°F (180°C).
2. Halve chicken legs or breasts to make 16 pieces. Remove all visible fat. Dredge in flour.
3. In a large skillet, sauté bacon or salt pork until crisp. Drain bacon or pork on paper towel, leaving drippings in skillet. Add chicken to skillet in batches, cook, turning, about 10 minutes, until light brown.
4. In a large heavy 12 cup (3 l) casserole, layer chicken and bacon.
5. Add onions, potatoes, mushrooms, and garlic to skillet; sauté 5 minutes. Add parsley, thyme, bay leaf, salt, and pepper. Stir in brandy, warm, and flame immediately. Stir in wine and chicken stock. Bring to a boil, reduce heat and simmer 5 minutes; pour over chicken.
6. Cover and bake in oven for 1 hour.
7. At this point, the casserole may be refrigerated until the following day when fat congealed on top can be removed.
8. Return chicken casserole to preheated oven; bake at 350°F (180°C) for 1 hour longer, until chicken is almost falling off bones.

Makes 8 servings.

BASQUE CHICKEN

The original recipe calls for simmering on top of the stove. I find it much easier to pop it in the oven and forget it for twenty minutes—and so will you.

The olives, prosciutto, and tomatoes give this chicken a party look, and the garlic gives it that old French Provençal taste.

Serve with garlic croutons and pommes frites.

4	pieces chicken, legs or breasts, about 2 lb/1 kg total	4
¼ cup	olive oil	50 ml
½ tsp	salt	2 ml
¼ tsp	freshly ground black pepper	1 ml
⅛ tsp	cayenne pepper	0.5 ml
2	large onions, coarsely chopped	2
2	red or green peppers, coarsely chopped	2
8	thin slices prosciutto, chopped	8
3	cloves garlic, finely chopped	3
4	medium tomatoes, peeled, seeded, and coarsely chopped	4
12	large pitted olives (black, green, or both), halved	12
4	thin slices prosciutto, cut in strips	4

1. Preheat oven to 350°F (180°C).
2. With a sharp knife disjoint or cut each piece of chicken in half.
3. In a large ovenproof skillet or Dutch oven, heat oil. Add chicken a few pieces at a time; cook about 10 minutes, turning until lightly browned. As chicken browns, remove pieces to warm platter and season with salt, pepper, and cayenne.
4. Add onions, peppers, and prosciutto to skillet and cook, stirring frequently, about 10 minutes, until vegetables are softened.
5. Stir in garlic; cook 2 minutes longer.
6. Add tomatoes; bring to a boil, reduce heat, and simmer 5 minutes. Return chicken to skillet and spoon sauce over each piece.
7. Cover and bake in oven for 15 minutes. Remove cover and bake 20 minutes longer, or until chicken is tender.

Garnish with olives and prosciutto strips, and serve.

Makes 4 servings.

> *Place three or four fully open garden roses in a bud vase and put them in the guest bathroom to complete your decorations for the evening.*

PLUM SAUCE CHICKEN BREASTS

You may never have seen a purple cow, but when you make this, you are going to see a purple chicken. A beautiful, appetizing purple chicken.

It is truly elegant, and when decorated with green and yellow pepper halves, filled with extra plum sauce, it is exotic. Equally good served hot or cold.

Garnish with a single yellow oncidium orchid spray on a dark dinner platter or, if using a white or glass serving platter, garnish with a mauve dendrobium orchid.

8	half chicken breasts	8
¼ cup	all-purpose flour	50 ml
½ tsp	paprika	2 ml
½ tsp	salt	2 ml
¼ tsp	freshly ground black pepper	1 ml
pinch	cayenne pepper	pinch
¼ cup	sweet butter	50 ml
½ cup	dry white wine	125 ml

1. Bone and skin chicken breasts.
2. In a shallow dish combine flour, paprika, salt, pepper, and cayenne. Roll each breast half in flour mixture to coat it completely.
3. In a large skillet heat butter. Add chicken breasts. Cook, turning once or twice, for about 5 minutes, until lightly browned on all sides. Add wine, cover, and simmer for 5 minutes.
4. Transfer chicken pieces to a casserole. Pour pan juices over chicken. Set aside.

PLUM SAUCE:

8	blue Italian plums (1 cup/250 ml), pitted	8
2	slices fresh ginger root, chopped fine	2
2 tbs	brown sugar	25 ml
2 tbs	rice or wine vinegar	25 ml
2 tbs	soy sauce	25 ml
½ cup	cold water	125 ml
1 tbs	cornstarch	15 ml
½ tsp	cinnamon	2 ml

1. Preheat oven to 350°F (180°C).
2. In a food processor, finely chop plums and ginger. In a 4 cup (1 l) saucepan combine chopped plum mixture, brown sugar, vinegar, and soy sauce. Cook, stirring, over medium heat, about 5 minutes, until soft.

3. Combine water, cornstarch, and cinnamon; stir until smooth. Stir into plum mixture. Cook, stirring constantly, about 2 minutes, until thick.
4. Pour over chicken in casserole. Cover and bake in oven for 20 to 25 minutes, or until chicken is tender and no longer pink.

Makes 8 servings.

CHICKEN SAAG

If your friends love to linger over dinner, then this dish will be as good at ten as it was at eight.

Saag is the East Indian name for the spicy green vegetable purée that gives the dish its character. Serve it with all kinds of fruit chutneys and fresh melons—cranshaw, cantaloupe, honeydew—strewn with leaves of fresh mint.

8	half chicken breasts	8
5 cups	rich chicken stock	1.25 l
1	onion, quartered	1
2	stalks celery, including leaves	2
6	sprigs parsley	6
3	garlic cloves, peeled	3
½ lb	fresh spinach, washed, trimmed, and coarsely chopped	250 g
1	stalk broccoli, including stalk, washed, trimmed, and coarsely chopped	1
¼ cup	clarified butter	50 ml
1 cup	finely chopped onions	250 ml
1 tbs	finely chopped fresh ginger root	15 ml
1 tsp	salt	5 ml
½ tsp	ground coriander	2 ml
½ tsp	garam masala*	2 ml
¼ tsp	ground cumin	1 ml
¼ tsp	turmeric	1 ml
½ cup	sour cream	125 ml

*Garam masala, an Indian spice, can be purchased in specialty food shops.

1. In a large skillet or saucepan, combine 4 cups (1 l) chicken stock with the onion, celery, parsley, and garlic. Bring to a boil. Add chicken breasts and poach about 20 to 25 minutes, until tender. Remove from stock, cool, then skin and bone, but keep the breast halves in one piece. Return to cooking liquid to keep warm.
2. While chicken breasts are poaching, prepare sauce. In food processor or blender, combine ½ cup (125 ml) chicken stock and a handful of spinach; process until chopped. Add another handful of spinach and process. Repeat until all spinach has been chopped. Remove to a large bowl.
3. Add remaining ½ cup (125 ml) chicken stock to processor. Add broccoli in batches and chop. Add to spinach.
4. In a heavy skillet, heat clarified butter. Add onions; sauté until softened. Add ginger and continue to sauté until golden brown. Stir in salt, coriander, garam masala, cumin, and turmeric and sauté 2 minutes.
5. Stir in the spinach and broccoli mixture, bring to a boil, reduce heat, and simmer, uncovered, 20 to 25 minutes, until most of the liquid has evaporated.
6. Just before serving stir in sour cream. Do not reheat.

   To serve, arrange poached chicken breasts on attractive platter. Spoon sauce over.

Makes 8 servings.

THE MAHARAJA'S POLO PARTY

GARLICKY-SPICY-CRAB-DIP
with Crudités for dipping

CHICKEN SAAG
INDIAN RICE WITH CHOPPED SCALLIONS
WARMED, CRISPY LENTIL POMPADOMS*
PEACH CHUTNEY
and
FRESH MINT CHUTNEY

DICED TOMATOES, ONIONS, AND CUCUMBERS
with Hearty Tomato Dressing

MOUNDS OF SLICED MELON
BITE-SIZED BITS OF PAPAYA, STRAWBERRIES, AND KIWI
mixed together and sprinkled with mint leaves
PECAN BUTTERSCOTCH COFFEE CAKE

*Available at most Indian markets.

CHICKEN PARISIENNE

This is a divine casserole to take to the cottage or ski lodge with you. Do all the preparation and cooking before you go, and just heat and serve when you get there.

Take along lots of crusty breads which you can warm along with the chicken. Guests will love to dip it in the rich broccoli purée.

8	boneless half chicken breasts, cooked	8
1	bunch (1 lb/500 g) broccoli, broken into florets	1
½ cup	sour cream	125 ml
2 tbs	dry sherry	25 ml
1 tsp	lemon juice	5 ml
1½ tsp	salt	7 ml
½ tsp	white pepper	2 ml
¼ tsp	ground nutmeg	1 ml
2 tbs	sweet butter	25 ml
2 tbs	all-purpose flour	25 ml
½ tsp	dry mustard	2 ml
¾ cup	milk or light cream	175 ml
2	drops hot pepper sauce	2
1 cup	grated Parmesan cheese	250 ml
½ cup	whipped cream	125 ml

1. Preheat oven to 325°F (160°C).
2. In lightly salted boiling water cook broccoli about 7 minutes until just tender.
3. In a food processor combine broccoli, sour cream, sherry, lemon juice, 1 tsp (5 ml) salt, ¼ tsp (1 ml) white pepper, and nutmeg.
4. Pour purée into an 8 inch (20 cm) baking dish or pan. Layer chicken on top of broccoli purée.
5. In a small saucepan, melt butter over medium heat and blend in flour and mustard. Whisk in milk. Bring to a boil and continue whisking about 4 minutes, until sauce is thickened. Blend in remaining salt and pepper, hot pepper sauce, and ½ cup (125 ml) grated cheese.
6. Fold in whipped cream. Spoon sauce over chicken. Top with remaining grated cheese.
7. Bake in oven for 20 minutes, until heated through. Place under preheated broiler for 2 minutes until lightly browned.

Makes 4 servings.

LITTLE RED CHICKEN SUPPER

ZESTY SUMMERTIME SOUP

CHERRY CHICKEN

SWEET SCENTED RICE

STEAMED SUMMER VEGETABLES
with sweet butter

BLUEBERRIES IN LEMON MOUSSE

CARIBBEAN CHERRY CHICKEN WITH DARK RUM

This is a spring dish for the fresh cherry season and the time of the island festivals, bongo drums, and dark rum.

Unless you do your own cherry preserves, don't attempt this out of season. Canned cherries don't seem to make it.

4	pieces chicken, legs or breasts, about 2 lb/1 kg total	4
1 tsp	salt	5 ml
½ tsp	paprika	2 ml
2 tbs	vegetable oil	25 ml
1 tbs	sweet butter	15 ml
1 tbs	all-purpose flour	15 ml
1 tsp	granulated sugar	5 ml
¼ tsp	ground allspice	1 ml
¼ tsp	ground cinnamon	1 ml
¼ tsp	dry mustard	1 ml
2 cups	fresh cherries, pitted and halved	500 ml
1 cup	chicken stock	250 ml
1 cup	unsweetened crushed pineapple, including juice	250 ml
2 tbs	brown sugar	25 ml
2 tbs	dark rum	25 ml

1. Preheat oven to 350°F (180°C).
2. With a sharp knife, disjoint or cut each piece of chicken in half. Sprinkle chicken pieces with ½ tsp (2 ml) salt and paprika.
3. In a large skillet heat vegetable oil and butter. Add chicken pieces; cook, turning, about 10 minutes, until golden. Remove chicken to a shallow casserole or baking dish; set aside.

4. To pan drippings in skillet, stir in flour, sugar, allspice, cinnamon, and mustard. Add cherries, chicken stock, pineapple, brown sugar, and rum; mix well and bring to a boil.
5. Pour over chicken, cover, and bake in oven for 50 minutes or until tender. Remove cover and bake 10 minutes longer.

Makes 4 servings.

> *You are the host or hostess. You set the pace, and the guests take your actions as their cue. Although the kitchen expects leeway between courses, don't dawdle unexpectedly or take phone calls. A delicate sauce may curdle or a rare lamb turn out well done.*
>
> *Don't be afraid to mix dinner guests up. Inviting people for dinner is a lot like making a salad. A lot of different ingredients go into a bowl, and the net result is a wonderful time. Too much of the same thing makes for a boring salad and a dull evening.*

STUFFING FOR BIG AND LITTLE BIRDS

There is such a profusion of birds available in the markets today that one is at a loss how to deal with them all. I expect to walk in someday and find someone has packaged larks' tongues and blackbirds.

In any case, here are two very good stuffings for you to rely on. One is a big bird stuffing, one for tiny birds. Feel free to try variations of them.

BIG BIRD FRUIT STUFFING WITH APRICOTS AND PRUNES

Fruity and with just the right touch of sage, this one is guaranteed to bring back memories of holiday dinners at grandmother's house.

¼ cup	sweet butter	50 ml
1½ cups	thinly sliced onions	375 ml
½ cup	finely chopped celery	125 ml
½ cup	finely chopped celery leaves	125 ml
1	clove garlic, finely chopped	1
½ lb	sausage meat	250 g
1 cup	finely chopped prunes	250 ml
1 cup	finely chopped dried apricots	250 ml
2	large Spy apples, cored and finely chopped	2
7 cups	fresh breadcrumbs	1.75 l
½ cup	finely chopped fresh parsley	125 ml
1 tsp	dried sage	5 ml
1 tsp	dried thyme	5 ml
½ tsp	freshly ground black pepper	2 ml
1–2 tbs	water, if necessary	15–25 ml

1. In a large skillet, melt butter; add onions, celery, celery leaves, and garlic. Sauté 5 minutes, until onions are softened.
2. Add sausage meat and cook 8 to 10 minutes, until meat is no longer pink. Stir in prunes, apricots, and apples; sauté 5 minutes, stirring frequently.
3. In a large bowl combine breadcrumbs, parsley, sage, thyme, and pepper; stir in meat mixture; mix well. Add water if dressing is dry.

Use to stuff an 8 to 10 lb (4 to 5 kg) goose or a 10 to 12 lb (5 to 6 kg) turkey.

Makes 9 cups (2.25 l).

CASHEW STUFFING FOR CORNISH HENS OR QUAIL

This is one of my favorites as it uses two of my most adored ingredients: cashews and wild rice.

It can also be rolled into Supremes (page 145). If you have any left over, just bake it in the oven with a touch of butter, and enjoy.

½ cup	wild rice	125 ml
1 cup	water	250 ml
1 cup	chopped unsalted cashews	250 ml
1 cup	chicken stock	250 ml
4	strips cooked bacon, crumbled	4
2 tbs	sweet butter	25 ml
½ tsp	salt	2 ml
¼ tsp	freshly ground black pepper	1 ml
2 tbs	chopped chives	25 ml

1. In a saucepan, combine rice and water; bring to a boil, reduce heat, and simmer 30 minutes, until liquid is absorbed.
2. In a small skillet over low heat, combine cashews and stock. Cook 10 minutes, until liquid is absorbed.
3. In a bowl combine cashew mixture, cooked rice, bacon, butter, salt, pepper, and chives; mix well.

Use to stuff 2 Cornish hens or 4 to 6 quail.

Makes 2 cups (500 ml).

STUFFED ROAST CHICKEN, TURKEY, OR CORNISH HEN

1. Rinse and wipe bird. Remove any accessible clumps of fat from body cavity.
2. Stuff bird as desired just before cooking.
3. Fill neck cavity with stuffing; pull neck skin over dressing and secure flap of skin to back of bird with a skewer.
4. Preheat oven to 350°F (180°C).
5. Stuff back end (vent) of bird, taking care not to pack stuffing too tightly. Skewer or sew opening closed. (Use metal skewers, poultry pins, or coarse thread on a darning needle.) If vent is too large to close, cover opening and exposed dressing with buttered piece of foil. Fold wing tips back under bird, then tie wings and legs close to body.
6. Place bird breast side up on a rack in an open roasting pan. Brush skin with oil or soft butter. (Cover each Cornish hen with a strip of bacon to keep it moist.) Insert meat thermometer in thickest part of thigh. Cover loosely with lightly buttered foil.
7. Roast in oven for 2 to 2½ hours for a stuffed 3½ lb (1.5 kg) chicken; 4 hours for a stuffed 12 lb (6 kg) turkey; 45 minutes for a stuffed Cornish hen. Baste with pan drippings to help brown. The poultry is cooked when the internal temperature reaches 190°F (85°C), the leg joint moves when the drumstick is turned, and the juices run clear, not pink.
8. Place cooked bird on hot serving platter. Let stand about 15 minutes in a warm place to allow flesh to set and make carving easier.

STUFFED CHICKEN SUPREMES WITH HONEY SESAME GLAZE

These are skinned, boned, and stuffed chicken breasts that roll up into savory little packages for a great party platter. The thing is you have to skin them yourself because you will need to repackage them in the skin for cooking and serving. That means, start early in the day to do this. It's a bit time-consuming but the result is a very elegant main dish.

If you have never skinned a chicken breast before, remove skin first, then the meat—and discard the bones or save for stock.

The honey sesame sauce can be served either in a side dish as a gravy or poured over the Supremes as they make their party entrance in a beautiful golden color.

You have to baste often to achieve that color and to preserve the moisture of the Supremes, even though the cooking time itself is brief. So plan to stay with your Supremes until they are completed. Then, keep them at room temperature— they don't have to be oven hot.

8	large whole chicken breasts, about 4¼ lbs/2.25 kg total	8
¼ lb	lean ground beef	125 g
¼ lb	ground veal	125 g
¼ lb	ground pork	125 g
1	small onion, finely chopped	1
1	clove garlic, finely chopped	1
1	piece (1 inch/2.5 cm) ginger root, peeled and finely chopped	1
8	water chestnuts, finely chopped	8
2 tbs	fine dry breadcrumbs	25 ml
2 tbs	soy sauce	25 ml
½ tsp	salt	2 ml
¼ tsp	freshly ground black pepper	1 ml
½ cup	liquid honey	125 ml
2 tbs	sesame seeds	25 ml
1	head lettuce, shredded	1

1. Remove bones and skin from chicken breasts. Reserve skin. Cut breasts in half. With a mallet flatten breasts between sheets of wax paper, until they are paper thin.
2. In a skillet combine ground beef, veal, pork, onion, garlic, ginger root, and water chestnuts; cook, stirring, about 10 minutes, until meat is no longer pink and vegetables are softened. Stir in breadcrumbs, soy sauce, salt, and pepper. Blend well. Set aside and cool.
3. Preheat oven to 325°F (160°C).
4. Place ¼ cup (50 ml) filling on each chicken breast and roll up, tucking ends in to enclose filling. Completely wrap each breast in chicken skin and secure with a toothpick. Arrange in a shallow baking pan.

5. Combine honey and sesame seeds. Bake chicken in oven for 20 minutes, basting every 5 minutes with honey mixture until chicken is golden brown and tender.
6. Place Chicken Supremes on a platter of shredded lettuce and spoon remaining honey mixture over the chicken.

Makes 8 servings.

BEAUJOLAIS NOUVEAU PARTY

TINY MUSHROOM CAPS STUFFED
with Pecans and Cream

INDIVIDUAL POTS OF PEPPERCORN PÂTÉ WITH MADEIRA

STUFFED CHICKEN SUPREMES WITH HONEY SESAME GLAZE
garnished with Whole Plums in Port

RICE PILAF WITH PINE NUTS

PURÉED BROCCOLI WITH CRÈME FRAICHE

THREE SCOOPS OF MOUSSE
—MILK CHOCOLATE
—RICH PRALINE
—MOCHA

The first course could start with a Beaujolais Nouveau, French, or Canadian, followed by a Beaujolais Villages, French, or a Gamay Noir, either from Canada or from California.

If something more full-bodied than a Beaujolais Villages is desired, then a Moulin-à-Vent could be substituted.

For dessert, a sparkling Blanc de Blanc, very dry, would complement.

BRING ON THE DUCK

There is an elegance in serving duck, particularly in North America where the flights of wild waterfowl can still conjure the chill of autumn days and the commencement of the fall social season. That's why I have selected recipes that lend themselves to formal dinner parties.

Crisp, succulent birds prepared with an eye to color, accompaniment, and an ambiance of fall leaves, chrysanthemums, soups, mushrooms.

Of course, the ducks you will use are from the butcher, the ingredients from your local market, and the genius to pull it all together is you.

THANKSGIVING DINNER

CARPACCIO WITH MUSTARDY-MAYO SAUCE

WILD MUSHROOM SOUP

ROAST DUCK WITH FIG SAUCE
SWEET POTATO PUFF

ENDIVE AND CHEESE SALAD

BAKED PEARS IN RED WINE
WALNUT CHIFFON CAKE WITH RUM AND BUTTER SAUCE

The Thanksgiving meal could commence with a very light red, possibly a French Tavel Rosé or, if more body is desired, a Chateauneuf-du-Pape. If using Italian wines, try either a Bardolino or a Castelli Romani. California provides a Petit Sirah, or Canada a Gamay Noir.

The main course requires a more robust, fruitier wine, such as a Bordeaux, either St. Julien, Margaux, or Graves, represented by such wines as Chateau Talbot, Chateau Palmer, and Smith Haut Lafitte. Spain provides a number of Gran Reservas Riojas. California, an estate Cabernet Sauvignon.

The dessert wine could be any very dry white sparkling, from France, Italy, Spain, or North America.

At Thanksgiving, bundle up tall cornstalks and surround them with pumpkins, bushels of apples, and clusters of bittersweet. Make one of these displays especially large and impressive and put it just outside the front door to let your guests know they're in for a treat.

DUCK WITH FIG SAUCE

I like to quarter the duck before I bring it to the table. Duck is not easy to carve, so I get out the poultry shears and do the job when no one is watching. I often serve this on a platter with loads of baked apples slightly colored with cranberries.

4–5 lb	duck	2–2.5 kg
½ cup	raspberry vinegar	125 ml
1	large green apple	1
2	cloves garlic	2

FIG SAUCE:

8	dried figs	8
½ cup	port	125 ml
2 tbs	sweet butter	25 ml
¼ cup	water	50 ml
2	shallots, finely chopped	2
½ cup	chicken stock	125 ml

1. Clean duck and remove all excess fat. Pierce skin well. Put duck in a heavy plastic bag. Pour raspberry vinegar over duck, secure bag, and marinate overnight in refrigerator.
2. Preheat oven to 425°F (220°C).
3. Remove duck from marinade, reserving marinade. Cut apple into chunks and place in cavity with garlic. Place duck on roasting rack in shallow roasting pan and sear in oven for 30 minutes.

4. Reduce temperature to 350°F (180°C). Pierce duck again and roast, basting frequently with reserved raspberry vinegar, for 50 to 60 minutes, or until juices run clear when duck is pierced in thickest part of thigh.
5. While duck is roasting, cut figs in quarters and marinate in port for 45 minutes. Pour figs and port into a small saucepan. Add 1 tbs (15 ml) butter and water. Bring to a boil, reduce heat, cover and simmer 15 to 20 minutes, until figs are very soft.
6. In a medium skillet, melt remaining butter, add shallots; sauté until soft but not brown. Pour in remaining reserved vinegar and boil over high heat, until reduced by half. Add chicken stock and bring to a boil. Whisk in fig mixture and simmer 5 minutes.
7. To serve, cut duck in quarters, discarding apple and garlic, and arrange on attractive serving dish. Pour fig sauce over.

Makes 4 servings.

RASPBERRY VINEGAR

You can cruise through the markets these days and find all kinds of fruit-flavored vinegars, from blueberry to raspberry.
    But if you would rather just make up a small amount of each kind (because I find that is usually all you want), here's how to do it.

1 cup	raspberries	250 ml
1 cup	white wine vinegar	250 ml

1. Wash fruit and place in sterilized 2 cup (500 ml) Mason-type jar.* Pour vinegar over fruit. Let stand in dark place, at room temperature, for at least 2 weeks.
2. Pour off the vinegar into another sterilized jar or bottle and discard fruit.
3. Store vinegar in dry cupboard at room temperature for 2 to 3 months.
    Note: Bottle the vinegar in a sterilized jar or bottle with a noncorrosive stopper. A cork works very well. For gift giving, use an old wine bottle.

Makes about 1 cup (250 ml) vinegar.

VARIATIONS:

Strawberry Vinegar: Use strawberries in place of raspberries.
Blueberry Vinegar: Use blueberries in place of raspberries.

*See p. 347 for how to sterilize.

PLUM SAUCE DUCK

This comes to the table looking absolutely fabulous. A rich dark mahogany.
Serve with lightly fried Chinese noodles to help soak up the delicious sauce.

4–6 lb	duck	2–3 kg
	salt	
	freshly ground black pepper	
1 cup	water	250 ml
½ cup	plum sauce	125 ml
¼ cup	sherry	50 ml
¼ cup	light soy sauce	50 ml
2 tbs	sugar	25 ml
1 tbs	grated orange rind	15 ml
4	cloves garlic, finely chopped	4
3	green onions, cut in 1 inch (2.5 cm) pieces	3
1 tbs	cornstarch	15 ml

1. Clean duck and pierce skin well in several places with a sharp knife or skewer. Season cavity with salt and pepper. Place duck in a large glass bowl. Combine water, plum sauce, sherry, soy sauce, sugar, orange rind, garlic, and green onions; pour over duck. Marinate at least 3 hours, or overnight in refrigerator.
2. Remove duck and reserve marinade.
3. Preheat oven to 425°F (220°C).
4. Place duck breast side up on a lightly greased roasting rack in a shallow roasting pan and sear for 30 minutes. Pierce duck again and baste with marinade.
5. Reduce temperature to 350°F (180°C) and continue to roast duck, basting and piercing often, for 1 hour, or until juices run clear when duck is pierced in thickest part of thigh.
6. When duck is almost cooked, combine cornstarch and 1 tbs (15 ml) cold water in a small saucepan, then stir in marinade. Bring to a boil, cook, stirring, about 2 minutes, until mixture thickens to a sauce. Serve sauce in a sauce dish.

Makes 4 servings.

THE VERSATILE VEAL

Veal is young, milk or corn-fed beef, but while beef will add flavor, veal absorbs whatever you choose to flavor it with, hence its delicacy and adaptability.

When one of my nieces asked me to cater her summer wedding, I decided on Roast Stuffed Veal en Gelée as the centerpiece of the meal.

SUMMER WEDDING LUNCHEON

NIBBLES WITH CHAMPAGNE
CURRY PUFFS
FINGER GNOCCHI
DATE AND CHEESE BITES
SHRIMP TOASTS

COLD CUCUMBER SOUP EMPRESS

SUMMER GREEN AND WHITE SCALLOP SEVICHE

ROAST STUFFED VEAL EN GELÉE
PASTA PRIMAVERA
CRUNCHY BROCCOLI SALAD

COEUR À LA CRÈME WITH STRAWBERRIES

ARGENTINE NUT MERINGUE WEDDING CAKE

Serve the appetizers with sparkling wine, preferably a Champagne, either French, Canadian, or American. Spain and Italy also have sparkling wines which are quite dry.

For the first course a white wine from France—either a Muscadet or a Sancerre. Or a Verdicchio di Castelli di Jesi or a Bolla Soave from Italy. A Rioja from Spain, or a Rodeo from Portugal. From California and Canada a Sevayl Blanc or a Reisling.

For the main course, a heavier white wine such as a white Burgundy from France: a Pouilly Fuissé or a Mersault. From Italy, Lacrima Christi, from Germany a Moeselle, or from Canada and the United States a white Chardonnay.

For dessert, a very sweet Vouvray.

For a wedding at home, swag white, pastel green, and pink ribbons over the doorways and mantels, leaving streamers long enough to reach the floor. Do the same for the bannisters and railings. At the points of each swag tie large bows of lace ribbon and tuck sprigs of baby's breath into each one.

Masses of white euphorbia in glass ginger jars around the room are all that are needed for the finishing touches.

Carry the white onto the table by placing three glass bowls with a single gardenia in each at the center of the table.

Roast Stuffed Veal en Gelée

This dish has the advantage of being served cold and therefore can be prepared ahead of time. Very important when you have something as momentous as a niece's wedding to prepare.

Ask your butcher to help by boning the breast of veal and wrapping with it a blanket of fat large enough to cover the roast while it is cooking.

For the platter I cut the gelée into tiny cubes and piled it around the roast so it will pick up light and shimmer and shake.

If you are doing a wedding, decide how many of these you have to make. Usually two eight-pound roasts will make enough for thirty to forty people. Beyond that, hand it all over to the caterer, but keep a firm hand on how the recipes are executed.

| 1 | boned breast of veal, 5 lbs/2.5 kg | 1 |

STUFFING:

1 lb	ground veal	500 g
¼ cup	all-purpose flour	50 ml
2 tbs	Madeira	25 ml
⅓ cup	milk	75 ml
1 tsp	dried savory leaves	5 ml
2 tsp	salt	10 ml
½ tsp	freshly ground black pepper	2 ml
1	egg, lightly beaten	1
¾ lb	fresh spinach	375 g
2 cups	grated carrot (4 medium)	500 ml
2 tbs	lemon juice	25 ml
1 tsp	dried rosemary leaves	5 ml
½ lb	fresh pork fat (barding fat)*	250 g
1 tbs	vegetable oil	15 ml
½ cup	dry white wine	125 ml

GLAZE:

2	packages (7 g each) unflavored gelatin	2
2	cans (10 oz/284 ml each) consommé	2
¼ cup	Madeira	50 ml
½ cup	mayonnaise (recipe p. 227)	125 ml

1. Open veal breast and lay skin side down on a cutting board.
2. To make Stuffing: Combine ground veal, flour, 2 tbs (25 ml) Madeira, milk, savory, 1 tsp (5 ml) salt, ¼ tsp (1 ml) pepper, and egg. Set aside.
3. In lightly salted water or in a steamer cook spinach. Squeeze out excess moisture and set aside.
4. Combine carrots, lemon juice, rosemary, 1 tsp (5 ml) salt, and ¼ tsp (1 ml) pepper. Spread evenly over veal, leaving 1 inch (2.5 cm) around all edges.
5. Preheat oven to 375°F (190°C).
6. Spread stuffing over carrots and top with layer of spinach. Roll up, jelly roll style.
7. Bard the veal: Cut the fresh pork fat into thin sheets. Lay them over the top and sides of veal roll. Tie in place with string.
8. Place seam side down on a rack in a shallow roasting pan. Roast in oven for 1 hour.

*Ask your butcher for barding fat.

9. Brush surface of roast with vegetable oil. Pour wine over roast. Roast, basting frequently, for 1½ hours longer.
10. Remove to platter, allow to cool. Wrap in plastic wrap or foil and refrigerate overnight.
11. Next day, prepare Glaze: In a saucepan sprinkle gelatin over ¾ cup (175 ml) cold consommé to soften. Stir over low heat until gelatin is dissolved. Stir in remaining consommé.
12. Pour 1¾ cups (425 ml) into a 9 inch (23 cm) square pan. Stir in ¼ cup (50 ml) Madeira. Refrigerate. Allow to set about 30 minutes, until jelled.
13. Stir mayonnaise into remaining consommé mixture. Beat until smooth. Chill until syrupy.
14. Unwrap veal roll, cut strings, remove, along with fat layer, and discard. Place veal on a platter. Spoon half mayonnaise mixture over it. Refrigerate 15 minutes until set, then spoon remaining mayonnaise mixture over veal roll.
15. With a knife cut jellied Madeira consommé into ½ inch (1 cm) cubes and spoon cubes around veal roll on a platter.

Makes 8 to 10 servings.

VEAL TENDERLOIN WITH MUSTARD SAUCE

This is a quick and easy dish to prepare.
Serve the veal on an elegant silver platter and ladle on great dollops of the creamy mustard sauce. Dot with parsley.

4	veal tenderloin slices, approximately 2 lb/1 kg total	4
1 tbs	sweet butter	15 ml
1 tbs	vegetable oil	15 ml
¼ cup	Dijon mustard	50 ml
½ cup	heavy or whipping cream	125 ml
2	egg yolks	2
¼ cup	dry white wine	50 ml
½ tsp	salt	2 ml
⅛ tsp	white pepper	0.5 ml

1. In a skillet heat butter and oil. Add veal tenderloin; sauté 5 to 7 minutes, or until no longer pink. Remove to warm serving platter and keep warm.
2. Combine mustard and ¼ cup (50 ml) cream, stir into skillet, scraping down any brown bits. Bring to boil, reduce heat, and simmer 2 minutes.

3. In a bowl, whisk together egg yolks, wine, salt, pepper, and remaining cream. Whisk into cream in skillet. Allow to heat through for about 2 minutes; do not boil.
4. Remove from heat. Pour sauce over veal and serve immediately.

Makes 4 servings.

Mail invitations at least four weeks before an important party, or even earlier at certain times of year.
   Remember coat and boot racks for the winter months.
   Consider valet parking if you live on a narrow street, if the weather is bad, or if you have an older crowd. This will be much appreciated by your guests.

CREAMY VEAL AND MUSHROOM RAGOUT

This is a versatile little dish that you can make anytime, freeze, and take with you to your ski chalet for a weekend gathering.
   The rich gravy gives you an excuse for whipping up baby dumplings to serve to guests who are cold and ravenous from the slopes.
   This perfect supper has made me the hit of many a winter party.

3 lb	stewing veal, cut in 1½ inch (3.5 cm) cubes	1.5 kg
¼ cup	all-purpose flour	50 ml
2 tsp	salt	10 ml
1 tsp	dried thyme	5 ml
½ tsp	freshly ground black pepper	2 ml
⅓ cup	sweet butter	75 ml
2 tbs	vegetable oil	25 ml
2	medium onions, coarsely chopped	2
1	clove garlic, coarsely chopped	1
½ cup	Marsala or sweet sherry	125 ml
½ cup	beef stock	125 ml
1 tbs	tomato paste	15 ml
¼ cup	heavy or whipping cream	50 ml
20	medium mushrooms, thinly sliced	20
2 cups	green peas	500 ml

1. In a bowl, combine flour, salt, thyme, and pepper; coat veal cubes with flour mixture.
2. In a large skillet or Dutch oven, heat 2 tbs (25 ml) butter and oil. Add veal; cook, stirring, about 10 minutes.

3. Add onions and garlic; cook 5 to 10 minutes, until softened.
4. Stir in Marsala, stock, and tomato paste. Cover and cook over low heat 45 minutes, or until veal is tender. Stir in 2 tbs (25 ml) butter and cream.
5. In a skillet, heat remaining butter, add mushrooms, sauté about 4 minutes.
6. Fold mushrooms and peas into veal mixture. Cook 10 minutes longer, until peas are tender.

Makes 6 servings.

STUFFED BREAST OF VEAL

This is one of the most useful dishes you can make for those Sunday dinners that somehow get out of hand: more people coming than you originally expected.
The grated potato and onion stuffing is a welcome surprise, and the natural juices from the roast form the basis for a delicious gravy.

STUFFING:

4	potatoes, peeled and grated	4
1	small onion, finely chopped	1
1	egg, slightly beaten	1
2 tbs	soft sweet butter	25 ml
1 tbs	all-purpose flour	15 ml
1 tsp	salt	5 ml
¼ tsp	freshly ground black pepper	1 ml

ROAST:

4 lb	breast of veal, with pocket for stuffing	2 kg
1	clove garlic, cut in half	1
1	medium onion, finely chopped	1
1	stalk celery, finely chopped	1
1	clove garlic, finely chopped	1
¼ cup	water	50 ml
½ tsp	salt	2 ml
½ tsp	paprika	2 ml
½ tsp	dried rosemary leaves	2 ml
¼ tsp	freshly ground black pepper	1 ml
½ cup	Chili Sauce (recipe p. 367)	125 ml
¼ cup	white wine or chicken stock	50 ml

1. To prepare Stuffing: Squeeze grated potatoes dry in paper towel. In a large bowl, combine potatoes, onion, egg, butter, flour, salt, and pepper; mix well. Set aside.

2. Preheat broiler.
3. Rub surface and inside pocket of veal with cut surfaces of garlic halves. Spoon stuffing into pocket. Tie roast in several places to hold together.
4. In bottom of roasting pan, place chopped onion, celery, chopped garlic, and water. Place roast on onion mixture in roasting pan. Sprinkle with salt, paprika, rosemary, and pepper. Spread Chili Sauce over top. Place roast under broiler 6 inches (15 cm) from heat and broil about 5 minutes, until top is browned.
5. Turn broiler off and set oven at 350°F (180°C). Cover roast and bake for 2 hours, until meat is tender and no longer pink. Remove to a platter and keep warm.
6. Place roasting pan on top of stove. Add wine to pan juices, bring to a boil, scraping down bits and deglazing pan. Reduce heat and simmer, stirring, about 2 minutes, until reduced slightly.
7. Slice roast and spoon pan juices on top.

Makes 6 servings.

A formal Valentine's dinner party. Swag long bolts of crimson moiré over mantles, mirrors, and sideboards throughout the house. Wrap white lace ribbon around the moiré. Place single red roses in crystal bud vases and place them everywhere. Make one or two spectacular arrangements of red roses in silver champagne buckets. The odd cherub here and there would complete the atmosphere.

VEAL CHOPS FORESTIÈRE

Try hard to find the chanterelles. If you can't, you can use ordinary white mushrooms. But chanterelles make this dish really special.
Serve with fresh buttered noodles.

4	veal chops, 1½ inch (4 cm) thick	4
½ tsp	salt	2 ml
¼ tsp	freshly ground black pepper	1 ml
2 tbs	sweet butter	25 ml
1 tbs	vegetable oil	15 ml
½ cup	slivered prosciutto	125 ml
1 lb	chanterelles	500 g
3	shallots, coarsely chopped	3
2	green onions, coarsely chopped	2
1	clove garlic, finely chopped	1
1 cup	chicken or veal stock	250 ml

1. Sprinkle chops with salt and pepper. In a large skillet, heat butter and oil; sauté chops 5 to 7 minutes on each side, until well browned but medium rare inside. Transfer chops to warm serving platter and keep warm.
2. To the same skillet, add prosciutto; stir-fry 2 minutes, until slightly crisp. Remove with slotted spoon and set aside.
3. Add chanterelles to the same skillet; sauté 3 to 4 minutes, until lightly browned.
4. Add shallots, green onions, and garlic. Cook 2 minutes longer.
5. Stir in stock. Simmer, stirring, 6 to 8 minutes, until reduced by half.
6. Stir prosciutto into sauce. Spoon over chops and serve.

Makes 4 servings.

Fill a large white mixing bowl with ten or twelve pomegranates for a bold display of red and white.

SWEETBREADS AU PORTO

This recipe has won over people who have avoided sweetbreads up to tasting time. It is a favorite of mine.

Both sweetbreads and sauce can be made ready early in the day so that final preparation takes only minutes.

I serve this with a light Saffron Rice.

2 lb	veal sweetbreads	1 kg
1 tbs	lemon juice	15 ml
½ cup	sweet butter	125 ml
2	onions, finely chopped	2
1 cup	thinly sliced mushrooms	250 ml
pinch	*each* of thyme, salt, and freshly ground black pepper	pinch
¼ cup	all-purpose flour	50 ml
1 cup	beef stock	250 ml
½ cup	Port	125 ml
	all-purpose flour, salt, and freshly ground black pepper	

1. In a bowl of ice water soak the sweetbreads for 30 minutes. Drain and place in large saucepan. Pour boiling water over to cover. Add lemon juice, bring to a boil, reduce heat, cover, and simmer 10 minutes, until tender.
2. Drain and cool immediately in ice cold water. Remove all connective tissue and membrane. Slice into ½ inch (1 cm) slices. Set aside.
3. In a medium saucepan melt ¼ cup (50 ml) butter. Add onions and sauté until softened. Add mushrooms, thyme, salt, and pepper; sauté until mushrooms are lightly brown.
4. Sprinkle flour over mixture and stir until all is absorbed. Slowly add stock, stirring constantly over medium heat until smooth. Add Port and bring to a boil, reduce heat, cover, and simmer 10 minutes.
5. While sauce is simmering, dredge sweetbread slices in flour seasoned with salt and pepper. In a large skillet melt remaining butter. Add sweetbreads and sauté in batches, if necessary, about 4 minutes, turning until golden brown on both sides.
6. Remove to a warm serving platter, cover to keep warm. Serve sauce with sweetbreads.

Makes 6 servings.

WINES

Order red wines two weeks before and allow them to settle, especially if they are vintage.
White wines are easily chilled in a laundry tub or rental tub.

WIENER SCHNITZEL

I keep this in mind when time is tight and serve it with Chunky Provençal Sauce.

6	veal scallops (4 oz/125 g each)	6
½ tsp	salt	2 ml
¼ tsp	white pepper	1 ml
¼ cup	all-purpose flour	50 ml
2	eggs, lightly beaten	2
1 cup	fine dry breadcrumbs	250 ml
2 tbs	sweet butter	25 ml
2 tbs	vegetable oil	25 ml

1. With a mallet lightly pound veal scallops between sheets of waxed paper until paper thin. Sprinkle both sides with salt and pepper. Dredge with flour.
2. Dip in beaten eggs, then coat with breadcrumbs and tap lightly with flat edge of knife to make crumbs stick.
3. Refrigerate 1 hour so that crumbs dry and adhere.
4. In a large skillet, heat butter and oil. Add 2 scallops, cook, turning once, for 5 minutes, until crumbs are golden and crisp. Place on hot platter. Keep warm. Cook remaining scallops. Serve immediately.

Makes 6 servings.

Variation:
Chicken Schnitzel: Use halved, skinned, and boned chicken breasts in place of the veal scallops.

CHUNKY PROVENÇAL SAUCE

Provençal refers to the South of France, where garlic grows wild and the people think they invented tomatoes. This is the perfect sauce for Wiener Schnitzel or Chicken Schnitzel. So chunky and rich, it can be served hot or cold.

2 tbs	olive oil	25 ml
1	medium onion, thickly sliced	1
2	cloves garlic, minced	2
½ lb	mushrooms, thickly sliced	250 g
6	large ripe tomatoes, peeled and chopped	6
¼ cup	sliced pitted black olives	50 ml
¼ cup	sliced pitted green olives	50 ml
1 tbs	tomato paste	15 ml
1 tsp	dried oregano	5 ml
1 tsp	salt	5 ml
1 tsp	freshly ground black pepper	5 ml

1. In a large skillet, heat oil. Add onion and garlic; sauté for 5 minutes.
2. Stir in mushrooms; cook about 7 minutes, until all liquid disappears and mushrooms are golden brown.
3. Stir in tomatoes, black and green olives, tomato paste, oregano, salt, and pepper. Bring to a boil, reduce heat, and simmer, uncovered, for 20 minutes.

Makes 4 servings.

PARSLEY, MINT, ROSEMARY, AND LAMB

Succulent cuts of tender lamb are available year-round, but to me, lamb is spring.

It is synonymous with great bowls of daffodils and tulips on the table, fresh herbs just budding.

I find myself humming a little descant of "Parsley, mint, rosemary, and lamb" to the tune of "Scarborough Fair."

Beyond lamb roasts, I have given you a number of recipes for Indian curries, which is another role this meat is perfectly suited for. Try them all any time of year, but especially in the spring, when the world drips with wet lilac and honey.

SHOPPING LIST FOR INDIAN COOKING:

Coriander   *Marjoram leaves*
Cumin   *Thyme leaves*
Turmeric   *Coconut*
Red pepper   *Garam masala*
Imported curry powder

LAMB CALCUTTA

The shreds of coconut and the chunks of apple make this a very sweet and gentle curried lamb.
Serve with your favorite chutney and my Sweet Rice.

2 lb	lean boneless lamb, cut in 1 inch (2.5 cm) cubes	1 kg
¼ cup	olive oil	50 ml
2	large apples, peeled, cored, and coarsely chopped	2
2	large onions, coarsely chopped	2
1	clove garlic, finely chopped	1
2 tbs	all-purpose flour	25 ml
1 tbs	curry powder	15 ml
½ tsp	salt	2 ml
½ tsp	dried marjoram	2 ml
½ tsp	dried thyme	2 ml
1½ cups	beef stock	375 ml
½ cup	dry red wine	125 ml
1	lemon, grated rind and juice	1
½ cup	raisins	125 ml
¼ tsp	ground cloves	1 ml
¼ cup	shredded coconut	50 ml
2 tbs	sour cream	25 ml

1. In a large skillet, heat 2 tbs (25 ml) oil; add lamb cubes, half at a time. Cook, turning, about 10 minutes, until lightly browned. Remove to a warm dish and keep warm. Repeat with remaining lamb.
2. In the same skillet, heat remaining oil. Add apples, onions, and garlic. Sauté about 5 minutes, until softened. Stir in flour, curry powder, salt, marjoram, and thyme. Cook, stirring, for 3 minutes.
3. Gradually stir in stock, wine, lemon rind and juice, raisins, cloves, and browned lamb cubes. Bring to a boil, reduce heat, cover, and simmer 20 to 30 minutes.
4. Stir in coconut. Cover and simmer 15 minutes longer.
5. Just before serving, blend in sour cream.

Makes 6 servings.

VEGETABLE PATÉ WITH DIJON MAYONNAISE

CURRIED CARROT AND LEEK SOUP WITH GARLIC CROUTONS
ROAST LEG OF LAMB WITH CANDIED ORANGES AND PEPPERS

BARLEY CASSEROLE

MIXED GREEN SALAD WITH CLASSIC DRESSING

CHEESE TRAY

LEMON SOUFFLE

This is a red wine menu. If using French wines, start with Châteauneuf-du-Pape and follow with a fruitier red wine such as a Chambertin or a Richebourg. For Italian wines, start with Torgiano Rubesco Reserva and follow with either an estate Barolo or a Brunello di Montalcino.

For Spanish wines try a young Rioja followed by an estate Rioja such as a Cune Imperial Gran Reserva 1960.

With California wines, start with a Barbera, followed by a Cabernet Sauvignon.

ROAST LEG OF LAMB WITH CANDIED ORANGES AND PEPPERS

This is three recipes in one, and the accompanying garnish and sauce can be used with chicken or with pork and do the same marvelous things for them—but not quite as excitingly.

Be prepared to spend a little time on this. You will earn a huge reward in happy guests.

GLAZED ORANGES AND PEPPERS:

1 cup	granulated sugar	250 ml
½ cup	corn syrup	125 ml
1 cup	water	250 ml
2	oranges, cut into ¼ inch (6 mm) slices	2
2	red peppers, cut in ¼ inch (6 mm) rings	2

ROAST LEG OF LAMB:

1	leg of lamb, 5–6 lb (2.5–3 kg)	1
¼ cup	olive oil	50 ml
¼ cup	lemon juice	50 ml
1 tbs	grainy mustard	15 ml
1 tsp	salt	5 ml
¼ tsp	freshly ground black pepper	1 ml
2 cups	dry white wine	500 ml

163

ORANGE PEPPER SAUCE:

¼ cup	sweet butter	50 ml
3	shallots, finely chopped	3
1	small onion, finely chopped	1
2	cloves garlic, finely chopped	2
	grated rind of ¼ orange	
1 tbs	lemon juice	15 ml
1	dried hot chili pepper, broken in pieces, seeds removed	1
½ tsp	salt	2 ml
2 tbs	all-purpose flour	25 ml
¾ cup	dry red wine	175 ml
¾ cup	water	175 ml

1. To prepare Glazed Oranges and Peppers: In a medium saucepan combine sugar, corn syrup, and water. Bring to a boil, reduce heat, and simmer 10 minutes.
2. Add orange slices and pepper rings. Bring to a boil, reduce heat, and simmer 10 to 15 minutes, until translucent. With a slotted spoon, remove and place orange and pepper rings on a plate to cool.
3. To prepare Roast Leg of Lamb: Place lamb in a roasting pan. Combine oil, lemon juice, mustard, salt, and pepper. Brush ½ of mixture on lamb. Pour remainder over lamb, cover, and marinate overnight, brushing occasionally with marinade.
4. Preheat oven to 400°F (200°C). Insert roast meat thermometer in thickest part of roast.
5. Roast in marinade in oven for 20 minutes. Pour all drippings and marinade from pan and discard.
6. Reduce oven temperature to 350°F (180°C), pour wine over lamb, and roast 1 hour, basting fequently with wine from pan. Remove lamb from oven, but do not turn off oven. Pour off pan juices, reserving 1 cup (250 ml) for sauce.
7. To prepare Orange Pepper Sauce: In a saucepan heat butter, add shallots, onion, and garlic; sauté about 5 minutes, until softened. Add orange rind, lemon juice, chili pepper, and salt; mix well. Stir in flour.
8. Stir in wine and water; cook, stirring occasionally, for 20 minutes, until thickened. Stir in reserved pan juice. Strain sauce.
9. Pour ½ Orange Pepper Sauce over lamb in roasting pan. Return lamb to oven and roast about 1 hour longer, basting frequently with sauce until meat thermometer registers 150°F (65°C), or medium rare.
10. Remove roast to warm platter and let stand 10 minutes to firm. Garnish lamb with Glazed Oranges and Pepper Rings. Pour remaining sauce in sauce pot and serve with lamb.

Makes 8 servings.

BARBECUED BUTTERFLY LAMB

I serve this with brown rice and sautéed red onions. I add a summer salad of blanched green beans and broccoli, raw zucchini, sliced or diced tomatoes, raw onion slices, and fresh mushrooms, all tossed with my Tomato Vinaigrette.

One tip: Make sure the knife you use for slicing and crisscrossing is super sharp.

1	butterflied leg of lamb, 4–6 lbs (2–3 kg)	1
2	large cloves garlic, coarsely chopped	2
½ cup	dry red wine	125 ml
¼ cup	olive oil	50 ml
¼ cup	lemon juice	50 ml
¼ cup	Dijon mustard	50 ml
¼ cup	chopped fresh mint leaves	50 ml
1 tbs	dried rosemary leaves	15 ml
1 tbs	dried oregano	15 ml
¼ tsp	freshly ground black pepper	1 ml

1. Place lamb in a large glass dish.
2. In a bowl combine garlic, wine, oil, lemon juice, mustard, mint, rosemary, oregano, and pepper; mix well. Pour over lamb. Cover and marinate in refrigerator for several hours or overnight. Turn lamb over in marinade several times so it is well coated.
3. Remove lamb from marinade, reserving marinade.
4. Before barbecuing, with a sharp knife score fat with crisscross lines to prevent meat from curling. Place lamb on barbecue grill 4 to 5 inches (10 to 12.5 cm) above hot coals. Barbecue lamb for 40 to 45 minutes, turning every 10 minutes and basting frequently with reserved marinade, until lamb is cooked to the desired doneness.
5. Allow roast to stand 10 minutes to set juices. With a very sharp knife, slice thinly and serve.

Makes 8 to 10 servings.

LAMB BASTED

I couldn't resist the pun. You can use a boned shoulder or a leg of lamb for this. If you use the leg, I suggest you get the butcher to bone it.

I like to start this the day before because I can let the roast cool and skim off all the fat.

1	boned shoulder or leg of lamb, 4–5 lb (2–2.5 kg)	1
2	cloves garlic, halved	2
1 tsp	salt	5 ml
1 tsp	freshly ground black pepper	5 ml
½ tsp	chili powder	2 ml
½ tsp	dry mustard	2 ml
¼ tsp	ground ginger	1 ml
1 tsp	lemon juice	5 ml
1 cup	tomato sauce	250 ml
½ cup	dry red wine	125 ml
	beef stock	

1. Preheat oven to 500°F (260°C).
2. With the point of a knife cut 4 slits in surface of lamb and insert pieces of garlic in slits. Combine salt, pepper, chili powder, mustard, and ginger. Sprinkle over surface of lamb. Place roast on a rack in a roasting pan. Sprinkle with lemon juice. Insert roast meat thermometer in thickest part of roast. Roast in oven for 20 minutes.
3. Reduce oven temperature to 300°F (150°C). Combine tomato sauce and wine; brush over roast. Return lamb to oven and roast, basting frequently with tomato mixture, for 2 to 2½ hours until meat thermometer registers 150°F (65°C) or medium rare.
4. Pour any liquid in bottom of pan into a measuring cup. Skim off fat. Add enough beef stock to make 2 cups (500 ml). Taste and season with salt and pepper if desired. Heat and serve as "jus" with lamb.

Makes 8 servings.

> *Braid a wreath of cedar or pine rope around the base of a silver three-candle candelabra. Decorate with small gold balls, thin gold ribbon, and walnuts.*

SWEDISH LAMB ROAST

There are all kinds of surprises in this very pretty lamb, not the least of which is a cup of coffee with cream and sugar.

The candied carrots are another bonus: you can adjust the number of carrots used to the number of guests you have invited.

I should add a note here about how to serve roasts. There is nothing quite so awkward as an inexperienced person trying to carve at table. I am not bad, but I still won't do it. I always let the roast cool down, carve in the kitchen and then warm everything up at the last moment.

1	leg of lamb, 4–5 lb (2–2.5 kg)	1
½ tsp	salt	2 ml
¼ tsp	freshly ground black pepper	1 ml
1	medium onion, thinly sliced	1
8	medium carrots, thickly sliced	8
1 cup	beef stock	250 ml
1 cup	very strong coffee	250 ml
½ cup	heavy or whipping cream	125 ml
1 tbs	sugar	15 ml

1. Preheat oven to 425°F (220°C).
2. Sprinkle lamb with salt and pepper. Insert roast meat thermometer in thickest part of roast. Place in roasting pan; sprinkle sliced onion around lamb. Roast in oven for 30 minutes.
3. Reduce oven temperature to 350°F (180°C). Add carrots and stock to pan. Roast 30 minutes longer.
4. Combine coffee, cream, and sugar; baste lamb, and roast 20 minutes longer, or until meat thermometer registers 150°F (65°C) or medium rare.
5. Remove roast to warm serving platter, let stand 10 minutes to make carving easier. Surround with carrots. Serve warm pan sauce in sauce boat.

Makes 6 to 8 servings.

INDIAN LAMB CHOPS IN A SNAPPY YOGURT MARINADE

The marinade makes these lamb chops. Let them soak in it until your guests are ready to have you barbecue.

12	loin lamb chops, ¾ inch/2 cm thick	12
	salt and freshly ground black pepper	
1 cup	yogurt	250 ml
1 tbs	crushed coriander seeds	15 ml
2 tsp	ground cumin	10 ml
1 tsp	garam masala*	5 ml
1	red onion, coarsely chopped	1
2	cloves garlic, finely chopped	2
1	lime, grated rind and juice	1
1	slice (½ inch/1 cm) ginger root, peeled and chopped	1
¼ tsp	hot pepper sauce	1 ml
	coarsely ground black pepper	

1. Arrange lamb chops in a shallow baking dish and season with salt and pepper. Combine yogurt, coriander, cumin, garam masala, onion, lime rind and juice, ginger root, and hot pepper sauce. Pour over lamb and allow to marinate, covered in refrigerator, overnight.
2. Broil or grill chops 5 minutes on each side or until cooked to desired doneness. Top with coarsely ground black pepper.

Makes 6 servings.

SPICY LAMB CHOPS IN A TOMATO ROSEMARY MARINADE

Somewhere someone tasted a tomato and said, "Needs Rosemary!" So here it is. The classic Tomato Rosemary Marinade for lamb chop barbecues and grills.

12	loin lamb chops, ¾ inch/2 cm thick	12

MARINADE:

½ cup	tomato paste	125 ml
½ cup	vegetable oil	125 ml
2 tbs	soy sauce	25 ml
2 tbs	red wine vinegar	25 ml
4	cloves garlic, finely chopped	4
1 tbs	dried rosemary leaves	15 ml
1 tsp	salt	5 ml
½ tsp	coarsely ground black pepper	2 ml

*Can be purchased in specialty food shops.

1. Arrange lamb chops in a shallow baking dish.
2. Combine tomato paste, oil, soy sauce, vinegar, garlic, rosemary, salt, and pepper. Pour over lamb chops and marinate, covered, overnight in refrigerator.
3. Broil or grill 5 minutes on each side, or until cooked to desired doneness.

Makes 6 servings.

MOUSSAKA

This is a wonderful prepare-ahead dish and can be easily reheated wherever you want to take it, provided there is an oven nearby.

3	medium eggplants (2 lb/1 kg each) unpeeled	3
⅓ cup	all-purpose flour	75 ml
½ cup	vegetable oil	125 ml
¼ cup	sweet butter	50 ml

TOMATO SAUCE:

1 cup	red wine	250 ml
¼ cup	tomato paste	50 ml
1	bay leaf	1
¼ tsp	dried thyme	1 ml
¼ tsp	dried marjoram	1 ml

MEAT SAUCE:

3	medium onions, finely chopped	3
2	cloves garlic, finely chopped	2
2 lb	ground lamb	1 kg
½ cup	chopped fresh parsley	125 ml
1½ tsp	salt	7 ml
½ tsp	cinnamon	2 ml
½ tsp	freshly ground black pepper	2 ml

CHEESE SAUCE:

3 tbs	sweet butter	45 ml
3 tbs	all-purpose flour	45 ml
2 cups	milk	500 ml
½ tsp	salt	2 ml
¼ tsp	ground nutmeg	1 ml
2	eggs, well beaten	2
1 cup	ricotta cheese	250 ml
½ cup	fine dry breadcrumbs	125 ml
¼ cup	grated Parmesan cheese	50 ml

1. Cut eggplants crosswise into ½ inch (1 cm) slices. Dredge with flour. In a large skillet heat ¼ cup (50 ml) oil and 2 tbs (25 ml) butter. Brown half eggplant slices on both sides. Remove and drain on paper towel.
2. To skillet add remaining oil and butter; brown remaining eggplant slices. Remove and drain on paper towel.
3. To make Tomato Sauce: Pour wine into small saucepan. Simmer over low heat until volume is reduced by half to ½ cup (125 ml). Stir in tomato paste, bay leaf, thyme, and marjoram. Simmer 5 minutes. Remove bay leaf. Set tomato sauce aside.
4. To make Meat Sauce: To the same skillet used for cooking eggplant, add onions, garlic, and lamb; cook, stirring, about 10 minutes, until onion is softened and lamb is no longer pink. Stir in Tomato Sauce, parsley, salt, cinnamon, and pepper. Cover and simmer, over low heat for 20 minutes, or until most of the liquid is absorbed. Set meat sauce aside.
5. To make Cheese Sauce: In a saucepan, heat butter and flour; mix well. Whisk in milk, salt, and nutmeg. Cook, whisking constantly, about 5 minutes, until thickened. Stir a little of the hot sauce into the beaten eggs and then whisk egg mixture back into sauce. Stir in ricotta cheese.
6. Preheat oven to 350°F (180°C).
7. To assemble: Over the bottom of a 9 × 13 inch (23 × 33 cm) baking pan sprinkle breadcrumbs. Arrange eggplant slices over breadcrumbs. Spread meat mixture over eggplant and top with cheese sauce. Sprinkle Parmesan cheese over all.
8. Bake in oven for 45 minutes, until bubbly and golden brown. Allow to cool slightly before cutting.

   Moussaka may be prepared a day ahead and reheated.

Makes 10 servings.

HERE'S THE BEEF

Beef is one of the great meats of the world. Since we cannot deal here with everything from Boeuf Bourgignon to Beef Wellington, I have tried to select a variety of beef recipes that stress the unusual and in one case the elevated: the filet roast of beef with pepper sauce.

The two brisket recipes are great main course dishes for taking to the country or cottage for weekends away.

The chili con carne is so different it makes all other chili recipes seem wrong or at least a little out of step.

The cabbage rolls are fit to serve to kings, but their true appeal is filling in as a delicious surprise for a ski weekend party or an in-town impromptu buffet.

BRISKET IN GINGERALE

This takes patience but is well worth it.

Since my guests have always exclaimed over the glazed carrots, I have allowed two for each person. If you have some brisket left over the next day, you are in for a treat, either hot with gravy or cold with horseradish sauce.

4–5 lb	beef brisket	2–2.5 kg
2	cloves garlic, finely chopped	2
1 tsp	paprika	5 ml
1 tsp	salt	5 ml
½ tsp	freshly ground black pepper	2 ml
¼ cup	prepared mustard	50 ml
1	large onion, finely chopped	1
8	carrots, cut in 2 inch (5 cm) pieces	8
2 tbs	water	25 ml
1	bottle (24 oz/750 ml) gingerale	1

1. Preheat oven to 450°F (230°C).
2. Rub brisket with garlic, paprika, salt, pepper, and mustard. Place brisket in heavy roasting pan. Sprinkle onion on top of brisket. Place carrots around brisket. Add water to pan.
3. Bake brisket in oven for 45 minutes. Remove from oven and drain off all fat.
4. Lower oven temperature to 300°F (150°C). Baste meat with ¼ cup (50 ml) gingerale. Bake, uncovered, for 20 minutes. Remove from oven; pour off liquid in pan and reserve.
5. Baste again with ¼ cup (50 ml) gingerale, return to oven, and continue baking for 20 minutes.
6. Repeat baste and drain procedure every 20 minutes for another 3 hours 20 minutes, until all of gingerale is used and beef is very tender. In a bowl pour off all gingerale drippings and reserve for gravy.
7. Remove brisket, cool, wrap; remove carrots to a small container, cover; refrigerate brisket and carrots overnight. Pour remaining pan juices into bowl, place in refrigerator overnight so that fat layer that rises to the top will harden. Lift off fat layer and discard.
8. Preheat oven to 350°F (180°C).
9. Slice brisket and arrange slices in a shallow casserole. Pour reserved pan juices over top. Place carrots around meat. Cover and reheat in oven about 30 minutes, or until heated through.

Makes 8 servings.

GERMAN POT ROAST

Again an unusual ingredient gives this dish its special zing. It's the crushed gingersnaps that do it. Makes a great winter party dish.

Once it is done, I carve it, then let it sit in the gravy till it's time to heat and serve.

4 lb	beef brisket	2 kg
2 tsp	salt	10 ml
4	cloves garlic, finely chopped	4
1	piece (1½ inch/3.5 cm) ginger root, peeled and finely chopped	1
2 cups	red wine vinegar	500 ml
1 cup	water	250 ml
½ cup	dry vermouth	125 ml
⅓ cup	granulated sugar	75 ml
2	onions, finely chopped	2
8	whole cloves	8
2	bay leaves	2
2 tsp	pickling spice	10 ml
1 tsp	whole black peppercorns	5 ml
½ tsp	dry mustard	2 ml
2 tbs	vegetable oil	25 ml
4	gingersnaps, crushed	4

1. Rub brisket all over with salt. In a large bowl place brisket; sprinkle garlic and ginger root over top.
2. Combine vinegar, water, vermouth, sugar, onions, cloves, bay leaves, pickling spice, peppercorns, mustard, vegetable oil. Pour marinade over brisket. Cover tightly and refrigerate overnight, turning once.
3. Remove brisket from marinade and reserve 2 cups (500 ml) of marinade. Pat meat with paper towels. In a Dutch oven, heat oil; add brisket and cook, turning once or twice, for about 10 minutes, until brown.
4. Preheat oven to 350°F (180°C). Pour reserved marinade over brisket; cover and bake in oven for 2 to 3 hours, or until meat is tender.
5. Let stand 10 minutes to firm. Remove meat to board and slice. Cover and refrigerate until required. Place pan juices in refrigerator until fat layer hardens.
6. Preheat oven to 300°F (150°C).
7. Arrange brisket slices in 8½ × 12½ inch (21 × 31 cm) shallow casserole. Remove fat from pan juices and strain juices into a saucepan. Add crushed gingersnaps. Bring to a boil, reduce heat, and simmer 2 minutes, until thickened. Pour over brisket slices.
8. Reheat in oven about 15 minutes, until hot. Serve immediately.

Makes 8 servings.

ORIENTAL BEEF SHISH KEBABS

I marinate these tidbits before I go out, knowing they will take only moments to prepare when my guests arrive. Serve with cooked rice vermicelli, chopped mint, shredded lettuce, and Dipping Sauce.

2 lb	beef sirloin steak	1 kg
⅓ cup	vegetable oil	75 ml
1 tbs	sesame oil	15 ml
1 tbs	granulated sugar	15 ml
1 tbs	soy sauce	15 ml
1 tbs	toasted sesame seeds	15 ml
1	clove garlic, finely chopped	1
1 tsp	salt	5 ml
½ tsp	freshly ground black pepper	2 ml
¼ tsp	five-spice powder*	1 ml
	toasted sesame seeds	

1. Cut beef into 2 × 1 × ¼ inch (5 cm × 2.5 cm × 5 mm) slices. Place in a glass bowl.
2. Combine vegetable oil, sesame oil, sugar, soy sauce, sesame seeds, garlic, salt, pepper, and five-spice powder. Pour over meat; cover and marinate for 3 to 4 hours in refrigerator.
3. Thread meat onto wooden or metal skewers, 6 inches (15 cm) long. (Soak wooden skewers in a pan of warm water, 1 hour before using.) Barbecue, grill, or broil, turning once, about 6 minutes or until meat is medium rare.
4. Sprinkle with additional sesame seeds. Serve with dipping sauce.

DIPPING SAUCE:

½ cup	water	125 ml
¼ cup	fish sauce*	50 ml
1	small clove garlic, finely chopped	1
½ tsp	granulated sugar	2 ml
¼ tsp	lemon juice	1 ml
dash	hot pepper sauce	dash

In a bowl, combine water, fish sauce, garlic, sugar, lemon juice, and hot pepper sauce; mix well.

Makes 6 servings.

*Available in Chinese specialty stores.

CABBAGE ROLLS

I can't think of a better dish to make, freeze, and hold for those occasions when you want to ask the whole crowd in and you haven't prepared a thing.

I often serve a bowl of sour cream on the side, along with skewered mushrooms.

The dark raisins and almonds add to the special taste and help produce the deep, dark sauce.

1	large head cabbage (24 medium leaves)	1
	boiling water	
2 lb	lean ground beef	1 kg
1 cup	long grain rice	250 ml
1	egg, well beaten	1
½ cup	water	125 ml
1	large onion, finely chopped	1
1	small clove garlic, finely chopped	1
2 tsp	salt	10 ml
½ tsp	freshly ground black pepper	2 ml
2	large carrots, thinly sliced	2
2	stalks celery, thinly sliced	2
½ cup	raisins	125 ml
12	whole almonds	12
1 cup	lightly packed brown sugar	250 ml
½ cup	lemon juice	125 ml
1	can (28 oz/796 ml) Italian tomatoes	1
1	can (10 oz/284 ml) tomato soup	1
	sour cream	

1. With a sharp knife remove core of cabbage and discard. In a large saucepan of lightly salted boiling water, place cabbage. Bring to a boil and boil 5 minutes. Remove leaves, 1 at a time, being careful not to break them. Drain leaves on paper towel.
2. Preheat oven to 350°F (180°C).
3. In a large bowl combine beef, rice, egg, water, onion, garlic, salt, and pepper; mix well. Place heaping tablespoons of filling in middle of each cabbage leaf, fold edge over, turn in sides, and roll up tightly.
4. In a shallow baking or roasting pan, layer carrots and celery. Arrange cabbage rolls over this "bed" of vegetables. Spread raisins, almonds, and brown sugar over rolls. Pour on lemon juice and tomatoes. Cover and bake in oven for 2 hours.
5. Remove cover and bake 1 hour longer, until cabbage rolls are tender. Serve with sour cream.
   Cabbage rolls freeze well.

Makes 24 cabbage rolls.

BEST EVER CHILI CON CARNE

It's the chocolate that makes this taste so different and definitive.

Every time I have served this down through the years, I have had to pass out recipes. I serve this with bowls of grated Cheddar cheese, chopped raw onion, and green peppers. Cornmeal muffins are the perfect scoopers.

2 lb	lean ground beef or beef cubes	1 kg
2½ cups	dry kidney beans	625 ml
¼ cup	olive oil	50 ml
3	cloves garlic, finely chopped	3
2	stalks celery, finely chopped	2
2	large onions, finely chopped	2
1	green pepper, finely chopped	1
1	can (28 oz/796 ml) plum tomatoes	1
2–3 tbs	chili powder	25–45 ml
1 tbs	brown sugar	15 ml
2½ tsp	salt	12 ml
1 tsp	ground cumin	5 ml
½ tsp	freshly ground black pepper	2 ml
½ tsp	dried oregano	2 ml
¼ tsp	cayenne pepper	1 ml
1	square (1 oz/28 g) bittersweet chocolate	1

1. In a large kettle, cover kidney beans with water. Soak overnight.
2. Drain off water. Cover beans with fresh boiling water 1 inch (2.5 cm) over top of beans. Return to a boil, reduce heat, cover, and simmer 40 minutes, until tender. Drain water from beans, reserving 2 cups (500 ml) cooking water.
3. In a large skillet, heat oil; add garlic, celery, onions, and green peppers. Sauté about 5 minutes, until softened. Add beef and cook, stirring, 10 minutes, until beef is no longer pink.
4. Transfer meat mixture to beans in kettle. Stir in tomatoes, chili powder, brown sugar, salt, cumin, pepper, oregano, cayenne, chocolate, and reserved water from kidney beans. Bring to a boil, cover, and simmer, stirring frequently, for 1 hour.
5. For thicker chili, remove lid and simmer until desired thickness.
   Chili may be refrigerated to be reheated later, or it may be frozen.

Makes 8 servings.

BEEFCAKES IN SOUR CREAM DILL SAUCE

This is not truly a hamburger, although it may seem to be parading as one. Once you get the sour cream with dill sauce over it, your beef has a whole new personality—one your guests will applaud.

1½ lb	lean ground beef	750 g
½ cup	sour cream	125 ml
1	clove garlic, finely chopped	1
½ tsp	salt	2 ml
¼ tsp	freshly ground black pepper	1 ml
2 tbs	sweet butter	25 ml

1. In a bowl combine beef, sour cream, garlic, salt, and pepper. Cover and refrigerate 15 minutes before shaping patties.
2. Divide into 6 portions and with hands form them into patties. In a skillet, heat butter. Cook patties, turning once, for 10 minutes, until lightly brown on the outside, pink on the inside.
3. Set patties on a warm platter and keep warm.

SOUR CREAM DILL SAUCE:

1 cup	sour cream	250 ml
1	clove garlic, finely chopped	1
2 tbs	chopped fresh dill, or 2 tsp (10 ml) dried dill	25 ml
½ tsp	granulated sugar	2 ml

1. In a small saucepan combine sour cream, garlic, dill, and sugar. Stir in juice from platter of cooked patties.
2. Heat sauce to simmering and serve over patties.

Makes 6 patties.

THE GREAT AMERICAN EPICUREAN HAMBURGER

Hamburger patties made epicurean by a gourmet sauce.

2 lb	lean ground beef	1 kg
¼ cup	chili sauce	50 ml
¼ cup	light or table cream	50 ml
2 tbs	Worcestershire sauce	25 ml
½ tsp	salt	2 ml
¼ tsp	freshly ground black pepper	1 ml
1 tbs	sweet butter	15 ml

1. In a bowl, combine beef, chili sauce, cream, Worcestershire sauce, salt, and pepper. Divide into 8 portions and with hands shape into patties.
2. In a large skillet, heat butter, cook patties, turning once, for 10 minutes, until light brown on the outside and pink on the inside.
3. Set patties on a warm platter and keep warm.

SAUCE:

2	green onions, finely chopped	2
¼ cup	red wine	50 ml
1 tbs	tomato paste	15 ml
¾ cup	heavy or whipping cream	175 ml

1. Return skillet to heat. To drippings in skillet add green onions; sauté 3 to 4 minutes, until softened.
2. Stir in red wine and tomato paste and simmer about 1 minute, or until reduced by half. Stir in cream. Simmer, stirring, 2 to 3 minutes, or until as thick as gravy. Spoon over patties.

Makes 8 patties.

SALMON MOUSSE IN ARTICHOKE BOTTOMS
With Remoulade Sauce

HOT CHÈVRE SALAD WITH BACON BITS

FILLET ROAST OF BEEF WITH PEPPER SAUCE

SKEWERED MUSHROOMS WITH OREGANO

POMMES FRITES

RICH CHOCOLATE CAKE

This is essentially a red wine dinner. The starting wine could be a very light red from France, a Beaujolais—or a Bardolino from Italy, a very young Rioja from Spain, a Zinfandel from California, or a Pinot Noir from Canada.

For the main course, a robust wine should be used, such as one of the major French Bordeaux, ranging from Chateau Latour to Chateau Haut-Brion and Chateau Leoville-Barton. Less expensive French wines could include Chateau Petit Village, a Chateau Pavie, or even go to a Crozes-Hermitage.

No wine is recommended for the dessert.

FILLET ROAST OF BEEF

The special combination of herbs and spices in this recipe can be used on lamb, veal, and pork roasts and chops. You might want to make a double batch, so that you can put one in a covered jar or shaker for later use. Keep in a dry, cool spot.

4½ lbs	beef fillet	2 kg
2 tbs	dried oregano	25 ml
1 tbs	dried thyme	15 ml
1 tbs	celery seed	15 ml
1 tbs	dried marjoram	15 ml
1 tbs	garlic powder	15 ml
1 tbs	coarse salt	15 ml
1 tbs	cracked green or black peppercorns	15 ml

1. In a bowl or jar, combine oregano, thyme, celery seed, marjoram, garlic powder, salt, and peppercorns. Rub seasoning mix on all sides of fillet to coat fillet completely. (Store any remaining mixture in a tightly covered container in a cool, dry cupboard for up to 6 months.)
2. Place beef on a plate, cover lightly with waxed paper. Allow to stand in refrigerator for 1 to 2 hours.
3. Preheat oven to 425°F (220°C).
4. Place fillet on rack of shallow roasting pan and roast in oven for 10 minutes.
5. Reduce heat to 325°F (160°C) and roast for another 30 minutes, until rare, or 40 minutes, until medium rare.
6. Remove to a warm platter. Let stand 10 minutes before slicing.
   Serve with Pepper Sauce.

Makes 10 to 12 servings.

PEPPER SAUCE

It's nice to see your daughter following in your footsteps when it comes to a career. It is sometimes a bit disturbing when you catch her using her feminine wiles to get her way with men.

I could never have gotten this recipe out of Jimmy, one of the owners of Auberge Gavroche, but my daughter did. It's a beautiful shiny sauce with galaxies of green, pink, and black peppercorns floating in it. Looks great, tastes better.

It can be served as well with steaks, hamburgers, and lamb chops.

1 tbs	sweet butter	15 ml
3	shallots, finely chopped	3
2 tbs	brandy	25 ml
1 tsp	Dijon mustard	5 ml
½ tsp	black peppercorns, lightly crushed	2 ml
½ tsp	*each* drained, whole green and pink peppercorns	2 ml
½ cup	heavy or whipping cream salt	125 ml

1. In a small skillet heat butter. Add shallots and sauté 4 minutes, until softened.
2. Add brandy and flame. Stir in mustard, peppercorns, and cream. Bring to a boil, reduce heat, and simmer, stirring, 4 to 5 minutes, until thickened.
3. Taste and season with salt.

Makes 4 to 6 servings.

> *For a child's garden birthday party, prepare individual packages of treats and prizes, using unusual inexpensive toys and curios found in any Chinatown. Wrap them in bright Chinese paper and suspend them from the trees in the yard at heights that the children can reach themselves. Hang colorful Chinese streamers and lanterns everywhere.*

TIME FOR PORK

Can a creature that finds truffles be all bad?

So many taboos surround different kinds of meat, many of them related to dietary laws established before butchering became the technically excellent art it is today.

Some Sikhs won't touch beef. Some Jews and Arabs won't touch pork. So if you're having Sikhs in for dinner, stay away from beef. If religious Jews and Muslims, don't serve pork. For the rest of the world, choose the main course dish that suits the season and the situations best.

ROAST PORK WITH APRICOTS AND PRUNES

This recipe is a veritable orchard of fruits, and I recommend an austere accompaniment of oven-roasted potatoes and purée of spinach.

4 lb	boneless pork loin roast	2 kg
¼ cup	lemon juice	50 ml
¼ cup	honey	50 ml
2 tbs	chopped fresh parsley	25 ml
2 tsp	dry mustard	10 ml
½ tsp	salt	2 ml
2	cloves garlic, finely chopped	2
1 cup	chicken stock	250 ml
1 cup	dried apricots	250 ml
1 cup	pitted prunes	250 ml
2½ cups	dry white wine	625 ml
½ cup	heavy or whipping cream	125 ml
1 tbs	brown sugar	15 ml
1 tbs	Dijon mustard	15 ml
2 tbs	softened sweet butter	25 ml
2 tbs	all-purpose flour	25 ml
½ tsp	white pepper	2 ml

1. Preheat oven to 425°F (220°C). Combine lemon juice, honey, parsley, dry mustard, salt, and garlic. Brush roast with mixture and place in a lightly oiled roasting pan. Insert meat thermometer. Pour chicken stock around roast. Roast 20 minutes to sear.
2. Baste with pan juices, reduce temperature to 325°F (160°C), and roast 1½ to 2 hours, basting often with pan juices, until meat thermometer registers an internal temperature of 170°F (80°C) and meat is no longer pink. (If pan liquids evaporate, add ½ cup (125 ml) chicken stock or water to keep roast moist.)
3. Let roast stand 15 minutes before carving.
4. Meanwhile, in a medium saucepan, combine apricots, prunes, and wine. Bring to a boil, reduce heat, cover, and simmer 20 minutes, or until fruit is tender.
5. With a slotted spoon, remove the fruit from the cooking liquid and reserve.
6. To the liquid in the saucepan add cream, brown sugar, and mustard. Stir and bring to a boil. Combine softened butter and flour; mix well. Stir into cream mixture; cook, stirring constantly, about 4 minutes, until thickened.
7. Stir in apricots and prunes and pepper. Serve with roast.

Makes 8 to 10 servings.

PORK WITH TOMATO AND RICE

A quick stove-top casserole for those busy days when you didn't expect so many things to happen. This dish almost cooks itself.
The tomato bits add color and that extra little bit of flavor.

2 tbs	vegetable oil	25 ml
1 lb	boneless pork, cut in cubes	500 g
1	medium onion, coarsely chopped	1
1	clove garlic, finely chopped	1
½ tsp	dried marjoram	2 ml
½ tsp	dried basil	2 ml
½ tsp	dried thyme	2 ml
½ tsp	salt	2 ml
½ tsp	freshly ground black pepper	2 ml
½ tsp	Worcestershire sauce	2 ml
½ tsp	soy sauce	2 ml
¼ tsp	chili powder	1 ml
1	tomato, coarsely chopped	1
¼ cup	dry sherry	50 ml
1½ cups	beef stock	375 ml
¾ cup	long grain rice	175 ml

1. In a large skillet with a lid, heat oil, add pork cubes; cook, turning, about 6 minutes, until brown.
2. Stir in onion and garlic and sauté about 5 minutes, until softened.
3. Stir in marjoram, basil, thyme, salt, pepper, Worcestershire sauce, soy sauce, and chili powder. Stir in tomato and sherry; cook 5 minutes.
4. Stir in beef stock and bring to a boil. Add rice, reduce heat, cover, and simmer about 20 to 25 minutes, until rice is tender.

Makes 4 servings.

TOURTIÈRE OR FRENCH CANADIAN CHRISTMAS PORK PIE

This is the traditional dish served after Midnight Mass on Christmas Eve.
Recipes for it are generations old, and no two are exactly the same.
This one was pried loose by my daughter from the mother of her best friend. It is a hearty nourishing pie and can be made either as a single large pie or as individual pies.
Be sure to serve homemade Chili Sauce with this.

3 lb	ground pork	1.5 kg
¼ lb	salt pork, diced	125 g
1	small onion, coarsely chopped	1
1	clove garlic, finely chopped	1
2 cups	beef stock	500 ml
2 tbs	celery leaves, finely chopped	25 ml
2 tbs	chopped fresh parsley	25 ml
1	small bay leaf	1
⅛ tsp	nutmeg	0.5 ml
⅛ tsp	dried chervil	0.5 ml
pinch	ground cloves	pinch
pinch	cayenne pepper	pinch
2	slices dry French bread, crumbed after crusts removed	2
	Lemon Tang Pastry (recipe p. 285) for 2 double-crust 9 inch (23 cm) pies	

1. In a large skillet fry salt pork about 7 minutes, until lightly browned.
2. Add onion and garlic; continue cooking for 3 minutes, until onion is softened.
3. Add ground pork, stock, celery leaves, parsley, bay leaf, nutmeg, chervil, cloves, and cayenne. Bring to a boil, reduce heat, and simmer, stirring occasionally, for 35 to 40 minutes, until pork is no longer pink.
4. Stir in breadcrumbs. Set aside to cool.
5. Preheat oven to 425°F (220°C).
6. Roll out pastry for 2 double-crust 9 inch (23 cm) pies. Fit pastry into pie plates and trim edges.
7. Spoon pork mixture into pie shells, spreading it well into the sides of pastry. Cover with pastry tops. Trim, seal, and flute edges. Cut steam vents.
8. Bake in oven for 15 minutes.
9. Reduce heat to 350°F (180°C) and continue to bake 25 to 30 minutes longer, until crust is golden.
10. Serve hot or freeze and reheat at serving time.

Makes 8 servings.

GLAZED CANADIAN BACON

A whole piece of Canadian bacon, which looks like a small boneless loin of pork and is sometimes known as back bacon, makes a great roast for a casual supper, particularly when it is slathered with the raisin glaze and then served with Russian mustard, fresh-baked muffins, and apple butter.

I sometimes substitute a boneless pork loin—fresh or smoked—for a deliciously different menu.

4 lb	piece Canadian bacon	2 kg
	Raisin Glaze	

1. Preheat oven to 325°F (160°C).
2. With a sharp knife cut bacon to within ½ inch (1 cm) of bottom into ½ inch (1 cm) slices, but do not cut through. Place on a rack in a shallow roasting pan. Pour water, ½ inch (1 cm) deep into pan to prevent drying. Bake in oven for 1¼ hours.
3. Prepare Raisin Glaze. Brush over bacon and between slices.
4. Return to oven for 30 minutes and brush occasionally with glaze, until browned and shiny.
5. Place on a serving platter. At serving time cut between slices and serve. Pour any remaining glaze into a sauce dish.

Makes 10 to 12 servings.

RAISIN GLAZE

½ cup	raisins	125 ml
½ cup	boiling water	125 ml
2 tbs	melted sweet butter	25 ml
1 tbs	molasses	15 ml
1 tbs	Worcestershire sauce	15 ml
1 tbs	Russian mustard	15 ml
2 tsp	grated fresh ginger root	10 ml
¼ tsp	ground cloves	1 ml
pinch	nutmeg	pinch

1. In a blender or food processor, combine raisins and water; process 30 seconds, or until puréed.
2. In a bowl, combine raisin purée, butter, molasses, Worcestershire sauce, mustard, ginger root, cloves, and nutmeg. Mix well.
3. Brush over Canadian Bacon (back bacon) roast, pork loin, or ham steaks.

Makes 1½ cups (375 ml).

BAKED PEARS IN RED WINE

8	*firm ripe pears*	8
1¼ cups	*granulated sugar*	300 ml
½ tsp	*grated lemon rind*	2 ml
4 cups	*dry red wine*	1 l
	whipped cream	

1. Preheat oven to 350°F (180°C).
2. Peel pears, but leave stems on. In a deep baking dish, mix together sugar, lemon rind, and wine. Place pears in dish. Cover and bake in oven, basting and turning frequently for 50 minutes, until fruit is tender.
3. Chill and use as a garnish for pork roast.

Makes 8 servings.

PEANUT PORK SATAY

The wonderful surprise in this elegant satay is that the cooked pork is rolled in chopped peanuts just before you serve it. The fun comes in the crunch.

If using as a main course, offer rice, bowls of chopped green onions, and chutneys. If as an hors d'oeuvre, hand around with drinks and napkins.

2 lb	boneless lean pork, cut into 1 inch (2.5 cm) cubes	1 kg
¼ cup	fruit chutney	50 ml
¼ cup	soy sauce	50 ml
2 tbs	peanut butter	25 ml
1 tbs	grated fresh ginger root	15 ml
2	cloves garlic	2
1	onion, quartered	1
	juice of 1 lime	
1 cup	finely chopped salted peanuts	250 ml

1. Place pork cubes in a glass bowl or heavy plastic bag.
2. In a food processor or blender combine chutney, soy sauce, peanut butter, ginger root, garlic, onion, and lime juice. Process until smooth. Pour over pork cubes. Toss to coat with sauce. Cover and marinate overnight in refrigerator.

3. Thread pork cubes on 12 skewers.* Grill over medium coals on barbecue, or broil under broiler about 4 inches (10 cm) from heat for 20 to 25 minutes, or until meat is no longer pink.
4. Roll skewers of meat in chopped peanuts and serve.

Makes 6 main course servings or 12 appetizers.

PORK MEDALLIONS WITH MUSTARD CREAM AND PEPPERCORNS GREEN

Forgive the attempt at a rhyme, but I've always thought recipes written down look like poetry.
   This one is sinfully easy to prepare and delivers a wonderful impact of texture and flavor. The mustard cream sauce is a thing of beauty to behold thanks to its delicate yellow cast.
   Serve with a potato casserole, so guests can sop up the extra sauce.

2	pork tenderloins, approx. 2 lbs (1 kg)	2
	flour, salt, and freshly ground black pepper	
⅓ cup	sweet butter	75 ml
2	shallots, finely chopped	2
⅓ cup	red wine vinegar	75 ml
2 cups	heavy or whipping cream	500 ml
1 tbs	drained green peppercorns	15 ml
⅓ cup	Dijon mustard	75 ml
½ tsp	salt	2 ml

1. Slice tenderloin into 1 inch (2.5 cm) pieces. With a mallet flatten between wax paper until ½ inch (1 cm) thick. Dredge in flour seasoned with salt and pepper, shaking off excess.
2. In a large skillet heat 3 tbs (45 ml) butter. Add pork; sauté about 5 minutes, turning, until lightly browned on both sides and no longer pink inside. Transfer to a warm platter and keep warm.
3. Add 1 tbs (15 ml) butter to skillet, add shallots; sauté about 3 minutes until softened.
4. Stir in vinegar and boil over high heat until reduced by ⅔. Stir in cream and peppercorns and simmer 5 minutes.
5. Remove from heat and whisk in mustard and remaining 1 tbs (15 ml) butter.
6. Season sauce with salt and pour over pork.

Makes 6 servings.

*If wooden skewers are used, soak them in a pan of water for about 1 hour before threading meat.

At Christmas time decorate the doorways and mantelpiece with thick garlands of cedar or pine rope. Decorate with real apples, nuts, holly, and pomegranates. Dozens of white candles around the rooms add to a feeling of Old World festivity.

On a large silver serving platter, build a tower of pineapples, starfruit, pomegranates, Mandarin oranges, and assorted nuts. Place sprigs of evergreen and cranberries around the base.

Placed on a sideboard, in front of a mirror, this display creates an elegant, luxurious Christmas mood.

ELEGANT CHRISTMAS BUFFET

LOBSTER SOUFFLE LOG

PEAR AND LEEK SOUP
with crumbled blue cheese

PORK LOIN WITH CHERRY ALMOND SAUCE

SPECIAL POTATO CASSEROLE
PURÉED BROCCOLI WITH CRÈME FRAICHE

ORANGE CRÈME CARAMEL

CHOCOLATE FONDANT CAKE
CREAMY CHEESECAKE
SPICY GINGERBREAD WITH APPLE TOPPING
COOKIE BASKET

With the Lobster Souffle Log and the soup, serve French Brut Champagne, Muscadet, or an Alsace Sylvaner; Californian or Canadian Rieslings or Selval Blanc.

With the main course, offer a French white Burgundy (a Montrachet or an ordinary Macon), a Portuguese white Dao, a Spanish white Rioja, or a Canadian or Californian Chardonnay or Riesling.

No dessert wine is recommended, unless a full-bodied French Sauterne or a Hungarian Takhai Aszu.

PORK LOIN WITH CHERRY ALMOND SAUCE

When this sits on a buffet, it almost preens, the cherries and the almond slivers give it such a wonderfully festive look. When you slice into it, you will see that the meat is almost as white as a turkey breast.

4–6 lb	boneless pork loin roast	2–3 kg
2	cloves garlic, cut into slivers	2
	salt, freshly ground black pepper, and dry mustard	
1 cup	imported cherry preserves	250 ml
¼ cup	red wine vinegar	50 ml
	grated rind of 1 orange	
1 tbs	lemon juice	15 ml
¼ tsp	salt	1 ml
¼ tsp	nutmeg	1 ml
pinch	ground cloves	pinch
pinch	freshly ground black pepper	pinch
¼ cup	slivered almonds	50 ml

1. Preheat oven to 325°F (160°C).
2. With tip of sharp knife make slits in pork roast; insert garlic slivers into slits. Rub roast generously with salt, pepper, and dry mustard.
3. Place on roasting rack in a shallow roasting pan and roast in oven 30 to 40 minutes per pound (500 g), or until meat thermometer inserted in center reaches 170°F (80°C) and pork is no longer pink.
4. While roast is cooking, make sauce. In a saucepan, combine cherry preserves, vinegar, orange rind, lemon juice, salt, nutmeg, cloves, and pepper. Bring to a boil, reduce heat, and simmer 1 minute.
5. Stir in almonds and remove from heat. Baste roast with sauce during last 30 minutes of cooking.
6. Let pork stand 15 minutes before carving to firm meat. Serve remaining sauce with roast.

Makes 8 servings.

WOKING AND TALKING

The great thing about a stir fry is that you might as well have everyone out into the kitchen to watch you put the dinner together and to chat while you work. Most stir fries take only a few minutes—if you've done all the preparation beforehand. Nearly everything for a stir-fry can be prepared the day before or well in advance of your tour de cuisine.

So, before we get into recipes, let's just review the steps to take care of before you hit the heat.

SHOPPING LIST FOR WOKING

Here is a list of the most commonly called for Chinese ingredients, which you can pick up these days in your supermarket or Chinese grocery store. If you also have a Chinese greengrocer, you are indeed in luck because you will discover all kinds of new and exciting vegetables to try.

Bamboo shoots
Blackbean paste
Chinese yellow lump sugar candy
Dried black mushrooms
Dried Chinese mushrooms
Dried hot chili peppers
Five-spice powder
Ginger root
Hoisin sauce
Hot pepper sauce

Oyster sauce
Peanut oil
Rice vinegar
Sake*
Sesame seeds
Sesame oil
Sherry*
Soy sauce
Water chestnuts

Depending where you live, you might probably need to pick these up in a liquor store.

Getting Ready to Wok

Assemble and prepare all the ingredients:

Cut vegetables into thin pieces or strips so they will cook quickly but still retain some "crunch."

Cut meat into thin strips for fast cooking.

Heat your wok (or skillet) at highest setting. Use peanut oil for stir-frying, as it has a relatively low smoking point.

Preparation for the Guests:

Invite them to wok over. Even if they can't, it brings up the subject, and you can tell them what you are planning. Before your guests arrive spread a few pieces of bright red cotton on your living room furniture, and if you have a Chinese objet d'art, feature it.

Use those little umbrella toothpicks for drinks that have fruit in them.

Burn a joss stick just before the guests arrive to approximate the Oriental atmosphere.

Serve a selection of hors d'oeuvres or finger foods from the Chinese Lantern Buffet Party (page 16).

When you invite your guests to pick up their drinks and join you in the kitchen, have one last simple treat waiting for them while they watch you perform your magic. I would suggest Finger Gnocchi. It is very easy to prepare and can be warmed in the oven in just a few moments.

How do you handle hot peppers? Very carefully!

The dried hot peppers in this shopping list and the jalapeño and other types of hot peppers you may have to chop or slice should be handled with gloves—literally. Gloves of the kind used to clean ovens.

The oils that seep out of these peppers can burn your skin, and if you touch your gloved hand to your eyes, you are in for a few minutes of excruciating pain, and up to a week of red eyes.

GON-BOW SHRIMPS (SHRIMPS WITH HOT SAUCE)

I like to sprinkle these with salt as soon as they come from the wok. If you like salt as much as I do, try that.
Serve with a dish of soft Chinese noodles and extra hot pepper sauce.

¾ lb	shrimps, shelled and deveined	375 g
1½ tsp	salt	7 ml
1	egg white, beaten	1
1 tbs	all-purpose flour	15 ml
2 tsp	cornstarch	10 ml
¼ tsp	baking powder	1 ml
1 cup	peanut oil	250 ml
6	green onions, thinly sliced	6
1 tsp	granulated sugar	5 ml
4 drops	drops hot pepper sauce	4 drops
	hot chili sauce	

1. Wipe shrimps with paper towel to dry thoroughly. Sprinkle with 1 tsp (5 ml) salt. In a shallow dish, combine egg whites and shrimps.
2. Combine flour, cornstarch, and baking powder. Sprinkle over shrimps and toss to coat well. Refrigerate 30 minutes.
3. In a wok heat oil. Deep-fry shrimps a few at a time, about 2 minutes, until golden brown. With a slotted spoon remove and drain on paper towel.
4. Pour all but 1 tbs (15 ml) oil out of wok. Add green onions and stir-fry for 1 minute.
5. Stir in sugar, hot pepper sauce, and shrimps. Toss all together. Serve immediately with hot chili sauce.

Makes 4 servings.

WOKING STICKS

Some, if not all of your friends, will have mastered dining with chopsticks. Simple bamboo sticks are best and easy to obtain. You can stir your wok with a couple of chopsticks too. Never use only one—it's bad form. Besides, you need two in nearly all recipes where you remove the meat and then add the vegetables.

SHRIMPS IN LOBSTER SAUCE

When I first got this recipe from Hazel Mah at her Imperiale Restaurant, I said to her in amazement, "You've left out the lobster sauce." She smiled and said, "But my dear Myra, there is no lobster in Shrimp in Lobster Sauce." Hmmm. You figure it out!

All I know is, it's a delicious dish. Maybe the way the shrimps and eggs work together give it that added lobster taste.

1 lb	small shrimps, shelled and deveined	500 g
2 tbs	peanut oil	25 ml
3	cloves garlic, finely chopped	3
4	green onions, thinly sliced	4
¼ lb	ground pork	125 g
1 tbs	soy sauce	15 ml
1 tbs	black bean paste	15 ml
1 tbs	sherry	15 ml
½ tsp	granulated sugar	2 ml
½ tsp	salt	2 ml
¼ tsp	freshly ground black pepper	1 ml
½ cup	water	125 ml
2 tsp	cornstarch	10 ml
2	eggs, well beaten	2

1. In a wok heat oil. Add garlic and green onions. Stir-fry 1 minute.
2. Add pork and stir-fry 3 to 4 minutes, until no longer pink.
3. Stir in shrimps and stir-fry 2 to 3 minutes, or until pink.
4. Combine soy sauce, black bean paste, sherry, sugar, salt, and pepper. Stir into wok.
5. Combine water and cornstarch, mix until smooth; stir into wok and cook about 8 minutes, until thickened.
6. Stir in eggs. Remove from heat immediately and serve.

Makes 4 servings.

BAY SCALLOPS WITH HOT AND SWEET RED PEPPER

The red of the peppers and the green and white of the scallions make this a pretty dish—and pretty delicious too.
Serve over Sesame Rice for a fluffy and full-flavored accompaniment.

1 lb	bay scallops	500 g
10	dried black mushrooms, or ½ oz (14 g) package	10
1	can (10 oz/284 ml) water chestnuts, drained	1
1	can (10 oz/284 ml) bamboo shoots, drained	1
2	sweet red peppers, cut in julienne strips	2
¼ cup	soy sauce	50 ml
¼ cup	rice vinegar	50 ml
2 tbs	brown sugar	25 ml
½ tsp	crushed dried hot chili peppers	2 ml
2	egg whites	2
2 tbs	cornstarch	25 ml
¼ cup	vegetable oil	50 ml
4	green onions	4

1. In warm water to cover, soak dried mushrooms for 30 minutes, until plumped. If water chestnuts are large, cut in half horizontally.
2. Combine water chestnuts, bamboo shoots, and red peppers. Combine soy sauce, rice vinegar, brown sugar, and chili peppers.
3. Drain and thinly slice mushrooms. Add to soy sauce mixture to absorb flavor.
4. In a large bowl, whisk egg whites and cornstarch. Add scallops and toss to coat well. Remove scallops to plate lined with waxed paper and refrigerate 30 minutes.
5. In a wok heat oil. Stir-fry scallops, a few at a time, for 1 minute, or until opaque. Remove and drain on paper towel.
6. Add water chestnut mixture. Stir-fry 2 minutes.
7. Add mushrooms, sauce, and scallops. Stir-fry 2 minutes.
8. Serve immediately. Garnish with green onions. Serve with Sesame Rice (page 220).

Makes 4 servings.

CHINESE LEMON CHICKEN

This is another of my favorite Chinese recipes from my friend, the fabled Hazel Mah.

I tried unsuccessfully for months to duplicate the taste in my own kitchen and then discovered Chinese yellow lump sugar candy was the secret ingredient. It can be purchased at most Chinese grocers.

4	whole chicken breasts, halved, skinned, and boned	4
2¾ cup	chicken stock	675 ml
1 lb	Chinese yellow lump sugar candy*	500 g
1½ cups	lemon juice	375 ml
1	lemon, halved lengthwise and thinly sliced	1
1 tsp	salt	5 ml
2	medium onions, thinly sliced	2
¼ cup	cornstarch	50 ml
¼ cup	water	50 ml
1	egg, slightly beaten	1
¼ cup	all-purpose flour	50 ml
¼ cup	vegetable oil	50 ml

1. In a saucepan, combine chicken stock, sugar candy, lemon juice, lemon slices, and salt. Heat to simmering, stirring about 10 minutes, until sugar candy is dissolved.
2. Add onions to sauce. Combine cornstarch and water; stir until smooth. Stir into lemon sauce. Cook, stirring constantly, about 3 minutes, until sauce is thickened.
3. Cut chicken breasts into bite-sized pieces.
4. Place beaten egg and flour in separate shallow dishes. Dip chicken pieces in egg and dredge with flour.
5. In a skillet heat oil. Add chicken pieces to a skillet a few at a time; cook 3 to 4 minutes. Remove to a warm platter; keep warm. Repeat with remaining chicken.
6. Place on a warm platter; pour sauce over chicken.

Makes 8 servings.

*Available in Oriental markets.

STIR-FRY CHICKEN WITH WALNUTS

If you prefer some other nut, feel free to add your own favorites: cashews, pecans, or peanuts. Just keep the quantities the same.
Serve this with hot buttered snowpeas.

1 lb	boneless chicken breasts, cut in 1 inch (2.5 cm) pieces	500 g
1	egg white, beaten until frothy	1
1 tbs	cornstarch	15 ml
1 cup	peanut oil	250 ml
1 cup	walnut halves	250 ml
2	dried hot chili peppers, broken in small pieces	2
4	cloves garlic, peeled and halved	4
3	pieces (½ inch/1 cm each) ginger root, peeled	3
1 tbs	soy sauce	15 ml
1 tbs	sherry	15 ml

1. In a glass bowl combine chicken and egg white. Sprinkle cornstarch on chicken and toss to coat well. Refrigerate 30 minutes.
2. In a wok heat oil. Deep-fry chicken a few pieces at a time, about 1 minute, or until golden brown. Remove from wok and drain on paper towel. Pour all but 2 tbs (25 ml) oil out of wok.
3. Add peppers, garlic, and ginger root; stir-fry 2 minutes. Remove with slotted spoon and discard.
4. Return chicken and walnuts to wok. Stir in soy sauce. Stir-fry 1 minute. Stir in sherry. Serve immediately.

Makes 4 servings.

GENERAL TSAO'S CHICKEN

The late, great general was both a political figure and a poet who lived in China, 155–220 A.D. He may owe his longevity (in those days) to his love of good food.
   Here's his recipe for chicken to prove it!

1 lb	boneless chicken breasts, cut in 1 inch (2.5 cm) pieces	500 g
3 tbs	soy sauce	45 ml
1 tbs	cornstarch	15 ml
1	egg white, beaten until frothy	1
1 cup	vegetable oil	250 ml
3	dried hot chili peppers, broken in half	3
2	cloves garlic, finely chopped	2
1	piece (1 inch/2.5 cm) ginger root, peeled and finely chopped	1
1 tbs	white wine vinegar	15 ml
1 tbs	white wine	15 ml
1 tsp	cornstarch	5 ml
1 tbs	brown sugar	15 ml
1 tsp	sesame oil	5 ml
½ tsp	salt	2 ml

1. In a glass bowl, place chicken pieces. Combine 1 tbs (15 ml) soy sauce and 1 tbs (15 ml) cornstarch. Blend in beaten egg white. Pour over chicken and toss to coat well. Marinate in refrigerator for 1 hour.
2. In a wok heat oil. Deep-fry chicken, a few pieces at a time, about 1 minute, or until golden brown. Remove and drain on paper towel. Pour all but 2 tbs (25 ml) oil out of wok.
3. To the wok add chili peppers, garlic, and ginger; stir-fry 2 minutes.
4. In a small bowl, combine remaining soy sauce, vinegar, white wine, and 1 tsp (5 ml) cornstarch; mix until smooth. Stir in sugar, sesame oil, and salt. Pour into wok and cook, stirring, about 2 minutes, until thickened.
5. Return chicken pieces to wok. Mix well and serve immediately.

Makes 4 servings.

GINGER CHICKEN WITH SWEET RED PEPPERS AND CASHEWS

This is a very hearty stir fry and one that will give your guests a really satisfied feeling.

1 lb	boneless and skinless chicken breasts	500 g
¼ cup	soy sauce	50 ml
¼ cup	sake or dry sherry	50 ml
1 tbs	peanut oil	15 ml
1	piece (1½ inches/3.5 cm) ginger root, peeled and chopped	1
4	green onions, sliced	4
2	cloves garlic, finely chopped	2
3 tbs	water	45 ml
1 tbs	hoisin sauce	15 ml
½ tsp	salt	2 ml
⅛ tsp	freshly ground black pepper	0.5 ml
2	red peppers, cut in thin slices	2
2	green peppers, cut in thin slices	2
½ cup	toasted cashew nuts (see p. 120)	125 ml

1. With a sharp knife slice chicken on the diagonal into thin slices. In a bowl, combine soy sauce and sake; marinate chicken in mixture for 1 hour.
2. In a wok heat oil. Add ginger root, green onions, and garlic; stir-fry 2 minutes.
3. Drain chicken, reserving marinade; add chicken to wok and stir-fry 2 minutes, or until no longer pink. Stir in reserved marinade, water, hoisin sauce, salt, and pepper. Add red and green peppers. Cook 2 minutes longer.
4. Add cashew nuts. Toss and serve immediately.

Makes 4 servings.

GINGER PORK CUBES

This is best served hot from the skillet on toothpicks.

2 lb	boneless pork cut in 1 inch (2.5 cm) cubes	1 kg
¼ cup	vegetable oil	50 ml
1 cup	finely chopped onion	250 ml
1	large clove garlic, finely chopped	1
½ cup	soy sauce	125 ml
2 tbs	white vinegar	25 ml
¼ cup	chopped preserved ginger	50 ml

1. In a skillet suitable for table-top service, heat oil. Add pork and cook cubes, turning several times, for about 15 minutes, until brown.
2. Add onion and garlic; cook 5 minutes, until onion is softened.
3. Stir in soy sauce, vinegar, and ginger. Cover and simmer for 10 minutes.
4. Skewer cubes with toothpicks and serve from skillet.

Makes 3 to 4 dozen.

QUICK KOWLOON PORK

The addition of vegetables like spinach and grated carrots make this not only a delicious but a very pretty stir fry. If you have other vegetables you'd like to substitute, go ahead. Best bets are broccoli, asparagus, sliced zucchini.

½ lb	boneless lean pork, cut into thin strips	250 g
½ cup	chicken stock	125 ml
¼ cup	light soy sauce	50 ml
1 tsp	sugar	5 ml
1 tsp	rice vinegar	5 ml
¼ cup	vegetable oil	50 ml
4	stalks celery, sliced diagonally in 1 inch (2.5 cm) pieces	4
1	green pepper, cut in 1 inch (2.5 cm) pieces	1
4	fresh or dried wild mushrooms (shitake or white matsutake)* (soak dried in warm water to cover for 20 minutes)	4
2	carrots, scraped in long strips with potato peeler	2
3	green onions, cut in 1 inch (2.5 cm) pieces	3
2	cloves garlic, finely chopped	2
1 tbs	finely chopped fresh ginger root	15 ml
2	hot chili peppers	2
¼ lb	fresh spinach leaves	125 g

1. In a bowl, combine chicken stock, soy sauce, sugar, and rice vinegar and set aside.
2. In a wok heat 2 tbs (25 ml) oil. Add celery, green pepper, mushrooms, carrots, and green onions: stir-fry 4 minutes, until just tender-crisp. Remove and set aside.
3. Heat another 2 tbs (25 ml) oil in wok. Add garlic, ginger, and chili peppers and stir-fry about 1 minute, until fragrant.

*Wild mushrooms are available in Oriental markets.

4. Add pork and stir-fry 3 to 4 minutes, until pork changes color and is no longer pink.
5. Stir in stock mixture, bring to a boil, reduce heat, and simmer 5 minutes.
6. Add vegetables and spinach leaves and cook about 1 minute, just until heated through.

Makes 4 servings.

PORK WITH HOISIN SAUCE

This is a delicious recipe from Northern China. The meat is arranged on a bed of shredded green onions, which gives it a wonderfully fresh look and piquant flavor.
  For those who like it hot, put a pot of Chinese chili sauce on the table.

1½ lb	lean pork, cut into thin strips	750 g

MARINADE:

2 tbs	light soy sauce	25 ml
2 tbs	water	25 ml
1 tbs	sake	15 ml
1 tsp	sesame oil	5 ml
1 tsp	cornstarch	5 ml

SAUCE:

½ cup	water	125 ml
¼ cup	light soy sauce	50 ml
2 tbs	hoisin sauce	25 ml
2 tbs	sake	25 ml
2 tbs	sugar	25 ml
2 tbs	vegetable oil	25 ml
2 cups	shredded green onions	500 ml

1. Place pork in a glass dish. Combine soy sauce, water, sake, oil, and cornstarch. Pour over pork strips; toss and allow to marinate at least 20 minutes.
2. To make Sauce, combine water, soy sauce, hoisin, sake, and sugar; set aside.
3. In a wok heat oil. Add pork strips (in two batches if necessary) and stir-fry 4 to 5 minutes, until no longer pink. Remove to warm plate.

4. Add sauce to wok, stir, and bring to a boil. Return pork strips and toss well. Serve over shredded green onions.

Makes 4 to 6 servings.

RARE BEEF TENDERLOIN IN OYSTER SAUCE

A wonderful way to serve beef tenderloin. This is the only stir-fry for which I use both a frying pan and a wok. That allows me to give the beef just the few moments it needs to turn brown and delicious on the outside, while remaining blue and juicy on the inside. That's the way we like it at my house.

1 lb	beef tenderloin, cut in thin slices	500 g
¼ cup	oyster sauce	50 ml
¼ cup	cold water	50 ml
2 tbs	red wine	25 ml
1 tbs	soy sauce	15 ml
1 tsp	Worcestershire sauce	5 ml
½ tsp	granulated sugar	2 ml
½ tsp	cornstarch	2 ml
¼ tsp	freshly ground black pepper	1 ml
1	pkg (½ oz/14.2 g) dried mushrooms	1
3 tbs	vegetable oil	45 ml
4	green onions, thinly sliced	4
2	cloves garlic, finely chopped	2
1	can (10 oz/284 g) water chestnuts, cut in half	1
½ lb	snow peas (about 2 cups/500 ml)	250 g
1	medium carrot, thinly sliced	1

1. In a medium bowl, combine oyster sauce, water, wine, soy sauce, Worcestershire sauce, sugar, cornstarch, and pepper; mix until smooth. Add beef, cover and marinate 1 hour or overnight in refrigerator.
2. In a bowl, soak mushrooms in warm water to cover for 1 hour. Drain and thinly slice.
3. In a wok or skillet heat 2 tbs (25 ml) oil. Add onions and garlic, stir-fry about 2 minutes, until softened.
4. Add water chestnuts, snow peas, mushroom slices, and carrot. Stir-fry about 5 minutes, until carrot is tender-crisp.
5. With slotted spoon remove beef from marinade, reserving marinade. Drain beef on paper towel.
6. In a separate skillet heat remaining oil, add beef; stir-fry 1 to 2 minutes, until rare. Do not overcook.

7. Stir reserved marinade into vegetable mixture. Cook, stirring, about 2 minutes, until sauce is thickened.
8. Add beef to vegetable mixture; toss to combine. Serve immediately.

Makes 4 servings.

STIR-FRY BEEF AND PEPPERS

Another wonderful beef stir-fry, this one with sweet red peppers and hot chili peppers.

¾ lb	beef sirloin steak, 1 inch (2.5 cm) thick	375 g
¼ cup	peanut oil	50 ml
3	sweet red peppers, cut in thin strips	3
1	hot chili pepper, cut in thin strips	1
4	green onions, thinly sliced	4
1	can (10 oz/284 ml) bamboo shoots, drained	1
¼ cup	water	50 ml
1 tbs	hoisin sauce	15 ml
1 tsp	soy sauce	5 ml
1 tsp	sesame oil	5 ml
½ tsp	salt	2 ml
½ tsp	freshly ground black pepper	2 ml
1 tsp	cornstarch	5 ml

1. Partially freeze beef for easy slicing. With a sharp knife slice very thin slices across the grain.
2. In a wok heat 2 tbs (25 ml) peanut oil, add beef; stir-fry 5 minutes, until medium rare. Remove from wok to drain on paper towel.
3. Add remaining oil to wok. Add red peppers, hot chili pepper, green onions, and bamboo shoots; stir-fry for 3 minutes.
4. Combine water, hoisin sauce, soy sauce, sesame oil, salt, pepper, and cornstarch; mix until smooth. Stir into wok and cook, stirring, about 2 minutes, until thickened.
5. Return beef to wok and toss all together. Serve immediately.

Makes 4 servings.

SIDE EFFECTS

THE PASTAS

These excellent dishes of pasta are, to a degree, the mainstay of Italian cuisine, or at least what we consider the main dishes of the Roman cookery.

When you are planning them, please remember that while there are many acceptable dried packaged pastas on the market, none of them can compare with freshly made pasta from a pasta shop. Remember, also, fresh pasta takes only about 3 to 4 minutes to cook al dente.

Fettucine Verde Alla Crema

There is nothing devious about Italian cookery. The way to achieve a creamy pasta is to use cream in the recipe.

Variations can include adding smoked ham cubes or crumbled prosciutto, broccoli, peas, etc.

1 lb	fettucine	500 g
2 tbs	sweet butter	25 ml
2 cups	heavy or whipping cream	500 ml
1 tsp	salt	5 ml
	freshly ground black pepper	
1¼ cups	coarsely grated Parmesan cheese	300 ml
2 tsp	freshly chopped parsley	10 ml

1. In a large pot of salted boiling water, cook fettucine about 10 minutes, until al dente. Drain and set aside.
2. In a large skillet over medium heat, melt butter. Add cream and heat until cream begins to bubble. Season with salt and pepper.

3. Add fettucine to cream, toss and heat.
4. Gradually add 1 cup (250 ml) Parmesan cheese. Toss well and heat until cheese has melted. Sprinkle with remaining Parmesan cheese and parsley. Serve immediately.

Makes 4 to 6 servings.

PASTA WITH GORGONZOLA

SALMON SEVICHE

CRUSTY ROLLS WITH BRIE BUTTER

WARM RHUBARB CRISP
with unsweetened whipped cream

PASTA WITH GORGONZOLA

A sophisticated pasta dish using the classic blue cheese of Italy. I discovered this dish in a small restaurant in Paris where I had gone to have lunch by myself, away from business, away from any pressures.

½ cup	sweet butter	125 ml
½ cup	crumbled Gorgonzola	125 ml
1 cup	half-and-half cream	250 ml
2 tbs	Cognac	25 ml
3 tbs	tomato paste	45 ml
1 lb	small pasta shells	500 g
1 cup	freshly grated Romano cheese	250 ml
½ cup	chopped fresh basil	250 ml
2 tbs	finely chopped toasted walnuts (see p. 120)	25 ml
pinch	cayenne pepper	pinch

1. In a medium-size skillet heat butter. Stir in Gorgonzola cheese until melted. Stir in cream, Cognac, and tomato paste.
2. In a large pot of salted boiling water, cook pasta about 10 minutes, until al dente. Drain.

3. Pour sauce over shells; toss gently.
4. Sprinkle with Romano cheese; toss again.
5. Garnish with basil, walnuts, and cayenne pepper. Serve immediately.

Makes 4 servings.

THREE CHEESE MACARONI

Italian cooks often combine more than one or two of their marvelous cheeses to make a pasta dish in which you'll never miss the meat.
   This should be served hot from the oven while the cheese is still bubbling. It makes a truly satisfying vegetarian dinner when you add simple Tomato Provençale (baked tomatoes with garlic and breadcrumbs), as my youngest child, Matthew, will attest.

1 lb	macaroni	500 g
3 tbs	sweet butter	40 ml
1 cup	grated Parmesan cheese	250 ml
½ cup	grated Swiss cheese	125 ml
½ cup	grated Mozzarella cheese	125 ml
1 cup	heavy or whipping cream	250 ml
1 tsp	salt	5 ml
¼ tsp	white pepper	1 ml

1. In a large pot of salted boiling water cook macaroni about 12 minutes, until al dente. Drain.
2. Preheat oven to 400°F (200°C).
3. In a casserole, toss macaroni with butter. Stir in cheeses, cream, salt, and pepper. Bake in oven for 20 minutes, until top is golden brown.

Makes 4 to 6 servings.

FETTUCINE CARBONARA

This is my brunch pasta—because it has eggs and bacon in it.

6	slices bacon, chopped	6
1 lb	fettucine noodles	500 g
2 tbs	salt	25 ml
1	bay leaf	1
1	clove garlic, finely chopped	1
1 tbs	olive oil	15 ml
2	eggs, lightly beaten	2
2 cups	heavy or whipping cream	500 ml
½ tsp	salt	2 ml
¼ tsp	freshly ground black pepper	1 ml
2 oz	cooked ham, diced (2 slices)	50 g
	chopped fresh parsley	

1. In a medium-size skillet, sauté bacon until most of the fat has melted. Drain bacon on paper towel.
2. To a large pot of boiling water add salt, bay leaf, garlic, and olive oil. Cook fettucine about 10 to 12 minutes, until al dente. Drain, set aside, and keep warm.
3. In a large, heavy pot, combine eggs and cream; cook, stirring, about 4 minutes, until slightly thickened. Season with salt and pepper.
4. Remove from heat. Add fettucine, bacon, and ham; toss together.
5. Sprinkle with chopped parsley and serve.

Makes 4 to 6 servings.

RIGATONI WITH SAUSAGE AND MUSHROOMS

The little extra zip from the lemon rind makes this dish sparkle.

6 oz	rigatoni	185 g
3 tbs	olive oil	45 ml
1	clove garlic, finely chopped	1
2	Italian sweet sausages	2
1 tbs	chopped Italian parsley	15 ml
1 tsp	salt	5 ml
½ tsp	freshly ground black pepper	2 ml
2 cups	coarsely chopped fresh mushrooms (1 lb/500 g)	500 ml
1 tsp	grated lemon rind	5 ml
½ cup	heavy or whipping cream	125 ml
2 tbs	sweet butter	25 ml
	grated Parmesan cheese	

1. In a pot of salted boiling water, cook rigatoni about 10 minutes, until al dente. Drain.
2. In a large skillet, heat oil. Add garlic and sauté until golden. Press with a fork to release flavor and discard.
3. Skin sausages and shred into skillet. Add parsley, salt, and pepper. Cook and stir over medium heat about 10 minutes, until meat browns.
4. Stir in mushrooms, lemon rind, and cream. Simmer over medium heat 3 minutes.
5. Add pasta. Toss thoroughly, dot with butter, and cook over low heat for 2 minutes.
6. Serve with grated Parmesan cheese.

Makes 2 to 3 servings.

MARTINI FETTUCINE
(FETTUCINE WITH SMOKED SALMON, TOMATOES, AND GIN)

Years ago while traveling in Holland, I was served a marvelous concoction of tomatoes and gin as a soup. Those two flavors loomed so large in my mind I couldn't wait to get home to my kitchen to start experimenting. I got the soup down pat almost immediately, but this is the one I went on to, and I believe it is a magic invention. Try it and see.

¼ cup	sweet butter	50 ml
2	green onions, finely chopped	2
1	clove garlic, finely chopped	1
1	large tomato, diced	1
	salt	
	freshly ground black pepper	
¼ cup	gin	50 ml
2 cups	heavy or whipping cream	500 ml
1½ lb	spinach fettucine	750 g
¼ lb	smoked salmon, cut in julienne strips	125 g
¼ cup	chopped fresh parsley	50 ml
⅔ cup	freshly grated Parmesan cheese	150 ml

1. In a large skillet over medium heat, melt butter. Add onions and garlic; sauté about 4 minutes, until tender.
2. Stir in tomato. Season to taste with salt and pepper. Cook over high heat, stirring constantly, about 2 minutes, until saucy.
3. Stir in gin and cream; simmer until volume is reduced by half.
4. In a large pot of salted boiling water, cook fettucine noodles about 10 minutes, until al dente. Drain well.
5. Add noodles and salmon to cream mixture. Toss gently. Garnish with parsley and Parmesan cheese. Serve immediately.

Makes 6 servings.

PESTO SAUCE

Of course, with your favorite pasta dishes!
I also love to use this for sandwiches. Just spread it on a slice of toasted French bread, add a slice or two of peeled tomato, and top off with some grated Mozzarella. Put under the grill for a few moments and voilà.

1 cup	fresh basil leaves	250 ml
¼ cup	freshly grated Parmesan cheese	50 ml
6	cloves garlic	6
4	sprigs fresh parsley	4
½ cup	pine nuts	125 ml
½ tsp	salt	2 ml
½ cup	olive oil	125 ml

1. In a food processor or blender, combine basil, cheese, garlic, parsley, nuts, and salt. Process 10 seconds.
2. With machine running, gradually add olive oil. Continue to process 20 to 30 seconds, or until a smooth sauce forms.
3. Transfer to a covered container and store in refrigerator up to 4 weeks or in freezer.

Makes 1 cup (250 ml) sauce.

CLAM SAUCE MILANESE FOR LINGUINE

This section would not be complete without a clam sauce. So here it is—quick, simple, and completely in the Italian tradition. Clams are one of the few canned products I keep in my pantry.

⅓ cup	olive oil	75 ml
4	whole cloves garlic, peeled	4
1	can (10 oz/284 ml) baby clams	1
1 cup	chopped parsley	250 ml
1 cup	Salsa di Pomodoro (Recipe p. 340)	250 ml
1 lb	linguine noodles	500 g

1. In a medium saucepan, heat olive oil, add garlic; sauté about 7 minutes, until brown.
2. Drain clam liquid into saucepan; reserve clams. Bring liquid to a boil, reduce heat, and simmer 5 minutes. Remove and discard garlic.
3. Stir in clams and simmer 5 minutes longer.
4. Stir in Salsa di Pomodoro and simmer 30 minutes longer.

5. In large pot of salted boiling water, cook linguine about 10 to 12 minutes, until al dente. Drain. Add warm clam sauce and toss. Serve immediately.

Makes 8 servings.

SPAGHETTI ALLA RUSTICA

Alla rustica *usually means country or peasant style.*
 This time it means surprisingly simple, surprisingly delicious.

2	cloves garlic, peeled and crushed	2
6 tbs	olive oil	90 ml
1	can (1.75 oz/50 g) anchovy fillets in oil, chopped	1
½ tsp	freshly ground black pepper	2 ml
1 lb	spaghetti	500 g
3 tbs	chopped fresh parsley	45 ml
¼ cup	grated Parmesan cheese	50 ml

1. In a small skillet, fry garlic in oil until brown. Stir in anchovies and pepper and cook 5 minutes, until mixture resembles a smooth paste. Set aside.
2. In a pot of salted boiling water, cook spaghetti about 10 minutes, until al dente. Drain.
3. Pour sauce over spaghetti; toss well. Sprinkle with parsley and Parmesan cheese.

Makes 4 servings.

MALFATI IN MEAT SAUCE (PASTA BADLY FORMED)

It's true that's what it means, but the Italian housewives took what could have been a domestic disaster and turned it into a thing of beauty—taste-wise.
 I really want you to try it and see how great a sloppy-looking dish of pasta can be.

MALFATI:

1 lb	spinach	500 g
1½ cups	Ricotta cheese	375 ml
¼ cup	grated Parmesan cheese	50 ml
4	green onions, finely chopped	4
2	cloves garlic, finely chopped	2
1 tbs	chopped fresh basil, or 1 tsp (5 ml) dried	15 ml
¼ tsp	ground nutmeg	1 ml
2 tbs	all-purpose flour	25 ml
1	egg, slightly beaten	1

1. In a large saucepan of salted boiling water, cook spinach 5 minutes. Drain well and chop.
2. In a large bowl, combine spinach, ricotta cheese, Parmesan cheese, onions, garlic, basil, and nutmeg. Add flour and egg; mix well.
3. Cover and refrigerate 1 hour.

MEAT SAUCE:

1 lb	ground beef	500 g
1	medium onion, finely chopped	1
2	cloves garlic, finely chopped	2
1 cup	beef stock	250 ml
1	can (19 oz/540 ml) Italian plum tomatoes	1
½ cup	dry red wine	125 ml
2 tbs	chopped fresh basil, or 2 tsp (10 ml) dried	25 ml
1 tsp	dried oregano leaves	5 ml
½ tsp	salt	2 ml
¼ tsp	freshly ground black pepper	1 ml
6	drops hot pepper sauce	6
½ cup	freshly grated Parmesan cheese	125 ml
½ cup	all-purpose flour for dredging	125 ml

1. In a large skillet combine beef, onion, and garlic; cook, stirring, about 10 minutes, until beef is no longer pink and onion is softened.
2. Drain any fat from cooked beef mixture. Add beef stock, tomatoes, wine, basil, oregano, salt, pepper, and hot pepper sauce. Bring to a boil, reduce heat, and simmer, stirring occasionally, 20 minutes, until thickened.
3. With hands, shape Malfati mixture into fingers 2 × ½ inch (5 × 1 cm). Roll in flour and chill in refrigerator 15 minutes.
4. Preheat oven to 350°F (180°C).
5. In lightly salted boiling water cook Malfati fingers 3 to 4 minutes, until tender. With slotted spoon, remove from water and drain on paper towel.
6. Arrange in a shallow 8 cup (2 l) casserole or baking dish. Cover with meat sauce. Bake in oven for 15 minutes, until sauce is bubbly.
7. Sprinkle with Parmesan cheese and serve.

Makes 8 servings.

INTERESTING RICE

Why are we surprised that there are so many great rice dishes surfacing?
The whole Orient runs on rice!

COM RANG (FRIED RICE)

*Now this is a fried rice! I often serve it as a lunch dish with "hot" cucumber
sticks.*

1	3 egg omelette, cut into shreds	1
¼ cup	vegetable oil	50 ml
2	cloves garlic, finely chopped	2
3	green onions, chopped	3
6 cups	chilled cooked rice	1.5 l
½ lb	cooked ham, shredded	250 g
¼ lb	cooked shrimp, chopped	125 g
1	small carrot, shredded	1
½ cup	cooked peas	125 ml
½ tsp	salt	2 ml
¼ tsp	freshly ground black pepper	1 ml
	soy sauce	

1. Make omelette, and set aside.
2. In a large skillet heat oil; add garlic and green onions and cook 4 minutes,
   until tender.
3. Stir in rice, ham, shrimp, carrot, peas, and omelette. Heat thoroughly.
4. Season with salt and pepper. Serve immediately with soy sauce.

Makes 6 servings.

INDIAN RICE

I don't know how I happened to call this Indian Rice. I just know it has had its name and its place in my esteem for years. It is the combination of brandy-soaked raisins and pine nuts that endear it to me, as well as the warm, yellowy color it gets from the rich chicken stock.

2 oz	brandy, port, or sherry	60 ml
½ cup	raisins	125 ml
3 tbs	clarified butter	45 ml
1	medium onion, finely chopped	1
1	clove garlic, finely chopped	1
2 cups	long grain rice	500 ml
½ tsp	curry powder	2 ml
4 cups	rich chicken stock	1 l
½ cup	pine nuts	125 ml

1. In a small saucepan, warm brandy. Add raisins, remove from heat, and set aside.
2. In a large skillet, heat butter, add onion and garlic; sauté about 5 minutes, until soft.
3. Stir in rice and curry powder; sauté for 5 minutes, until rice is translucent.
4. Add stock, bring to a boil, reduce heat, cover, and simmer for 20 minutes.
5. Bring raisin mixture to a boil, reduce heat, and simmer 2 to 3 minutes, until liquid disappears.
6. Add to rice with pine nuts. Cover and continue to simmer about 7 minutes longer, until all liquid has disappeared.

Makes 6 servings.

VARIATION:
Coconut Rice: Use ½ cup (125 ml) flaked, unsweetened coconut in place of raisins.

SWEET-SCENTED RICE

Serve this rice with curries or spicy hot dishes like Chicken Molé, and the cinnamon, cloves, and cardamom will rise up and seduce your guests.

¼ cup	sweet butter	50 ml
1	medium onion, chopped	1
2 cups	long grain rice	500 ml
4 cups	chicken stock	1 l
4	cloves	4
4	cardamom seeds	4
12	peppercorns	12
2	cinnamon sticks (2 inch/5 cm long)	2
½ cup	slivered almonds	125 ml
¼ cup	raisins	50 ml

1. In a large skillet, melt butter. Add onion; sauté 7 minutes, until golden brown.
2. Stir in rice and coat well with butter. Add stock and bring mixture to a boil.
3. Transfer to a buttered 8 cup (2 l) casserole with a lid.
4. Preheat oven to 325°F (160°C).
5. In a small piece of cheesecloth, tie together cloves, cardamom seeds, peppercorns, and cinnamon sticks. Place in rice and cover.
6. Bake in oven for 25 minutes, until rice is tender.
7. Remove cheesecloth bag of spices. Before serving stir in almonds and raisins.

Makes 6 to 8 servings.

RICE PILAF WITH PINE NUTS

The lovely long grain rice brightened with the pimento, parsley, and pine nuts appeals to everyone. It looks festive, tastes like Christmas, and adds class to your menu of Stuffed Chicken Supremes.

⅓ cup	sweet butter	75 ml
2	cloves garlic, chopped	2
1	medium onion, chopped	1
1¼ cups	long grain rice	300 ml
2½ cups	chicken stock	625 ml
½ tsp	salt	2 ml
¼ tsp	white pepper	1 ml
½ cup	chopped pimento	125 ml
⅓ cup	pine nuts	75 ml
2 tbs	chopped parsley	25 ml

1. In a medium saucepan, heat butter. Add garlic and onion; sauté over medium heat for 10 minutes, until softened.
2. Add rice and cook 2 minutes longer.
3. Stir in chicken stock, salt, and pepper. Bring to a boil, reduce heat, cover, and simmer for 25 minutes, until all moisture is absorbed.
4. Remove lid and with a fork fluff rice. Stir in pimento, pine nuts, and parsley.

Makes 5 to 6 servings.

SPRING PADDY RICE

This is called spring because of the green of the young sweet peas.
This is an excellent side dish to serve with roasts—especially veal.

2 tbs	olive oil	25 ml
2 tbs	sweet butter	25 ml
1	medium onion, chopped	1
1½ cups	long grain rice	375 ml
3 cups	hot chicken stock	750 ml
1 tsp	salt	5 ml
½ tsp	white pepper	2 ml
3 cups	peas	750 ml
¼ cup	grated Parmesan cheese	50 ml

1. In a large skillet heat oil and 1 tbs (15 ml) butter. Add onion; sauté 5 minutes, until softened.
2. Add rice; cook 3 minutes longer, until translucent.
3. Stir in 2 cups (500 ml) stock, salt, and pepper. Bring to a boil, reduce heat, cover, and simmer 10 minutes.
4. Add remaining stock and peas; cook, covered, 10 minutes longer, or until rice is tender and dry. Stir in remaining butter and cheese.

Makes 6 to 8 servings.

SAFFRON RISOTTO

This should be served when the rice is at its creamiest—just as it is finished.
But my children are very fond of this as a leftover. They make it into patties and fry them up for a quick lunch. Naturally they refer to them as rice-burgers.

2 tbs	sweet butter	25 ml
1	medium onion, finely chopped	1
2 cups	Italian short grain rice	500 ml
¼ cup	dry white wine	50 ml
¼ tsp	saffron threads	1 ml
1 tsp	salt	5 ml
4½ cups	chicken stock	1.125 l
2 tbs	minced parsley	25 ml
½ cup	grated Parmesan cheese	125 ml

1. In a large skillet melt butter. Add onion; sauté about 5 minutes, until softened.
2. Stir in rice and mix until coated. Stir in wine, saffron, and salt. Cook about 5 minutes, until wine is absorbed.
3. Add 1 cup (250 ml) stock, bring to a boil, reduce heat, cover, and simmer about 10 minutes, until absorbed.
4. Continue adding stock 1 cup (250 ml) at a time, until rice is tender but firm.
5. Stir in parsley and cheese. Remove from heat and let stand covered 5 minutes before serving.

Makes 6 to 8 servings.

RISOVERDI (GREEN RICE)

This is perfect in both color and taste to serve with a shrimp curry. For a quick light supper for your friends, add a cheese sauce and a green salad.

2 tbs	olive oil	25 ml
2 tbs	sweet butter	25 ml
1 cup	minced green onions	250 ml
1 cup	minced parsley	250 ml
1½ cups	finely chopped raw spinach	375 ml
2 cups	long grain rice	500 ml
3½ cups	chicken stock	875 ml
1½ tsp	salt	7 ml
¼ tsp	white pepper	1 ml

1. In a large skillet heat oil and butter. Stir in onions, parsley, and spinach. Cover and cook over low heat 15 minutes.
2. Stir in rice and mix until coated. Add 2 cups (500 ml) stock, salt, and pepper. Cover and bring to a boil, reduce heat, and simmer for 15 minutes.
3. Add remaining stock and continue to simmer, covered, for 10 minutes more, until rice fluffs with a fork. Serve warm.

Makes 4 to 6 servings.

SAVORY MUSHROOM RICE

Check out the veal recipes with oodles of gravy and serve this rice with them. It is a natural sopper-upper.

It goes just as well with chicken dishes that are rich in sauce.

Another great thing about this dish is you don't have to watch it. Once it goes into the oven, simply set the temperature and timer and concentrate on other things.

2 cups	long grain rice	500 ml
¼ cup	sweet butter	50 ml
2	large onions, finely chopped	2
½ lb	mushrooms, thinly sliced	250 g
2½ cups	rich beef stock	625 ml
1 tsp	salt	5 ml

1. Preheat oven to 350°F (180°C).
2. In a large skillet, heat rice, stirring constantly, until it turns golden. Transfer to an 8 cup (2 l) casserole.
3. In the same skillet melt butter. Add onions and mushrooms; sauté 5 minutes, until tender. Add to rice. Stir in stock and salt; blend well.
4. Bake in oven for 1¼ hours, adding water if necessary to keep rice moist, until rice is tender.

Makes 8 to 10 servings.

RICE WITH SMOKED SALMON AND GREEN ONIONS

This is a beautiful dish to behold—and should be garnished in a subtle way.
I sometimes ring the border of the plate with tiny pink flowers that go with the pink of the salmon and the green of the onions.
Serve this one as a first course with a very elegant dinner.

3 cups	hot cooked long grain rice	750 ml
¼ cup	sweet butter	50 ml
1	small clove garlic, finely chopped	1
1 cup	heavy or whipping cream	250 ml
1 tbs	Dijon mustard	15 ml
½ lb	smoked salmon, diced	250 g
6	green onions, thinly sliced	6
½ cup	grated Parmesan cheese	125 ml
½ tsp	salt	2 ml
¼ tsp	freshly ground black pepper	1 ml

1. Prepare rice ahead.
2. In a large skillet, melt butter. Add garlic; sauté about 3 minutes, until softened.
3. Stir in cream and mustard; heat thoroughly. Add salmon and cook 1 minute.
4. Remove from heat, add rice. Toss to mix well.
5. Spoon immediately into a warm serving dish. Sprinkle with onions and cheese and toss again. Season with salt and pepper.

Makes 6 servings.

SESAME RICE

Quick, intriguing, yet simple. You'll enjoy the mixture of oil, onion, and garlic.

2 tbs	vegetable oil	25 ml
1	small onion, finely chopped	1
1	clove garlic, finely chopped	1
1 cup	long grain rice	250 ml
½ cup	sesame seeds	125 ml
2½ cups	chicken stock	625 ml
1 tbs	chopped fresh parsley	15 ml

1. In a saucepan heat oil, add onion and garlic, and sauté about 3 minutes, until softened.
2. Stir in rice and sesame seeds. Toss together and cook 3 minutes.
3. Stir in chicken stock. Bring to a boil, reduce heat, cover, and simmer 20 minutes, until tender and liquid is absorbed.
4. Sprinkle with parsley, fluff with a fork, and serve.

Makes 4 servings.

GRANOLA

Okay, so I grew up in the 1960s—the Kennedys and flower power and the invention of granola. This, however, is worth remembering and keeping. Just add milk and fresh fruit in season.

1 cup	honey	250 ml
½ cup	melted butter	125 ml
2 tbs	molasses	25 ml
2 tbs	milk	25 ml
1 tsp	salt	5 ml
4 cups	rolled oats	1 l
1 cup	All Bran	250 ml
1 cup	wheat germ	250 ml
1 cup	ground nuts	250 ml
1 cup	sunflower seeds	250 ml

1. Preheat oven to 250°F (130°C).
2. In a saucepan, combine honey, butter, molasses, milk, and salt. Bring to a boil, reduce heat, simmer 5 minutes.
3. In a large bowl, combine oats, All Bran, wheat germ, nuts, and seeds. Pour liquid over cereal.
4. Spread on a large baking sheet and bake in oven, stirring occasionally, for 45 minutes, until mixture is golden brown.

Makes 8 cups (2 l).

FRESH VEGETABLES

What can we do with a vegetable to enhance its flavor? Combine it with other foods at a table or serve it royally by itself? What spices can we use, what changes in texture and appearance can we make?

All these vegetables, with the possible exception of the cherry tomatoes and zucchini in basil butter, are quite changed and reorganized—for the better, I think you will agree.

CAULIFLOWER PURÉE WITH CRÈME FRAICHE

Purées are probably my favorite way to serve a vegetable.

The Cauliflower Purée presented here can work just as well with broccoli, carrots, spinach, or peas.

I like to serve these in peach halves or scooped-out green peppers.

1	large cauliflower, broken into florets, stems chopped	1
1 cup	crème fraiche	250 ml
2 tbs	sour cream	25 ml
⅔ cup	shredded Cheddar cheese	150 ml
½ tsp	nutmeg	2 ml
¼ tsp	white pepper	1 ml
	salt to taste	
2 tbs	sweet butter	25 ml

1. Preheat oven to 350°F (180°C).
2. In a large pot of salted boiling water cook cauliflower about 8 minutes, until tender. Drain well. Transfer to a food processor or blender.
3. Add crème fraiche; process until puréed. Pour into a buttered 8 cup (2 l) casserole.
4. Stir in sour cream, cheese, nutmeg, pepper, and salt. Dot with butter and bake in oven for 25 minutes, or until purée is steaming hot.

Makes 8 servings.

CRÈME FRAICHE

1 cup	heavy or whipping cream	250 ml
1 tbs	buttermilk	15 ml

1. In a container combine cream and buttermilk; stir well.
2. Cover and set aside at room temperature for 8 hours, until thickened, then chill.
   Keeps well in the refrigerator for 4 to 6 weeks.

Makes 1 cup (250 ml).

VARIATIONS:
Puréed Broccoli with Crème Fraiche: Substitute 2 lb (1 kg) broccoli (2 bunches).
Puréed Carrots with Crème Fraiche: Substitute 2 lb (1 kg) carrots, cut in 1 inch (2.5 cm) slices and cooked 15 minutes. Use ground ginger in place of nutmeg.
Puréed Green Beans with Crème Fraiche: Substitute 2 lb (1 kg) green beans, cut in pieces and cooked 12 to 15 minutes.
Puréed Turnip (Rutabaga) with Crème Fraiche: Substitute 2 large turnips, peeled and diced. Use ground cardamom in place of nutmeg.

Spinach Casserole

When you get tired of serving potatoes, switch to this spinach casserole. It probably has the same number of calories as the potato dishes, but it's so good!

The cottage cheese makes this hearty and a natural dinner companion to any grill.

2 lb	fresh spinach, chopped and cooked	1 kg
1 cup	cottage cheese	250 ml
¼ cup	sour cream	50 ml
3	eggs, lightly beaten	3
2 tbs	all-purpose flour	25 ml
½ tsp	nutmeg	2 ml
½ tsp	salt	2 ml

1. Preheat oven to 350°F (180°C).
2. Place spinach in paper towel and squeeze out excess moisture.
3. In a small casserole combine spinach, cottage cheese, sour cream, eggs, flour, nutmeg, and salt. Bake in oven for 30 minutes, stir mixture, continue to bake for another 30 minutes, until set.

Makes 4 servings.

Baked Eggplant Rolls

A light vegetarian supper or lunch all by itself. Or a great side dish to serve with small lamb kabobs or lambburgers.

2	medium eggplants	2
1 tsp	salt	5 ml
2	eggs	2
¼ cup	milk	50 ml
½ cup	all-purpose flour	125 ml
1 tsp	salt	5 ml
½ tsp	freshly ground black pepper	2 ml
1 cup	vegetable oil	250 ml

TOMATO SAUCE:

2 tbs	olive oil	25 ml
1	clove garlic, finely chopped	1
1	can (19 oz/540 ml) Italian plum tomatoes	1
¼ cup	chopped fresh basil	50 ml
½ tsp	salt	2 ml
¼ tsp	freshly ground black pepper	1 ml

STUFFING:

1½ cups	ricotta cheese	375 ml
4 tbs	freshly grated Parmesan cheese	50 ml
1	egg	1
8	black olives, finely chopped	8
½ tsp	salt	2 ml
¼ tsp	freshly ground black pepper	1 ml
pinch	nutmeg	pinch
	grated Mozzarella cheese	
	lemon wedges	

1. Slice each eggplant lengthwise into 8 slices, ¼ inch (5 mm) thick. Sprinkle with salt and let drain 1 hour in colander. Blot dry on paper towel to remove excess moisture.
2. In a bowl combine eggs and milk. In another bowl combine flour, salt, and pepper. Dredge eggplant slices in flour mixture, then dip in egg mixture.
3. In a large skillet heat oil, add eggplant slices in a single layer. Cook 4 minutes, turning, until golden brown on each side.
4. Remove from oil and drain on paper towel. Cool.
5. To make Sauce: In a saucepan heat olive oil; add garlic and sauté 3 minutes, until softened.
6. Add tomatoes, basil, salt, and pepper; cook, stirring, about 10 minutes, until slightly reduced.
7. Pour ¼ cup (50 ml) sauce onto bottom of 8½ × 12½ inch (21 × 31 cm) shallow baking dish.
8. To make Stuffing: In a bowl combine Ricotta and Parmesan. Beat in egg and fold in olives; chill 20 minutes. Stir in salt, pepper, and nutmeg.
9. Preheat oven to 350°F (180°C).
10. To assemble: Place 1 tsp (5 ml) of cheese mixture on one end of each eggplant slice and roll up. Arrange in baking dish, seam side down, tightly in rows.
11. Cover with remaining sauce, sprinkle with grated Mozzarella cheese, and bake in oven for 20 to 25 minutes, until cheese is melted and bubbling. Garnish with a lemon wedge.

Makes 4 servings.

ZUCCHINI WITH CHERRY TOMATOES IN BASIL BUTTER

The important thing to remember here is that the basil must be fresh and the tomatoes should be barely warmed through.

8	medium zucchini, cut into ½ inch (1 cm) slices	8
4 cups	cherry tomatoes, halved	1 l
¼ cup	sweet butter or margarine	50 ml
1 tbs	lemon juice	15 ml
1 tbs	chopped fresh basil	15 ml
1½ tsp	salt	7 ml
1 tsp	grated lemon rind	5 ml
⅛ tsp	freshly ground black pepper	0.5 ml
2 tbs	grated Parmesan chse	25 ml

1. In a pot of salted boiling water cook zucchini about 4 minutes, until tender crisp. Drain well and add tomatoes.
2. In a small saucepan, heat butter with lemon juice. Pour over vegetables and toss.
3. Season with basil, salt, lemon rind, and pepper. Cover and cook 2 to 3 minutes to heat the tomatoes.
4. Sprinkle cheese over top before serving.

Makes 12 servings.

ZUCCHINI SOUFFLE

This recipe is subtle; you can really taste the vegetable. It makes a marvelous accompaniment to any of the roast lamb recipes.

2 lb	zucchini, cut in 2 inch (5 cm) pieces	1 kg
1 cup	heavy or whipping cream	250 ml
⅓ cup	all-purpose flour	75 ml
4	eggs, lightly beaten	4
1 tsp	salt	5 ml
½ tsp	white pepper	2 ml

1. Preheat oven to 350°F (180°C).
2. In a pot of salted boiling water, cook zucchini 6 to 8 minutes, until tender crisp. Drain; place in a food processor or blender; purée until smooth.
3. Stir in flour, eggs, salt, and pepper. Pour into 1½ inch (3.5 cm) buttered gratin dish. Bake in oven for 45 minutes, or until top is golden brown. Serve immediately.

Makes 8 servings.

BAKED RATATOUILLE

This is a recipe for twelve people. Even if you are only having six or eight, make it up for twelve and keep the leftovers to use as a condiment. I like to chop all the ingredients to a uniform size for this beautiful casserole.

¼ cup	olive oil	50 ml
½ lb	mushrooms, coarsely chopped	250 g
2	medium onions, coarsely chopped	2
3	cloves garlic, coarsely chopped	3
3	medium zucchini, coarsely chopped	3
1	medium eggplant, coarsely chopped	1
2	tomatoes, coarsely chopped	2
1	can (5½ oz/156 ml) tomato paste	1
¾ cup	water	175 ml
¼ cup	chopped fresh parsley	50 ml
2 tsp	salt	10 ml
2 tsp	dried basil	10 ml
2	bay leaves	2
1 tsp	ground coriander	5 ml
¼ tsp	freshly ground black pepper	1 ml
¼ cup	fine dry breadcrumbs	50 ml
1 tbs	freshly grated Parmesan cheese	15 ml
1 tbs	chopped fresh parsley	15 ml

1. In a large skillet heat oil. Add mushrooms, onions, and garlic; sauté about 5 minutes, or until onions are soft.
2. Add zucchini and eggplant. Cook over medium heat 8 to 10 minutes.
3. Stir in tomatoes, tomato paste, water, parsley, salt, basil, bay leaves, coriander, and pepper.
4. Simmer over low heat about 1 hour, until sauce is thick and eggplant is soft. Transfer to a buttered 6 cup (1.5 l) casserole.
5. Preheat oven to 325°F (160°C).
6. In a small bowl combine crumbs, cheese, and parsley. Sprinkle on top of vegetable mixture. Bake in oven for 30 minutes, or until top is golden brown.

Makes 12 servings.

FESTIVE MUSHROOM ROLL

This eye-catching and appealing dish should be served with a flavored mayonnaise and sprinkled with chopped chives.

1½ lb	mushrooms, finely chopped	750 g
6	eggs, separated	6
¼ cup	soft sweet butter	50 ml
2 tbs	lemon juice	25 ml
1 tsp	salt	5 ml
½ tsp	freshly ground black pepper	2 ml
pinch	nutmeg	pinch
	chopped chives	
	Flavored Mayonnaise	

1. Oil a 10½ × 15 inch (25 × 37.5 cm) jelly roll pan and line with lightly oiled wax paper.
2. Preheat oven to 350°F (180°C).
3. Place chopped mushrooms in paper towel and wring out excess moisture.
4. In a large bowl beat egg yolks until fluffy. Stir in soft butter, mushrooms, lemon juice, salt, pepper, and nutmeg.
5. Beat egg whites until moist peaks form. Fold mushroom mixture into egg whites. Pour into prepared pan, smoothing surface.
6. Bake in oven for 20 minutes, until firm and lightly browned. Cool.
7. With the point of a knife cut around outside edges. Turn out onto fresh waxed paper and peel off waxed paper attached to bottom of baked mixture.
8. Starting at wide end, roll up jelly-roll fashion, using waxed paper to support baked mixture as it is rolled. Discard waxed paper.
9. Place seam side down on a long narrow platter. Sprinkle with chopped chives and serve with Flavored Mayonnaise.
10. May be prepared in advance, refrigerated for up to 2 days, and then reheated in a 350°F (180°C) oven for 10 minutes.
   Serve hot or at room temperature.

Makes 6 to 8 servings.

FLAVORED MAYONNAISE

This is light and delicious and can be augmented with Dijon mustard or any of your favorite herbs.

3	egg yolks	3
1 tbs	lemon juice	15 ml
½ tsp	salt	2 ml
⅛ tsp	white pepper	0.5 ml
pinch	dry mustard	pinch
pinch	cayenne pepper	pinch
1¼ cups	olive oil	300 ml

1. In a blender or food processor combine yolks, lemon juice, salt, white pepper, dry mustard, and cayenne; blend until smooth, about 1 minute.
2. With machine running, gradually pour in oil in a thin steady stream. Blend about 3 minutes, until thick.

Makes 2 cups.

BAKED MUSHROOM SQUARES

This recipe is versatile and cooperative as only mushrooms can be. Serve them as a side dish with your favorite curry or stew: I like to serve them with cabbage rolls. Or cut them into larger pieces and serve them as a main dish with sour cream and chopped chives.

¼ cup	sweet butter	50 ml
1	medium onion, finely chopped	1
½ cup	milk	125 ml
½ cup	cream	125 ml
1 cup	soft whole wheat breadcrumbs	250 ml
1 lb	mushrooms, chopped fine	500 g
1 tsp	salt	5 ml
¼ tsp	freshly ground black pepper	1 ml
2	eggs, well beaten	2

1. In a small skillet over medium heat, melt butter. Add onions and sauté for 10 minutes, stirring frequently.
2. In a large bowl, combine milk, cream, and breadcrumbs. Let stand for 10 minutes.
3. Preheat oven to 350°F (180°C).
4. Combine sautéed onion, breadcrumb mixture, mushrooms, salt, pepper, and eggs. Mix well. Pour into a buttered 8 inch (20 cm) square baking dish and bake in oven for 1 hour, until tester inserted in center comes out clean.
5. Cut into squares and serve hot.

Makes 6 servings.

SKEWERED MUSHROOMS WITH OREGANO

This is a recipe to prepare for any barbecue party. The oregano makes it a particularly good accompaniment for steaks.

The trick is to have the mushrooms at room temperature and then screw the skewer into them. That way they are much less likely to split.

1½ lb	medium mushrooms	750 g
¼ cup	olive oil	50 ml
3	cloves garlic, finely chopped	3
1 tsp	salt	5 ml
¼ tsp	freshly ground black pepper	1 ml
¼ tsp	oregano	1 ml

1. Wash and dry mushrooms. Thread onto wooden skewers with 4 to 5 mushrooms on each one. Set in a 9 × 13 inch (23 × 33 cm) glass baking dish.
2. In a small bowl combine oil, garlic, salt, pepper, and oregano. Pour over mushrooms; let stand 1 hour to marinate.
3. Remove skewers from marinade. Grill, broil, or barbecue for 8 to 10 minutes, until lightly browned.

Makes 4 servings.

VEGETABLE SWISS CHEESE PIE

You can make this with onions as well as broccoli or cauliflower. Or use a combination of all three vegetables. It does service as a side dish with roasts. Serve the pie bubbling hot from the oven in the pan you used for baking.

1	single pie crust for 9-inch (23 cm) pie	1
3 cups	coarsely chopped broccoli or cauliflower	750 ml
¼ cup	coarsely chopped walnuts	50 ml
2 cups	grated Swiss cheese	500 ml
1 tbs	all-purpose flour	15 ml
6	eggs, lightly beaten	6
1 cup	heavy or whipping cream	250 ml
4 drops	hot pepper sauce	4 drops
½ tsp	salt	2 ml
¼ tsp	freshly ground black pepper	1 ml

1. Line the bottom of a 9 inch (23 cm) pie plate or quiche dish with pie crust.
2. Arrange broccoli on pie crust and sprinkle walnuts on top.
3. Dredge cheese in flour and arrange over top of broccoli-nut mixture.
4. Preheat oven to 400°F (200°C).

5. In a small bowl, combine eggs, cream, hot pepper sauce, salt, and pepper. Pour over cheese and broccoli mixture.
6. Bake in oven for 15 minutes. Reduce heat to 325°F (160°C) and bake for 30 minutes, or until knife inserted near center comes out clean.

Makes 6 to 8 servings.

CARAWAY RED CABBAGE

Just shave your cabbage, peel the apples, insert your onions, and away it goes. Leave it on low simmer for as long as you like, or switch it off and reheat later. It is also good cold.

1	head red cabbage (about 1½ lb/750 g), finely shredded	1
¼ cup	red wine vinegar	50 ml
½ tsp	salt	2 ml
2 tbs	sweet butter	25 ml
1	Spanish onion, thinly sliced	1
2	apples, thinly sliced	2
½ cup	chicken stock	125 ml
2 tbs	brown sugar	25 ml
2 tsp	caraway seed	10 ml
½ tsp	freshly ground black pepper	2 ml

1. In a large bowl combine cabbage, vinegar, and salt. Let stand 5 minutes.
2. In a large skillet heat butter. Add cabbage, turning 2 to 3 times. Stir in onion, apples, stock, sugar, caraway, and pepper.
3. Cook, covered, over low heat for 1 hour, until cabbage is tender. Serve warm.

Makes 6 servings.

TURNIPS FRENCH CANADIAN STYLE

I serve this at Christmas with roast goose, or any other time of the year when I get a feeling for goose. It also goes well with lamb, pork, and turkey.

2 cups	cooked, mashed yellow turnips (rutabagas)	500 ml
1	egg, lightly beaten	1
2 tbs	sweet butter	25 ml
½ tsp	salt	2 ml
¼ tsp	freshly ground black pepper	1 ml
½ cup	finely shredded Cheddar cheese	125 ml
2 tbs	dry breadcrumbs	25 ml

1. Preheat oven to 400°F (200°C).

2. In a bowl, combine turnips, egg, butter, salt, and pepper; mix well. Pour into a 6 cup (1.5 l) souffle dish.
3. Combine cheese and breadcrumbs; sprinkle over top of turnips. Bake in oven for 20 minutes, until crumbs are golden.

Makes 4 servings.

VEGETABLE TEMPURA

I pile the peppers and the sweet potato pieces and zucchini on a plate beside my stove and then batter and fry as needed. And I invite guests to dip and fry for themselves on those informal evenings that are so pleasurable for everyone.

2	sweet potatoes	2
2	sweet green peppers	2
2	sweet red peppers	2
2	medium zucchini	2
1	small eggplant	1

BATTER:

2	egg yolks	2
2 cups	iced cold water	500 ml
2 cups	all-purpose flour	500 ml

DIPPING SAUCE:

¾ cup	dashi*	175 ml
3 tbs	light soy sauce	45 ml
3 tbs	mirin (sweet rice wine)	45 ml
1 cup	grated giant radish	250 ml
¼ cup	grated fresh ginger root	50 ml

DIPPING SALT:

2 tbs	curry powder	25 ml
2 tbs	salt	25 ml
	peanut oil for deep frying	

1. Peel sweet potatoes and slice in thin rounds. Cut green and red peppers into ½ inch (1 cm) strips. Cut eggplant in half lengthwise and then into ¼ inch (5 mm) slices. Cut zucchini into 2 × ½ inch (5 × 1 cm) sticks.

*Available at Japanese markets.

2. To make Batter: In a bowl combine egg yolks, water, and flour; stir well to make a thick batter.
3. To make Dipping Sauce: In a bowl combine dashi, soy sauce, mirin, radish, and ginger root. Mix well. Makes 2½ cups (625 ml).
4. To make Dipping Salt: In a small bowl combine curry powder and salt. Mix well. Makes ¼ cup (50 ml).
5. In a wok, heavy saucepan, or deep fryer, heat oil to 375°F (190°C). Dip vegetables, a few pieces at a time, in batter; slip into hot oil. Cook 2 to 3 minutes, until golden.
6. Remove with slotted spoon. Drain on paper towel.
7. Arrange deep-fried vegetables on individual plates or a warm platter. Serve with Dipping Sauce and Dipping Salt.

Makes 8 to 10 servings.

CRUNCHY BROCCOLI STIR FRY

This recipe is perfect to serve with Chinese Roast Pork in combination with a rice dish.

1	bunch broccoli (2 lb/1 kg)	1
2 tbs	vegetable oil	25 ml
2	cloves garlic, finely chopped	2
½ cup	chicken stock	125 ml
1 tbs	lemon juice	15 ml
2 tsp	oyster sauce	10 ml
½ tsp	salt	2 ml
¼ tsp	freshly ground black pepper	1 ml
¼ tsp	dry mustard	1 ml
2 tbs	toasted sesame seeds	25 ml

1. Cut florets off stems and cut stems into 1 inch (2.5 cm) pieces. In a large skillet heat oil. Add broccoli florets and stems and garlic. Stir until broccoli is coated with oil.
2. Stir in stock, lemon juice, oyster sauce, salt, pepper, and dry mustard. Bring to a boil, reduce heat, cover, and cook 3 minutes, until broccoli is tender-crisp.
3. Sprinkle with toasted sesame seeds at serving time.

Makes 4 to 6 servings.

CHINESE VEGETABLES

There's a lot, aside from bean sprouts, that represent the Chinese kitchen garden. And the seasonings give them that Oriental tang.

¼ cup	vegetable oil	50 ml
3 cups	broccoli florets	750 ml
1 cup	diagonally cut carrot slices	250 ml
1 cup	diagonally sliced green beans	250 ml
1 cup	cauliflower florets	250 ml
1	large green pepper, cut into 1 inch (2.5 cm) pieces	1
2 cups	coarsely shredded cabbage	500 ml
1 cup	whole small mushrooms	250 ml
1 cup	bean sprouts	250 ml
2 tbs	oyster sauce	25 ml
½ tsp	sesame oil	2 ml
½ cup	beef stock	125 ml
¼ cup	soy sauce	50 ml
1 tbs	cornstarch	15 ml

1. In a large skillet or wok, heat oil. Add broccoli and carrots. Stir-fry 2 to 3 minutes.
2. Add beans, cauliflower, green pepper, cabbage, mushrooms, sprouts, oyster sauce, sesame oil, and beef stock. Cover and steam for 1 minute.
3. Combine soy sauce and cornstarch; mix until smooth. Blend into vegetables; cook, stirring, about 2 minutes, until thickened.

Makes 8 servings.

VEGETABLE FRITTATA

Here is a vegetable omelette from Italy that can be used not only for lunch or brunch, but as a first course when you are entertaining.

2 tbs	olive oil	25 ml
1 tbs	sweet butter	15 ml
1	medium onion, chopped	1
6	medium mushrooms, sliced (½ cup/125 ml)	6
½ cup	thinly sliced zucchini	125 ml
¼ cup	chopped red pepper	50 ml
1 tsp	salt	5 ml
¼ tsp	freshly ground black pepper	1 ml
1 tsp	chopped fresh basil, or ¼ tsp (1 ml) dried	5 ml
pinch	cayenne pepper	pinch
6	eggs	6
½ cup	pitted black olives, halved	50 ml
¼ cup	Tomato Sauce (recipe p. 340)	50 ml

1. Preheat oven to 350°F (180°C).
2. In an ovenproof skillet heat oil and butter. Add onions; sauté 5 minutes, until softened.
3. Add mushrooms, zucchini, and red pepper and sauté 5 minutes, until vegetables are softened.
4. Stir in salt, pepper, basil, and cayenne. Beat eggs until frothy. Pour over vegetables. Spoon olives and Tomato Sauce over top.
5. Bake in oven for 15 minutes, or until set.
   Serve at once, cut in wedges.

Makes 4 servings.

SWEDISH LAMB ROAST
with Sweet Roasted Carrots

SPECIAL POTATO CASSEROLE

PURÉED BROCCOLI WITH CRÈME FRAICHE

WINTER FRUIT BASKET OF PEARS AND TANGERINES

QUEEN ELIZABETH CAKE

SPECIAL POTATO CASSEROLE

This recipe is easily reheatable and goes with just about any kind of main course. Serve it with roasts or with one of the heartier salads.

6	medium potatoes, cooked in jackets, peeled, and cubed	6
⅓ cup	chopped green onions	75 ml
1 cup	sour cream	250 ml
1½ cups	grated Cheddar cheese	375 ml
1 cup	chicken stock	250 ml
1 cup	light cream	250 ml
½ tsp	salt	2 ml
¼ tsp	freshly ground black pepper	1 ml
¼ cup	sweet butter	50 ml
¾ cup	crushed cornflakes	175 ml

1. Preheat oven to 350°F (180°C).
2. In a 9 × 13 inch (23 × 32 cm) baking dish or casserole arrange potato cubes. Sprinkle green onion over top.
3. In a mixing bowl combine sour cream, cheese, stock, light cream, salt, and pepper. Pour over potatoes.
4. In a small saucepan, melt butter. Stir in cornflakes. Spread on top of potato mixture.
5. Bake in oven for 30 minutes, until heated through and lightly browned.

Makes 6 to 8 servings.

MASHED POTATO AND ONION SOUFFLE

Let me explain that here I am not using the term "souffle" in its technical sense. This recipe does not depend on timing or the ability of egg whites to rise and stay put. It does, however, have that marvelous souffle texture and is great to serve with any recipe that has a lot of gravy.

3 cups	mashed potatoes	750 ml
1 tbs	soft sweet butter	15 ml
3 tbs	light cream	45 ml
3	eggs, separated	3
1	medium onion, finely chopped	1
2 tsp	chopped chives	10 ml
1 tsp	chopped fresh parsley	5 ml
1 tsp	salt	5 ml
½ tsp	freshly ground black pepper	2 ml

1. Preheat oven to 350°F (180°C).
2. In a large bowl beat butter and cream into potatoes by hand. Add yolks one at a time, beating after each addition. Stir in onion, chives, parsley, salt, and pepper.
3. Beat egg whites until stiff but not dry. Fold into potato mixture.
4. Spoon into a buttered 6 cup (1.5 l) souffle dish. Bake in oven for 30 minutes, or until puffy and brown on top.

Makes 6 servings.

SWEET POTATO PUFF

I love sweet potatoes the way I love pumpkin, and a puréed sweet potato has something comforting, deep, and rich about it that is irresistible.
Try this one at your next dinner party and see how your guests react to the smooth texture and sweet, orangey flavor.

3 cups	cooked and puréed sweet potatoes (3 medium)	750 ml
¼ cup	soft sweet butter	50 ml
2 tbs	brown sugar	25 ml
½ tsp	cinnamon	2 ml
½ tsp	ground ginger	2 ml
¼ tsp	ground cloves	1 ml
4	eggs	4
⅓ cup	orange juice	75 ml
2 tbs	dark rum	25 ml
1 tsp	grated orange rind	5 ml
½ cup	dry breadcrumbs	125 ml
1 tsp	salt	5 ml
¼ tsp	freshly ground black pepper	1 ml
2 tbs	chopped pecans	25 ml
	Crème Fraiche (recipe p. 222)	
	freshly ground black pepper	

1. In a bowl combine sweet potato, butter, brown sugar, cinnamon, ginger, and cloves; mix well.
2. Beat eggs with orange juice, rum, and orange rind. Stir into sweet potato mixture. Stir in half the breadcrumbs, salt and pepper.
3. Preheat oven to 375°F (190°C).
4. Butter a 6 cup (1.5 l) souffle dish; sprinkle with remaining breadcrumbs. Pour sweet potato mixture into dish. Sprinkle with pecans.
5. Place souffle dish in large pan; pour in hot water to halfway up sides of souffle dish. Bake in oven for 1 hour, or until a tester inserted in the center comes out clean.

6. Serve immediately before souffle deflates. Serve with Crème Fraiche and gratings of black pepper.

Makes 6 to 8 servings.

PERFECT POMMES FRITES (FRENCH FRIES)

Thanks to my friend Jean Michel, owner of Auberge Gavroche, I can pass along this recipe to you.
    These are the definitive French fries. Your friends will love them, though they may wind up hating you three pounds later.
    Serve these with steak, roasts, burgers, or just because. . . .

8	large potatoes, peeled	8
4 cups	cooking oil	1 l
	salt to taste	

1. Cut potatoes into long strips about ¼ inch (5 mm) wide. Rinse with cold water (to get rid of starch) and dry well.
2. In a deep skillet or deep fryer, heat oil to 250°F (120°C). Blanch potatoes for 6 minutes in hot oil, remove, and drain on paper towel.
3. Increase heat of oil to 350°F (180°C). Cook potatoes for 4 minutes, until golden brown. Drain on paper towel.
4. Sprinkle with salt to taste.

Makes 6 servings.

LATKES (CRISP POTATO PANCAKES)

These are so delicious I always make lots of them and serve with pots of applesauce and thick sour cream. They go like, well, like hotcakes.
    Latkes also make a great nosh for a cocktail party, but if you use them this way, be sure to make them bite-size.

4	medium potatoes, peeled	4
2 tbs	finely chopped onion	25 ml
2	eggs, well beaten	2
2 tbs	all-purpose flour	25 ml
1 tsp	baking powder	5 ml
1 tsp	salt	5 ml
¼ tsp	freshly ground black pepper	1 ml
¼ cup	vegetable oil	50 ml
	sour cream and applesauce	

1. In a large bowl of ice water, chill peeled potatoes for 2 hours. Grate coarsely. Place grated potatoes in a tea towel and press excess moisture from potatoes, until quite dry.
2. In a large bowl, combine potatoes, onion, eggs, flour, baking powder, salt, and pepper; mix well.
3. In a large skillet, heat oil. Drop potato mixture, 2 tbs (25 ml) at a time into hot oil. Cook 5 minutes, over moderate heat, on each side until golden brown.
4. Serve with sour cream and applesauce.

Makes 6 servings.

APPLESAUCE

4	medium MacIntosh apples, unpeeled, quartered, and seeds removed	4
¼ cup	water	50 ml
¼ cup	granulated sugar	50 ml
pinch	cinnamon	pinch

1. In a heavy saucepan combine apples and water. Cook over medium heat 15 to 20 minutes, until apples are soft. Transfer to a Mouli or press through a sieve to strain out skin.
2. Stir in sugar and cinnamon. Chill.

Makes 1 cup (250 ml).

BARLEY CASSEROLE

My favorite companion for this dish is Barbecued Butterfly Lamb, but this barley dish is good with almost any of the spicy fish dishes, curries, or sweet and sours.

½ lb	mushrooms	250 g
¼ cup	sweet butter	50 ml
1	large onion, finely chopped	1
1 cup	pearl barley	250 ml
1 tsp	salt	5 ml
½ tsp	freshly ground black pepper	2 ml
2 cups	chicken stock	500 ml

1. Preheat oven to 350°F (180°C).
2. Slice mushroom caps thinly and chop stems.
3. In a large skillet melt butter, add onion; sauté 3 to 4 minutes, until tender.
4. Stir in mushrooms. Cook 4 to 5 minutes.
5. Mix in barley, salt, and pepper and brown lightly, mixing well with mushrooms and onions.
6. Transfer to a buttered 4 cup (1 l) casserole. Stir in stock. Cover casserole and bake in oven for 25 minutes, until barley is tender.

Makes 6 servings.

THE STAFF OF LIFE

BREADS AND MUFFINS

These are the sweet side of the staff of life. Little rolls and loaves that don't usually employ yeast, though there are a few with it in here.

These offerings are sliced and broken and buttered and slipped under and around fillings and spreads.

I don't know why it is, but even the most self-disciplined dieters will allow themselves a slice or two of pecan bread (buttered, of course) when they won't touch the other goodies on the tea table.

PECAN BREAD

When this bread is made with pecans and onions, it is a wonderful bread to serve with salads and soups and lots of fresh butter.

In its sweet version, minus the onions, it is good for formal dinners. I like to pass plates of it with the dessert cheese tray.

1 tsp	granulated sugar	5 ml
½ cup	lukewarm milk	125 ml
1	envelope active dry yeast	1
3–3½ cups	all-purpose flour	750–875 ml
1 cup	whole wheat flour	250 ml
2 tsp	salt	10 ml
⅓ cup	water	75 ml
¾ cup	finely chopped onion*	175 ml
¼ cup	soft sweet butter	50 ml
1 cup	coarsely chopped pecans	250 ml
	cornmeal	

*If serving with dessert cheeses, substitute ¾ cup (175 ml) currants for the onions.

1. In a small bowl, dissolve sugar in milk. Sprinkle in yeast. Let stand 10 minutes, then stir well.
2. In a large bowl, combine 1 cup (250 ml) all-purpose flour, all the whole wheat flour, and salt. Add yeast mixture and stir 2 minutes, until well blended.
3. In a small skillet heat butter, add onions; sauté 5 minutes, until softened. Add onion mixture to flour mixture.
4. Stir in more all-purpose flour (2–2½ cups/500–625 ml) to make a dough which leaves the side of the bowl.
5. On a lightly floured surface, knead dough until smooth. Place in a well-greased bowl, turning so that dough is greased all over. Cover and let rise in a warm place for 1 hour, or until doubled.
6. Preheat oven to 425°F (220°C).
7. On a lightly floured surface punch dough down; knead 2 to 3 minutes.
8. Cut in half and shape each half as an oval loaf, about 10 inches (25 cm) long.
9. Sprinkle baking sheet with cornmeal and place loaves on sheet. Let rise, uncovered, in a warm place for 20 minutes. Slash tops diagonally. Bake in oven for 25 to 30 minutes, until loaves sound hollow when tapped on top.

Makes 2 loaves.

OATMEAL BREAD

Because this recipe makes two loaves, I make the first one plain to serve with soups and the second one with currants and cinnamon to go with cheeses.

2 tbs plus 2 tsp	granulated sugar	35 ml
½ cup	lukewarm water	125 ml
2	envelopes active dry yeast	2
3 cups	rolled oats	750 ml
2½ cups	boiling water	625 ml
½ cup	molasses	125 ml
1 tbs	salt	15 ml
¼ cup	shortening	50 ml
½ cup	cold water	125 ml
6 cups	all-purpose flour	1.5 l
2 tbs	melted sweet butter	25 ml

1. In a cup combine 2 tsp (10 ml) sugar and lukewarm water; stir to dissolve. Sprinkle yeast over and let stand 10 minutes, then stir well.
2. In a large bowl, combine rolled oats, boiling water, molasses, remaining sugar, salt, and shortening and stir to blend. Add cold water to oatmeal mixture and stir until lukewarm.

3. Stir in yeast mixture. Add half of the flour and beat with a wooden spoon until well blended. Add enough of remaining flour, mixing first with spoon then with hands, to make a firm but not stiff dough.
4. Turn out onto a floured board and knead about 8 minutes, until elastic.
5. Put in a greased bowl, cover with a damp cloth, and let rise in a warm place about 1 hour and 15 minutes, until double in bulk.
6. Punch down and let rise again, about 45 minutes to an hour, until double. Punch down.
7. Grease two 9 × 5 inch (23 × 13 cm) loaf pans. Divide dough into 2 equal parts and shape each into a loaf. Place in prepared pans. Brush tops with melted butter and let rise in a warm place about 1 hour, until double.
8. Preheat oven to 425°F (220°C). Bake for 15 minutes, then reduce temperature to 375°F (190°C) and continue to bake 45 minutes, or until loaves sound hollow when tapped on top. Cool on racks.

Makes 2 loaves.

VARIATION:
Oatmeal Fruit Loaf: Before shaping portions of dough into loaves, roll each portion to form a 9 inch (23 cm) wide rectangle. For each loaf combine 2 tbs (25 ml) brown sugar, ½ cup (125 ml) raisins or currants, and 1 tsp (1 ml) cinnamon. Sprinkle over surface of rectangle, roll up and tuck in ends, and place in prepared pan. Continue as recipe directs.

SPREADS FOR TEATIME TOAST

These butters should be spread right on the bread with the crusts removed and put under the grill for a moment to meld the taste of the spread and the toast together. It is a powerful union.

For other times, keep in pots and put out for use with an assortment of other breads and muffins.

HONEY BUTTER TOAST

½ cup	soft sweet butter	125 ml
½ cup	honey	125 ml
12	slices bread, crusts removed	12
	cinnamon	

1. Preheat broiler.
2. In a bowl, cream butter and honey. Toast bread on one side under broiler. Turn and partially toast second side.
3. Spread second side with honey-butter mixture. Sprinkle with cinnamon. Continue toasting until golden brown.

Store any unused portion of honey butter in refrigerator. Keeps up to 1 week.

Makes 12 slices.

LEMON TOAST

½ cup	granulated sugar	125 ml
¼ cup	soft sweet butter	50 ml
	grated rind and juice of ½ lemon	
10	slices bread, crusts removed	10

1. Preheat broiler.
2. In a bowl, cream sugar, butter, lemon rind, and juice. Toast bread on one side under broiler.
3. Turn and partially toast second side. Spread second side with lemon-butter mixture and continue toasting until golden brown.
4. Cut slices into halves or quarters and serve immediately.
5. Store any unused portion of lemon butter in refrigerator. Keeps up to 1 week.

Makes 10 slices.

CHERRY BUTTER

½ cup	soft sweet butter	125 ml
¼ cup	imported cherry preserves	50 ml

In a small dish cream together butter and cherry preserves. Makes ¾ cup (175 ml).

VARIATIONS:

Raspberry Butter: Use Seedless Raspberry Jam (recipe p. 349) in place of imported cherry preserves.

Strawberry Butter: Use Strawberry Jam (recipe p. 349) in place of imported cherry preserves.

JALAPEÑO CORNBREAD AND MUFFINS

Serve with spicy chili con carne or pack lots of rare roast beef slices into a corn muffin and top with your favorite relish.

This recipe came to me via my friend Ethel, a super cook who got it from her friend Leya, a terrific chef, who got it from her friend. . . .

1 cup	yellow cornmeal	250 ml
½ cup	all-purpose flour	125 ml
1 tsp	baking powder	5 ml
½ tsp	baking soda	2 ml
½ tsp	salt	2 ml
3	eggs	3
¾ cup	milk	175 ml
¼ cup	vegetable oil	50 ml
1 cup	corn niblets	250 ml
1 cup	shredded sharp Cheddar cheese	250 ml
¼ cup	finely chopped jalapeño peppers*	50 ml

1. Preheat oven to 400°F (200°C).
2. Lightly grease a 9 × 5 inch (23 × 12 cm) loaf pan.
3. Combine cornmeal, flour, baking powder, baking soda, and salt.
4. In a bowl lightly beat eggs; stir in milk and oil. Add corn, cheese, and peppers; mix well.
5. Stir dry ingredients into liquid until evenly mixed. Do not beat. Pour batter into prepared loaf pan.
6. Bake in oven for 35 to 40 minutes, until toothpick inserted in center comes out clean. Let cool in pan 10 minutes, then remove to a wire rack.

Makes 1 loaf.

VARIATION:
Jalapeño Corn Muffins: Spoon batter into lightly greased 12 cup muffin pan to fill each cup ⅔ full. Bake in a 400°F (200°C) oven for 20 to 25 minutes, or until toothpick inserted in center comes out clean. Let cool 10 minutes before inverting and cooling on wire rack.

Makes 12 medium muffins.

*Look for these at greengrocers or in produce departments.

HOT BLUEBERRY MUFFINS

Nothing is quite as satisfying as reaching into a basket lined with a colorful napkin, picking up a hot muffin, and breaking it open. As the steam pours out, so does the wonderful aroma of fresh blueberries. Just take a moment to slather on beaten butter and then bite. Mmmmmmmmuffins.

2 cups	all-purpose flour	500 ml
1 tbs	baking powder	15 ml
2 tbs	granulated sugar	25 ml
½ tsp	salt	2 ml
½ cup	cold sweet butter	125 ml
1	egg, lightly beaten	1
1 cup	milk	250 ml
1 cup	fresh blueberries	250 ml

1. Preheat oven to 400°F (200°C).
2. In a large mixing bowl, combine flour, baking powder, sugar, and salt. With a pastry blender or 2 knives, cut in butter.
3. Make a well in dry ingredients; add egg, milk, and blueberries. Mix just until dry ingredients are moistened.
4. Spoon into 12 medium muffin cups to fill them ⅔ full. Bake in oven for 25 minutes, or until lightly browned. Remove from pans immediately.

Makes 12 medium muffins.

CARROT BRAN MUFFINS

A not-too-sweet muffin. You can fill it with thinly sliced smoked meats and top off with chili sauce for a quick sandwich snack.

But if you are in the mood for something sweet, serve this perfect muffin with butter and your own homemade preserves.

1 cup	100% bran cereal	250 ml
1 cup	milk	250 ml
2	eggs	2
1 cup	grated raw carrot	250 ml
¼ cup	vegetable oil	50 ml
1½ cups	all-purpose flour	375 ml
¼ cup	firmly packed brown sugar	50 ml
2 tsp	baking powder	10 ml
½ tsp	cinnamon	2 ml
½ tsp	salt	2 ml

1. Preheat oven to 400°F (200°C).
2. In a small bowl combine cereal and milk; let stand 10 minutes. Beat in eggs, carrot, and oil.
3. In a mixing bowl combine flour, sugar, baking powder, cinnamon, and salt. Make a well in the center and pour in bran mixture. Stir quickly and only until mixture is moistened.
4. Spoon into greased 12 cup muffin tins, filling each cup ⅔ full. Bake in oven for 20 to 25 minutes, until lightly browned. Let cool 5 minutes, then remove.

Makes 12 medium muffins.

SPICY FRUIT AND NUT BRAN LOAF

I have found my middle son, Harris, whipping up this loaf on a Sunday morning. He is the most health-conscious of my five children. But slices are wonderful topped with whipped cream cheese and homemade jam.

1 cup	100% bran cereal	250 ml
½ cup	milk	125 ml
½ cup	orange juice	125 ml
2	eggs	2
¼ cup	vegetable oil	50 ml
¼ cup	grated raw carrot	50 ml
1 cup	all-purpose flour	250 ml
½ cup	whole wheat flour	125 ml
½ cup	firmly packed brown sugar	125 ml
2 tsp	baking powder	10 ml
½ tsp	salt	2 ml
½ tsp	cinnamon	2 ml
¼ tsp	nutmeg	1 ml
¾ cup	chopped walnuts	175 ml
¼ cup	currants	50 ml
	grated rind of 1 orange	

1. Preheat oven to 350°F (180°C).
2. Grease and flour a 9 × 5 inch (23 × 12 cm) loaf pan.
3. In a small bowl combine cereal, milk, and orange juice; let stand 10 minutes. Beat in eggs, oil, and carrot.
4. In a mixing bowl combine flours, sugar, baking powder, salt, cinnamon, and nutmeg. Make a well in the center. Pour in bran mixture, walnuts, currants, and orange rind. Stir quickly and only until mixture is moistened.
5. Spoon into loaf pan. Bake in oven for 50 to 60 minutes, until lightly browned and tester inserted in center comes out clean.

Makes 1 loaf, 20 slices.

ZUCCHINI BREAD

Another way to use the ubiquitous zucchini. Combined with the flavors of cinnamon, walnuts or pecans, raisins, vanilla, and brown sugar, it becomes a taste-tempting bread that can be served simply sliced and lightly buttered.

2 cups	whole wheat flour	500 ml
1½ cups	firmly packed brown sugar	375 ml
2 tsp	baking soda	10 ml
1 tsp	ground cinnamon	5 ml
1 tsp	salt	5 ml
1 cup	raisins	250 ml
1 cup	walnut or pecan pieces	250 ml
3	eggs	3
1 cup	vegetable oil	250 ml
2 tsp	vanilla extract	10 ml
2 cups	shredded unpeeled zucchini (2 small)	500 ml
	whipped sweet butter	

1. Grease and flour a 9 × 5 inch (23 × 12 cm) loaf pan.
2. Preheat oven to 350°F (180°C).
3. In a bowl combine flour, sugar, baking soda, cinnamon, and salt. Stir in raisins and walnuts.
4. In a mixing bowl beat eggs, oil, and vanilla. Stir in dry ingredients. Carefully fold in zucchini to distribute evenly.
5. Spoon into loaf pan and bake in oven for 1½ hours, until a wooden toothpick inserted into the center comes out clean.
6. Cut in slices and serve with whipped butter.

Makes 1 loaf, 24 slices.

SWEET DECADENCE

PUDDINGS AND OTHER EGG AND CREAM DELIGHTS

Rich and soothing is how I would describe everything in this section.

These are the things you do with eggs and cream and fruit and cooking magic when you aren't whipping up cakes and pies and cookies. Your guests will declare it was well worth your excursion into this part of the dessert world.

LEMON CUSTARD PUDDING

Sweet and tart and simple. Serve this at the end of a meal that has been spicy and hot.

1 cup	milk	250 ml
1 cup	granulated sugar	250 ml
¼ cup	sweet butter	50 ml
4 tsp	all-purpose flour	20 ml
2	eggs, separated	2
	juice and grated rind of 1 lemon	

1. Preheat oven to 325°F (160°C).
2. In mixing bowl combine milk, sugar, butter, flour, egg yolks, lemon juice and rind; mix well.
3. Beat egg whites until stiff. Fold lemon mixture into egg whites.
4. Pour into buttered 4 cup (1 l) baking dish or individual custard cups.
5. Place in a larger baking dish. Pour warm water into larger dish halfway up sides of baking dish or cups.

6. Bake in pan of water in oven for 30 minutes, or until set.
7. Serve hot, at room temperature, or chilled.

Makes 4 to 6 servings.

ROSE'S RAISIN CINNAMON RICE PUDDING

This is a hand-me-down recipe from my dear friend Maralyn's mother, Rose. It has been a favorite with my son Milton for years.

½ cup	short grain rice	125 ml
4 cups	milk	1 l
¼ cup	granulated sugar	50 ml
2 tbs	sweet butter	25 ml
½ tsp	salt	2 ml
½ cup	raisins	125 ml
	cinnamon	
	granulated sugar	

1. In a saucepan of salted boiling water, boil rice 10 minutes. Drain.
2. In a large enamel pot combine partially cooked rice, milk, sugar, butter, and salt. Simmer, uncovered, stirring occasionally, about 1 hour, until milk is absorbed. Stir in raisins.
3. Transfer to a glass bowl. Sprinkle with cinnamon and sugar to coat top.
4. Cool and refrigerate until ready to serve.

Makes 4 to 6 servings.

SAUCE AMBROSIA

This is a rich custard sauce—filled with eggs and sugar and milk.
   When you come across the perfect fresh fruit and want to enhance it for friends who understand the need to be simple when faced with perfection, this is what you serve.

5	egg yolks	5
½ cup	granulated sugar	125 ml
2 tbs	Grand Marnier or Cointreau	25 ml
1 cup	heavy or whipping cream	250 ml
2 tbs	confectioner's or icing sugar	25 ml

1. In a mixing bowl beat yolks and sugar until thick and pale yellow.
2. Transfer to the top of a double boiler; with a rotary beater, beat over boiling water about 7 minutes, until thick and foamy.

3. Remove from heat; stir in Grand Marnier. Cover; cool, and refrigerate for at least 1 hour.
4. Whip cream until soft peaks form and beat in confectioner's sugar. Fold into chilled yolk mixture. Serve over fresh fruit or transfer to sauce bowl and serve with fresh fruit.

Makes 4 to 6 servings.

SWEDISH CREAM

This is very close to Crème Fraiche, except that gelatin holds it together. It is equally rich and can serve all the purposes of Crème Fraiche.

2	envelopes unflavored gelatin	2
½ cup	cold water	125 ml
2 cups	cream	500 ml
¾ cup	granulated sugar	175 ml
1 tsp	vanilla	5 ml
2 cups	sour cream	500 ml
	fresh berries	
	grated orange rind	

1. Sprinkle gelatin over water to soften.
2. In a medium-size saucepan over medium heat combine cream and sugar. Heat to simmering.
3. Stir softened gelatin and vanilla into cream mixture.
4. Cool in refrigerator about 20 minutes, or until mixture is partially set.
5. Stir in sour cream, pour into 4 cup (1 l) mold. Chill at least 2 hours, until firm.
   Serve with fresh berries and garnish with grated orange rind.

Makes 6 servings.

COEUR À LA CRÈME WITH STRAWBERRIES

This cream is a true winner and there is nothing like it for ending an informal dinner or lunch in fresh strawberry time. Your guests will dip their berries in it most happily.

1½ cups	ricotta cheese	375 ml
1	package (8 oz/250 g) cream cheese	1
½ cup	sour cream	125 ml
2 tsp	sweet butter	10 ml
¾ cup	confectioner's or icing sugar	175 ml
1½ quarts	fresh strawberries	1.5 l

1. In a mixer bowl combine ricotta and cream cheese; beat until fluffy. At lower speed gradually add sour cream, butter, and sugar.
2. Line a heart-shaped (coeur) basket or mold with cheesecloth. Pack cheese mixture into lined container. Place on a plate or pan to catch any drippings from the basket or mold. Chill 4 hours in refrigerator. Invert onto a serving plate. Carefully remove mold and cheesecloth and surround with berries.

Makes 8 to 10 servings.

CHOCOLATE CREAM

Smooth and elegant, this blends rich flavors into a cool and creamy dream. Try it on friends who are not too worried about their weight.

2	bars (4 oz/113 g) German Sweet Chocolate	2
⅓ cup	Bourbon, Cognac, rum, or strong coffee	75 ml
2 tbs	water	25 ml
⅓ cup	granulated sugar	75 ml
2 cups	heavy or whipping cream	500 ml
1 tsp	vanilla	5 ml

1. In a double boiler over hot, not boiling, water combine chocolate, Bourbon, and water. Cook, stirring constantly, until chocolate is melted and mixture is smooth.
2. Add sugar, cream, and vanilla; stir until well blended. Remove from heat. Chill in refrigerator several hours or overnight.
3. In a mixer bowl beat chocolate cream until soft peaks form.
4. Serve immediately in sherbet glasses, or freeze and serve at a later date.

Makes 6 to 8 servings.

THREE MOUSSE MIXUP: MILK CHOCOLATE, PRALINE, AND MOCHA

You'd think they'd all basically have the same recipe, wouldn't you? Well, they don't. There is enough variation in each to make it necessary to follow three separate recipes. Three lovely mousses, different shades of brown and different tastes, each one more delightful than the next—until you come back to the first.

MILK CHOCOLATE MOUSSE

1	envelope unflavored gelatin	1
½ cup	granulated sugar	125 ml
pinch	salt	pinch
1½ cups	milk	375 ml
1	square unsweetened chocolate	1
¼ tsp	vanilla	1 ml
1 cup	heavy or whipping cream	250 ml
	grated chocolate	

1. In a saucepan combine gelatin, sugar, and salt. Stir in milk and chocolate. Cook over low heat, stirring constantly, until gelatin and sugar are dissolved and chocolate has melted.
2. Remove from heat and stir in vanilla. Beat with whisk until flecks of chocolate disappear.
3. Whip cream. Fold into chocolate mixture. Turn into a 3 cup (750 ml) mold.
4. Chill at least 2 hours, until firm. Unmold onto a serving plate or serve from mold. Garnish with grated chocolate.

Makes 8 servings.

RICH PRALINE MOUSSE

PRALINE POWDER:

¾ cup	unblanched almonds	175 ml
1½ cups	granulated sugar	325 ml
½ tsp	cream of tartar	2 ml

MOUSSE:

2	eggs	2
2	egg yolks	2
⅓ cup	granulated sugar	75 ml
¼ cup	light rum	50 ml
1	envelope unflavored gelatin	1
¼ cup	cold water	50 ml
1 tbs	lemon juice	15 ml
1 cup	heavy or whipping cream	250 ml

1. To make Praline Powder: In a heavy saucepan combine almonds, sugar, and cream of tartar. Heat over medium heat, stirring occasionally, until mixture reaches a deep amber color.
2. Pour into a lightly oiled jelly roll pan. When hard, break up, and in a blender or food processor grind to a powder.
3. Store in a covered container at room temperature.
4. To make Mousse: In a mixer bowl at high speed beat eggs and egg yolks about 5 minutes, until thick and yellow-colored.
5. Add sugar gradually and continue to beat until light and fluffy. Fold in rum. Set aside.
6. In a small saucepan sprinkle gelatin over water and lemon juice and let sit for 5 minutes to soften.
7. Place pan over low heat, for about 3 minutes, stirring, until gelatin dissolves. Carefully fold the dissolved gelatin into egg mixture until completely blended.
8. Fold in ¼ cup (50 ml) of the praline powder and chill about 20 minutes, until mixture begins to thicken.
9. Whip the cream until stiff; carefully fold into mousse mixture.
10. Spoon into an attractive crystal bowl and chill 3 hours before serving.

Makes 8 servings.

MOCHA MOUSSE

1	package (6 oz/180 g) semisweet chocolate pieces	1
¼ cup	hot strong coffee	50 ml
2 tbs	coffee liqueur	25 ml
4	egg yolks	4
4	egg whites	4
¼ cup	sugar	50 ml
½ cup	heavy or whipping cream	125 ml
	chocolate shavings	

1. In a blender or food processor combine chocolate pieces and coffee, process with on/off motion about 2 minutes, until smooth.
2. Add liqueur and egg yolks; blend 30 seconds.
3. In a mixer bowl at high speed, beat egg whites until soft peaks form. Gradually beat in sugar until stiff; fold into yolk mixture.
4. Whip cream until soft peaks form; fold into chocolate mixture.
5. Spoon into small chocolate pots or cups. Chill until serving time.
6. Garnish with dollops of whipped cream and chocolate shavings, if desired.

Makes 8 servings.

BANANAS FLAMBÉE

If you have an elegant chafing dish in your collection and if you feel very confident, go ahead and prepare these at the table. If not, just excuse yourself for a moment and return with the flaming bananas.

4	medium ripe but firm bananas	4
2 tbs	sweet butter	25 ml
1 tbs	lime juice	15 ml
½ cup	firmly packed brown sugar	125 ml
¼ tsp	*each,* cinnamon, cloves, allspice	1 ml
¼ cup	Cognac or dark rum, warmed	50 ml
	vanilla ice cream, optional	

1. Cut bananas in half lengthwise. In a large skillet, melt butter. Place bananas cut side down in butter. Sprinkle with lime juice and cook over medium heat about 5 minutes, until softened.
2. Combine brown sugar, cinnamon, cloves, and allspice. Sprinkle over bananas and continue to cook until sugar has melted.
3. Pour warmed Cognac or rum over bananas and ignite. Take to the table flaming if desired.
4. Serve with vanilla ice cream, if desired.

Makes 4 to 6 servings.

ORANGE CRÈME CARAMEL

A delightful variation on the traditional crème caramel. The addition of the orange rind gives it a light and lively zest all its own.

CARAMEL:

½ cup	granulated sugar	125 ml
1 tbs	water	15 ml

CUSTARD:

2 cups	milk	500 ml
2	eggs	2
2	egg yolks	2
¼ cup	granulated sugar	50 ml
1 tbs	grated orange rind	15 ml
1 tsp	vanilla	5 ml

1. To make Caramel: In a small saucepan combine sugar and water. Place over low heat. Allow sugar to melt, then allow to boil without stirring until the sugar caramelizes and is amber brown. Watch carefully to prevent its burning.
2. Pour immediately into a souffle dish. Turn dish around to coat the bottom and sides evenly with caramel.
3. To make Custard: In a saucepan scald milk.
4. In a bowl whisk together eggs, egg yolks, sugar, orange rind, and vanilla. Whisk in scalded milk.
5. Preheat oven to 325°F (160°C).
6. Pour custard into prepared souffle dish, cover with foil, and set into larger baking dish. Pour boiling water into larger dish to halfway up sides of souffle dish. Bake in oven for 40 to 50 minutes, or until just set. Let cool completely.
7. Serve at room temperature or refrigerate until serving time.
8. Turn out of dish onto a serving plate with deep sides just before serving.

Makes 4 to 6 servings.

LEMON CREAM CHEESE CREPES WITH APRICOT SAUCE

This is another of those complicated-seeming recipes that really takes only minutes to prepare—especially if you have everything ready ahead of time. Just smile confidently when you are congratulated and say, "It's nothing really."

CREPES:

2	eggs	2
1¼ cups	milk	300 ml
1 cup	all-purpose flour	250 ml
2 tbs	melted sweet butter	25 ml
pinch	salt	pinch

1. In food processor or blender combine eggs, milk, flour, melted butter, and salt. Process until smooth, scraping down sides. Refrigerate at least 1 hour or overnight. Batter should be the consistency of thick cream. If necessary, batter can be thinned with additional milk.
2. Heat a lightly buttered 6 to 7 inch (15 to 18 cm) crepe pan. Pour in ¼ cup (50 ml) batter for each crepe. Quickly spread, tilting pan back and forth until a layer of batter covers bottom of pan. Cook about 10 seconds, until surface dries.
3. With a round-tipped knife or spatula, flip over and cook about 10 seconds, until golden.
4. Layer between waxed paper or plastic wrap. Makes 16 crepes.

FILLING:

1	package (8 oz/250 g) cream cheese, softened	1
¼ cup	soft sweet butter	50 ml
¼ cup	granulated sugar	50 ml
1 tbs	grated lemon rind	15 ml
1 tsp	vanilla	5 ml

In a bowl, combine cream cheese, softened butter, sugar, lemon rind, and vanilla; beat until light and fluffy.

APRICOT SAUCE:

⅔ cup	apricot jam	150 ml
⅓ cup	orange juice	75 ml
2 tbs	sweet butter	25 ml
1 tbs	lemon juice	15 ml
1 tsp	grated lemon rind	5 ml

In a saucepan combine apricot jam, orange juice, butter, lemon juice and rind and cook until sauce comes to a boil. Stir well.

GARNISH:

⅓ cup	toasted slivered almonds	75 ml

1. Preheat oven to 350°F (180°C).
2. Spread about 2 tbs (25 ml) filling on each crepe. Roll loosely, arrange seam side down in a lightly greased shallow 8 × 12 inch (20 × 30 cm) baking dish. Cover with foil.
3. Bake in oven for 15 to 20 minutes, or until filling is warm and bubbling.
4. Pour half the sauce over crepes. Garnish with toasted almonds. Pass remaining sauce with crepes.

Makes 14 to 16 filled crepes.

BLUEBERRIES IN LEMON MOUSSE

Blue and yellow, a perfect summer dessert.

4	egg yolks	4
½ cup	granulated sugar	125 ml
6 tbs	lemon juice	75 ml
2 tsp	grated lemon rind	10 ml
2	egg whites	2
½ cup	heavy or whipping cream	125 ml
1 cup	fresh blueberries	250 ml

1. In the top of a double boiler before placing over hot water, beat egg yolks until thick and pale. Beat in sugar, lemon juice, and rind.
2. Place over boiling water; cook egg mixture, stirring, about 5 minutes until thick. Cool.
3. Beat egg whites until stiff and fold into cooled egg yolk mixture.
4. Whip cream and fold in, along with ¾ cup (175 ml) blueberries.
5. Spoon into stemmed glasses, garnish with remaining blueberries, and chill until serving time.
   Note: This dessert is best the day it is prepared.

Makes 5 to 6 servings.

A CHEESE TRAY BEFORE THE LEMON SOUFFLE

My selection of cheese would center around some of my favorites, like French Brie, English Stilton, Cambozola, St. André, and Bonifaz.
These can be prettied up by surrounding them with grapes and other fruits that you have dipped in lightly beaten eggs and rolled in confectioner's or icing sugar.

LEMON SOUFFLE

This cool and frothy lemon dessert is a perfect ending to a rich and satisfying dinner. I serve it after the cheese tray; with its collar removed, it looks like a floating cloud.
This is perfect for when the table is relatively small, up to eight. For larger groups I serve a tray of lemon souffles in individual colored glass compotes. By candlelight the effect is quite dazzling.

1 cup	granulated sugar	250 ml
3	envelopes unflavored gelatin	3
6	egg yolks	6
1½ cups	water	375 ml
2 tsp	grated lemon rind	10 ml
¾ cup	lemon juice	175 ml
6	egg whites	6
⅓ cup	granulated sugar	75 ml
2 cups	heavy or whipping cream, whipped	500 ml

1. Cut a piece of waxed paper long enough to fit a little more than once around a 4 cup (1 l) souffle dish and fold it in half lengthwise. Wrap it around souffle dish, extending it 4 inches (10 cm) above the top of the dish. With string, tie it tightly in place.
2. In a medium-sized heavy saucepan combine ⅔ cup (150 ml) sugar and gelatin.
3. Beat egg yolks slightly, blend in water; stir into gelatin mixture.
4. Cook over medium heat, stirring constantly, until mixture is about to come to a boil and begins to thicken. Do not boil.
5. Remove from heat, cool. Stir in lemon rind and juice.
6. In the refrigerator, chill mixture about 30 minutes, until it mounds slightly when spooned.
7. In a large bowl, beat egg whites until frothy. Gradually beat in remaining sugar and continue beating until stiff and glossy.

8. Fold whites into gelatin mixture, then fold in whipped cream. Pour into prepared souffle dish.
9. Chill 2 to 3 hours, until firm. Remove collar when ready to serve.

Makes 8 servings.

PEARS SWIMMING IN RASPBERRY PURÉE

This is an elegant way to serve the delicate pear. Make up a little extra purée when you are building your supply, or use Seedless Raspberry Jam (page 349).

1½ cups	water	375 ml
1½ cups	sugar	375 ml
3	firm, ripe pears, peeled and halved	3
½ tsp	vanilla	2 ml
1 tsp	cornstarch	5 ml
2 tbs	cold water	25 ml
2 cups	raspberries	500 ml
2 tbs	Kirsch	25 ml
	toasted slivered almonds	

1. In a saucepan combine water and sugar. Bring to a boil; cook 5 minutes.
2. Reduce heat, add pears and vanilla; simmer 15 minutes, until fruit is tender but firm.
3. In refrigerator, chill for 1 hour.
4. In a saucepan, combine cornstarch with cold water. Stir in raspberries. Bring to a boil, reduce heat, and simmer 3 minutes.
5. Press raspberry sauce through a sieve to remove seeds, stir in Kirsch.
6. Spoon a puddle of sauce onto each dessert plate. With a slotted spoon remove pears from syrup and place on raspberry sauce. Sprinkle with toasted almonds.

Makes 6 servings.

SUMMERTIME BUFFET

SOLE WITH ALMONDS AND GRAPES

MACARONI WITH THREE CHEESES

DILLY CUCUMBERS AND ONIONS

STRAWBERRIES ROMANOFF

PECAN PUFFS

STRAWBERRIES ROMANOFF

The Romanoffs may have disappeared without a trace, but they left many mementos behind. With this delicious mixture, you can toast the tsar or toast the revolution.

2 cups	strawberries, washed and hulled	500 ml
1 cup	confectioner's or icing sugar	250 ml
¾ cup	freshly squeezed orange juice	175 ml
2 tbs	Cointreau	25 ml
1 cup	heavy or whipping cream	250 ml

1. In a large bowl combine berries, sugar, orange juice, and Cointreau.
2. Refrigerate, stirring occasionally, for 1 hour.
3. Whip cream until soft peaks form. Fold into berries. Serve immediately.

Makes 4 to 6 servings.

STRAWBERRY FOOL

This is partly an ice cream, but the result is much richer. Keep a few berries on hand to decorate the top of the bowl, or place a red, red rose on top.

2 cups	fresh strawberries, washed and hulled	500 ml
2 oz	Grand Marnier	50 ml
2 tbs	granulated sugar	25 ml
¾ cup	vanilla ice cream	175 ml
2 cups	heavy or whipping cream	500 ml

1. In a blender or food processor, with on/off motion, blend strawberries 30 seconds, until puréed. Transfer mixture to a sieve and press through twice so all seeds are removed.
2. Place purée back in blender or food processor. Gradually add Grand Marnier, sugar, and ice cream; blend 2 minutes, until smooth.
3. Add cream; process 1 minute longer, until cream is fully whipped.
4. Pour into serving dish, cover, and chill 1 to 2 hours, until set.
5. Garnish with fresh strawberries.

Makes 4 to 6 servings.

PRUNES IN MULLED WINE

Leave the prunes soak overnight in all the goodness of the wine.

1 lb	pitted prunes	500 g
2 cups	red Bordeaux or Burgundy	500 ml
1 cup	granulated sugar	250 ml
	rind of 1 orange	
3	cloves	3
1	cinnamon stick	1
1 tsp	lemon juice	5 ml
3	oranges, peeled, sliced, and pitted	3
½ cup	freshly squeezed orange juice	125 ml

1. In a medium bowl combine prunes and wine. Allow to soak for 8 to 10 hours, or overnight.
2. In a large saucepan combine prunes, wine mixture, sugar, orange rind studded with cloves, cinnamon stick, and lemon juice. Simmer 15 minutes.
3. Fold in orange slices and juice. Refrigerate for at least 3 hours, until chilled.
4. Serve cold as a dessert or drain and serve with roasts.

Makes 8 to 10 servings.

TARTS AND COOKIES

There are some quick and simple recipes here and some decidedly tricky ones. Just take your time in choosing which to try when.

Iced, rolled in confectioner's sugar, sprinkled with candy chips, whatever, these little offerings dance out, show their costumes, and are as entertaining as they are delectable.

FUDGY BROWNIES WITH MOCHA FROSTING

All right, so you and your guests will have to do a few extra laps around the block. It's worth them just to sink your teeth into these fudgy brownies.

I slather the brownies with Mocha Frosting, then sprinkle nuts over one half of the frosting and coconut over the other, mainly because my family is divided on the merits of the two garnishes.

3	squares (3 oz/84 g) unsweetened chocolate	3
¾ cup	sweet butter	175 ml
1½ cups	granulated sugar	375 ml
¾ cup	all-purpose flour	175 ml
1 tsp	baking powder	5 ml
3	eggs	3
1 tsp	vanilla	5 ml
½ cup	chopped nuts or dessicated coconut (optional)	125 ml
	Mocha Frosting	
	additional chopped nuts and dessicated coconut, optional	

1. Preheat oven to 350°F (180°C).
2. In the top of double boiler, over simmering water, melt chocolate and butter. Set aside to cool for about 10 minutes.
3. In a bowl combine sugar, flour, and baking powder. Make a well in the center. Add eggs, vanilla, and chocolate mixture. Beat for 1 minute. Fold in nuts or coconut, if desired.
4. Pour into a buttered 8 inch (20 cm) square baking pan. Bake in oven for 20 to 25 minutes, until tester inserted in center comes out clean. Cool. Spread with Mocha Frosting. Sprinkle nuts over half and coconut over the other half, if desired.

Makes 48 squares.

VARIATION:
Dust with confectioner's or icing sugar instead of frosting.

MOCHA FROSTING

⅓ cup	soft sweet butter	75 ml
1	egg yolk	1
1½ cups	confectioner's or icing sugar	375 ml
1 tbs	cocoa	15 ml
2 tbs	very strong coffee, cooled	25 ml
½ tsp	vanilla	2 ml

1. In a bowl, cream butter and egg yolk until fluffy. Stir in half the sugar.
2. Combine cocoa and coffee. Beat into butter mixture alternately with remaining sugar.
3. Beat well until smooth and creamy. Stir in vanilla.

Makes 2 cups (500 ml) frosting.

VARIATION:
Orange Frosting: Use 2 tbs (25 ml) fresh orange juice and the grated rind of 1 orange in place of the coffee and cocoa.

CHOCOLATE CHIP BARS

Here it is! Chips and coconut over a rich shortbread base that puts the old-fashioned chocolate chip cookie to shame.

BASE:

1½ cups	all-purpose flour	375 ml
⅓ cup	firmly packed brown sugar	75 ml
¾ cup	cold sweet butter	175 ml

FILLING:

2	eggs	2
1 cup	firmly packed brown sugar	250 ml
1 tsp	vanilla	5 ml
3 tbs	flour	45 ml
½ tsp	baking powder	2 ml
¼ tsp	salt	1 ml
1 cup	flaked desiccated coconut	250 ml
½ cup	chopped walnuts	125 ml
1 cup	chocolate chips	250 ml

1. Preheat oven to 350°F (180°C).
2. To make Base: In a bowl combine flour and brown sugar. With a pastry blender or 2 forks, cut in butter until mixture resembles coarse crumbs.
3. Press into bottom of ungreased 8 × 12 inch (20 × 30 cm) pan and bake in oven for 10 to 15 minutes, or until lightly golden. Set aside.
4. To make Filling: In same bowl lightly beat eggs. Stir in brown sugar and vanilla. Stir in flour, baking powder, and salt until well blended. Add coconut, walnuts, and chocolate chips; mix well. Spread over baked crust.
5. Return to oven and bake 15 to 20 minutes, or until golden. Cool and cut into 2 inch (5 cm) squares.

Makes 24 squares.

Nanaimo Bars

With coffee after dinner, or especially with a warm and intimate afternoon tea, Nanaimo Bars are one of the most perfect taste charmers yet.

Base:

½ cup	sweet butter	125 ml
2	squares semisweet chocolate	2
¼ cup	granulated sugar	50 ml
1	egg	1
1 tsp	vanilla	5 ml
1¾ cup	graham cracker crumbs	425 ml
1 cup	flaked dessicated coconut	250 ml
½ cup	chopped nuts	125 ml

Filling:

¼ cup	soft sweet butter	50 ml
2 tbs	vanilla custard powder	25 ml
2 cups	confectioner's or icing sugar	500 ml
¼ cup	milk	50 ml

Topping:

3	squares semisweet chocolate	3
1 tbs	sweet butter	15 ml

1. Preheat oven to 350°F (180°C).
2. To make Base: In a double boiler or a saucepan over low heat combine butter, chocolate squares, sugar, egg, and vanilla. Stir until melted.
3. Remove from heat and stir in graham cracker crumbs, coconut, and chopped nuts.
4. Press mixture into an 8 inch (20 cm) square pan and bake in oven for 10 to 15 minutes, or until set. Cool.
5. To make Filling: In a bowl, cream butter and custard powder until smooth. Stir in sugar and milk until smooth and soft enough to spread. Add a few drops of milk if needed. Spread over cooled base.
6. To make Topping: Melt chocolate squares and butter. Spread over filling. Chill until set, then cut into 2 inch (5 cm) squares.

Makes 16 squares.

LEMON COCONUT SQUARES

This is a bar of great appeal, thanks to a buttery oatmeal base, oodles of raisins, and lots of lively lemon.

½ cup	all-purpose flour	125 ml
¼ cup	brown sugar	50 ml
¼ tsp	baking powder	1 ml
pinch	salt	pinch
¾ cup	rolled oats	175 ml
⅓ cup	cold sweet butter	75 ml
2	eggs	2
¾ cup	firmly packed brown sugar	175 ml
1 tbs	lemon juice	15 ml
	grated rind of ½ lemon	
¾ cup	flaked dessicated coconut	175 ml
¾ cup	raisins	175 ml

1. Preheat oven to 350°F (180°C).
2. In a bowl combine flour, brown sugar, baking powder, salt, and rolled oats. Cut in butter until mixture resembles coarse crumbs.
3. Press into a lightly greased 8 inch (20 cm) square pan and bake in oven for 10 to 15 minutes, or until a light golden brown.
4. Meanwhile in the same bowl combine eggs, brown sugar, lemon juice and rind. Stir in coconut and raisins.
5. Spread over baked crust and return to oven for 20 to 25 minutes, or until topping is golden.
6. Let cool before cutting into 3 inch (7.5 cm) squares.

Makes 16 squares.

BUTTER PECAN TURTLES

Where the name "turtles" came from I will never know. These are a lot faster than turtles as they move off the plate and into the mouth.

2 cups	all-purpose flour	500 ml
1¾ cups	firmly packed brown sugar	425 ml
1½ cups	soft sweet butter	375 ml
1 cup	pecan pieces	250 ml
1 cup	chocolate chips	250 ml

1. In a bowl combine flour and 1 cup (250 ml) brown sugar. With a fork stir in ½ cup (125 ml) butter until mixture resembles coarse crumbs.
2. Press into bottom of a lightly greased 12 × 8 inch (30 × 20 cm) pan. Sprinkle with pecans. Set aside.
3. Preheat oven to 350°F (180°C).

4. In a saucepan combine 1 cup (250 ml) butter and ¾ cup (175 ml) brown sugar; cook over medium heat, stirring constantly until mixture boils. Continue stirring and boil 1 minute, or until mixture blends; pour over prepared base.
5. Bake for 15 to 20 minutes or until surface is bubbly.
6. Remove from oven and immediately sprinkle chocolate chips evenly over surface.
7. Let stand 1 minute to melt. Spread chocolate with fork.
8. Cool completely until chocolate is set. Cut into 2 inch (5 cm) squares when cool.

Makes 24 squares.

CHEWY RASPBERRY SQUARES

When I had a gourmet food store, we could never make enough of these super shortbread-based bars with the raspberry topping.

¾ cup	sweet butter	175 ml
¾ cup	granulated sugar	175 ml
2	eggs, separated	2
1½ cups	all-purpose flour	375 ml
½ cup	chopped walnuts	125 ml
1 cup	raspberry jam	250 ml
½ cup	flaked desiccated coconut	125 ml

1. Preheat oven to 350°F (180°C).
2. In a bowl, cream butter and ¼ cup (50 ml) sugar until light and fluffy. Beat in egg yolks. Stir in flour until blended.
3. Spread evenly in lightly greased 8 inch (20 cm) square pan and bake in oven for 15 to 20 minutes, or until golden.
4. While crust is baking, in mixer bowl beat egg whites until foamy.
5. Gradually beat in remaining ½ cup (125 ml) sugar until stiff peaks form and meringue is glossy. Gently fold in walnuts.
6. Spread raspberry jam over crust layer, sprinkle evenly with coconut. Cover with meringue, spreading evenly.
7. Return to oven and bake 25 to 30 minutes, or until lightly golden.
8. Cool completely before cutting into 1 × 2 inch (2.5 × 5 cm) bars.

Makes 32 bars.

MISSISSIPPI PECAN TREATS

If you like pecan pie you will love these bars.

I like to serve these with unsweetened, fresh blueberries, strawberries, raspberries, peaches, or apricots, or a combination.

CRUST:

1 cup	all-purpose flour	250 ml
¼ cup	granulated sugar	50 ml
½ tsp	baking powder	2 ml
¼ tsp	salt	1 ml
½ cup	cold sweet butter	125 ml

TOPPING:

2	eggs	2
1 cup	firmly packed brown sugar	250 ml
¼ cup	sweet butter, melted and cooled	50 ml
1 tsp	vanilla	5 ml
1 cup	chopped pecans	250 ml

1. To make Crust: Preheat oven to 350°F (180°C).
2. In a bowl, combine flour, sugar, baking powder, and salt. With a pastry blender or 2 forks cut in butter until it resembles coarse crumbs.
3. Press into the bottom of an ungreased 8 inch (20 cm) square pan and bake in oven for 10 to 15 minutes, or until golden.
4. To make Topping: In a bowl lightly beat eggs. Stir in brown sugar, melted butter, and vanilla. Stir in pecans.
5. Spread over baked crust and return to oven for 20 to 25 minutes, or until puffed, golden, and almost set in center.
6. Cool completely. Cut into 2 × 1 inch (5 × 2.5 cm) bars.

Makes 32 bars.

CRISP BRANDY CONES

This is a deluxe way to serve ice cream or flavored whipped cream. I sometimes add strawberries, raspberries, or blueberries to the whipped cream.

If you fill the cones with ice cream, pop them in the freezer until you are ready to serve.

½ cup	molasses	125 ml
½ cup	sweet butter	125 ml
1 cup	all-purpose flour	250 ml
½ cup	granulated sugar	125 ml
1 tsp	ground ginger	5 ml
1 tbs	brandy	15 ml

1. Preheat oven to 300°F (150°C).
2. Line 2 baking sheets with parchment paper or lightly oil.
3. In a medium saucepan heat molasses to boiling point. Stir in butter until melted. Gradually add flour, sugar, and ginger, stirring constantly. Remove from heat. Stir in brandy.
4. Drop mixture about 2 tbs (25 ml) at a time, at least 2 inches (5 cm) apart onto prepared baking sheets. Using back of a spoon, spread to a 5 inch (12 cm) circle.
5. Bake in oven for 12 to 15 minutes, or until cookies stop bubbling. Cool slightly.
6. With fingers roll into cone shapes. If they become too hard to roll, reheat in oven for a few minutes.
7. Cool on wire rack.

Makes 2 dozen cones.

RUM BALLS

These you just mix, roll into balls, and store for three days before serving. Everything that goes into them is so sinfully good they don't need heat.

½ lb	vanilla wafers, crushed	250 g
1 cup	confectioner's or icing sugar	250 ml
2 tbs	cocoa	25 ml
1 cup	finely chopped pecans	250 ml
¼ cup	light corn syrup	50 ml
¼ cup	rum	50 ml
	confectioner's or icing sugar	
60	pecan halves, optional	60

1. In a large bowl combine wafer crumbs, sugar, and cocoa. Add chopped nuts, syrup, and rum; stir until well blended and stiff.

2. Shape into 1 inch (2.5 cm) balls. Let stand 1 hour.
3. Roll each ball in confectioner's sugar to coat and press a pecan half into each ball, if desired.
4. Store in a tightly covered container in a cool, dry place. Set aside 3 days before serving to allow flavors to mellow.

Makes 5 dozen.

BLACK AND WHITE MERINGUES

You hardly know you've eaten these That's the old meringue trick—something bite-sized that turns out to be a concentrated drop of flavor.

4	squares semisweet chocolate	4
1 cup	chopped nuts	250 ml
3	egg whites	3
pinch	salt	pinch
1 tbs	vinegar	15 ml
1 cup	granulated sugar	250 ml
1 tsp	vanilla	5 ml

1. Preheat oven to 250°F (130°C).
2. Line 2 baking sheets with parchment paper or lightly oil.
3. In a food processor with grater blade, or with hand grater, grate chocolate squares. In a bowl combine grated chocolate and nuts; set aside.
4. In a mixer bowl beat egg whites until frothy. Add salt and vinegar and continue beating.
5. Gradually add sugar and beat until stiff peaks form and meringue is glossy.
6. Fold in vanilla, then chocolate-nut mixture.
7. Drop by teaspoonful about 2 inches (5 cm) apart onto prepared baking sheets.
8. Bake in oven for 30 minutes, or until firm and quite dry. Cool 1 minute before removing from pan.
9. Remove to a wire rack to cool and dry. Store in an airtight container.

Makes 8 dozen meringues.

GINGERBREAD COOKIES

These can be made into perfect old-time Christmas tree decorations simply by putting holes in them with a straw before baking.
  The dough or can be frozen for future use.

5 cups	all-purpose flour	1.25 l
1½ tsp	baking soda	7 ml
1 tsp	ground ginger	5 ml
1 tsp	ground cinnamon	5 ml
½ tsp	ground cloves	2 ml
½ tsp	salt	2 ml
1 cup	shortening	250 ml
1 cup	granulated sugar	250 ml
1	egg	1
1 cup	molasses	250 ml
2 tbs	vinegar	25 ml

1. Combine flour, soda, ginger, cinnamon, cloves, and salt.
2. In a mixing bowl, cream shortening, add sugar, and beat until light and fluffy. Stir in egg, molasses, and vinegar; beat well. Add dry ingredients and mix just until blended.
3. Divide dough into 3 portions, wrap, and refrigerate about 3 hours.
4. Preheat oven to 375°F (190°C).
5. Line cookie sheets with parchment paper or lightly oil.
6. On a lightly floured surface, roll dough to about ⅛ inch (3 mm) thickness. Cut into desired shapes and place on prepared cookie sheets. Bake in oven for 5 to 6 minutes, or until firm. Cool 1 minute, then remove to wire rack.
7. Cool, then decorate, if desired, with Decorating Icing.

Makes 5 dozen.

DECORATING ICING

2 cups	confectioner's or icing sugar	500 ml
2–4 tbs	water	25–50 ml
	food coloring (optional)	

1. Sift the sugar into a bowl. Stir in the water a tablespoonful at a time, until mixture reaches the desired consistency and is smooth.
2. Add food coloring, as desired.
3. Put the icing into a wax paper cone or decorating tube fitted with a writing tip and decorate the cookies.

Makes about 1 cup (250 ml).

PALM LEAVES

I serve these regularly with coffee after a rich dessert.

1½ cups	all-purpose flour	375 ml
1 cup	cold sweet butter	250 ml
½ cup	sour cream	125 ml
2 cups	granulated sugar	500 ml

1. Place flour in a bowl. With a pastry blender or two forks partially cut in butter to form coarse crumbs. Stir in sour cream.
2. Knead briefly until mixture sticks together. Form into a ball, wrap in waxed paper, and chill in refrigerator for 2 hours.
3. Cut in half. Sprinkle sugar generously on pastry canvas or working surface. Roll out half the dough. Sprinkle generously with sugar.
4. Continue to roll to form a 10 inch (25 cm) square, about ⅛ inch (3 mm) thick. Sprinkle top with sugar.
5. Lightly mark a center line in dough. Roll each side over twice to meet in the center. Fold these two thick sides together.
6. Repeat with other ½ of dough.
7. Wrap each roll in waxed paper and refrigerate 1 hour or freeze ½ hour.
8. Preheat oven to 425°F (220°C).
9. Line 2 baking sheets with parchment paper.
10. With a sharp knife, cut each roll in ½ inch (1 cm) pieces. Dip both sides of each piece in sugar and place at least 3 inches (7 cm) apart on prepared baking sheets.
11. Bake 6 to 7 minutes, or until sugar is caramelized on underside of cookie.
12. Turn leaves over and bake another 4 to 5 minutes, or until evenly caramelized and golden on both sides. Cool on wire racks.

Makes 40 cookies.

ALMOND WAFER ROLLS

These are intriguing-looking rolled almond cookies which approximate the traditional sweet offered at the end of a Chinese dinner. Wonderfully crisp and almondy.

2	egg whites	2
½ cup	granulated sugar	125 ml
⅓ cup	all-purpose flour	75 ml
¼ cup	melted sweet butter	50 ml
¼ cup	finely chopped blanched almonds	50 ml
¼ tsp	almond extract	1 ml

1. Preheat oven to 450°F (230°C).
2. Line 2 cookie sheets with parchment paper or oil lightly.
3. In a mixer bowl beat egg whites until stiff. Fold in sugar. Then fold in flour, butter, almonds, and almond extract until well blended.
4. Drop batter by heaping teaspoonfuls at least 3 inches (7 cm) apart onto cookie sheets. Spread batter with the back of a spoon to make thin rounds 2 to 3 inches (5 to 7 cm) in diameter.
5. Bake in oven for 3 to 4 minutes, or until golden brown around the edges.
6. With a metal spatula, loosen immediately from cookie sheet. Use fingers to shape quickly into loose rolls.
7. Cool on a wire rack. Store in an airtight container.

Makes 2 dozen.

LACE WAFERS

Make something rich enough and thin enough and bake it hot enough—and voilà, lace!

These look so elegant I line a silver cookie basket with a white linen napkin to serve them in.

¼ cup	shortening	50 ml
¼ cup	corn syrup	50 ml
⅓ cup	firmly packed brown sugar	75 ml
½ cup	all-purpose flour	125 ml
½ cup	finely chopped walnuts or pecans	125 ml

1. Preheat oven to 375°F (190°C).
2. Line baking sheets with parchment paper or oil lightly.
3. In a small saucepan combine shortening, corn syrup, and sugar. Stir constantly over medium heat until mixture starts to boil.
4. Remove from heat and stir in flour and nuts. Drop mixture by the tablespoon at least 3 inches (7 cm) apart onto prepared cookie sheets.
5. Bake in oven for 5 to 6 minutes, or until edges of cookies are lightly brown.
6. Remove from oven and let cool for only 30 seconds. With metal spatula remove carefully to wire rack to cool. Store in airtight container.

Makes 2 dozen.

An English Garden Tea Party. Create nosegays of pink heather, paperwhite narcissus, and silver roses. Tie each nosegay with an eight-inch piece of antique lace trim, easily found at flea markets and antique fairs.

Make one nosegay for each guest to take home. Long after the flowers are gone they will have the lace trim as a reminder of that pleasant afternoon.

PECAN PUFFS

These look gorgeous for your afternoon tea parties and tempt even the dieter.

½ cup	sweet butter	125 ml
¼ cup	granulated sugar	50 ml
1 tbs	vanilla	15 ml
1 cup	finely chopped pecans	250 ml
1 cup	cake and pastry flour	250 ml
	confectioner's or icing sugar	

1. Preheat oven to 300°F (180°C).
2. Line 2 cookie sheets with parchment paper or lightly oil.
3. In a bowl, cream butter and sugar until light and fluffy. Stir in vanilla. Add nuts and flour, stir until evenly blended.
4. Roll into small balls, 1 inch (2.5 cm) in diameter, and place on cookie sheets about 2 inches (5 cm) apart. Bake in oven for 30 to 40 minutes, or until lightly golden.
5. Place confectioner's sugar on a small plate. While baked puffs are hot, roll them in sugar.
6. Roll again in sugar when cold.

Makes 2 dozen.

DATE BALLS

These super-sweet little spheres can be rolled in three different coverings so you have a choice of looks.

1	egg, lightly beaten	1
1 cup	firmly packed brown sugar	250 ml
1 cup	dessicated coconut	250 ml
¾ cup	chopped pitted dates	175 ml
¼ cup	chopped pecans	50 ml
4–6	maraschino cherries, coarsely chopped	4–6
1 tbs	maraschino cherry juice	15 ml
½ tsp	vanilla	2 ml
½ tsp	almond extract	2 ml
	shredded desiccated coconut, chopped pecans, or graham cracker crumbs for coating	

1. In a heavy saucepan combine egg, brown sugar, coconut, dates, pecans, cherries, cherry juice, vanilla, and almond extract.
2. Cook over low heat, stirring frequently, about 25 to 30 minutes, or until thickened.
3. Cool until mixture can be handled. Shape into small balls ¾ inch (1.5 cm) in diameter.
4. Roll in either shredded coconut, chopped pecans, or graham cracker crumbs to coat well. Keep in covered container in refrigerator.

Makes 2 dozen.

BACHELOR BUTTONS

These are little sandwich cookies that are filled with dates.

1½ cups	all-purpose flour	125 ml
½ tsp	baking soda	2 ml
¼ tsp	salt	1 ml
½ cup	sweet butter	125 ml
½ cup	firmly packed brown sugar	125 ml
1	egg	1
1 tsp	vanilla	5 ml

DATE FILLING:

1 cup	chopped dates	250 ml
2 tbs	granulated sugar	25 ml
2 tbs	water	25 ml

1. Combine flour, baking soda, and salt.
2. In a mixer bowl cream butter and sugar until light and fluffy. Add egg and vanilla; beat well. Stir in dry ingredients until well blended.
3. Wrap dough in plastic wrap and chill for 1 hour.
4. To make Filling: In a small saucepan combine dates, sugar, and water. Cook over low heat about 10 minutes, until thick. Set aside.
5. Preheat oven to 350°F (180°C).
6. Line baking sheets with parchment paper or oil lightly.
7. On a lightly floured board roll half of dough out to about ¼ inch (5 mm) thick. Cut into 1 inch (2.5 cm) round shapes.
8. Place on prepared baking sheets and bake in oven 8 to 10 minutes, or until lightly brown.
9. Cool on wire racks. Repeat with remaining dough.
10. Spread a small amount of date filling on underside of 1 cookie and press another cookie onto it.

Makes 10 dozen 1 inch (2.5 cm) cookies or 5 dozen sandwiches.

Lemon Curved Cookies

Thin, buttery, and lemon rich, these are my choice to serve with Chocolate Mousse.

¼ cup	soft sweet butter	50 ml
½ cup	granulated sugar	125 ml
2	egg whites	2
¼ cup	all-purpose flour	50 ml
⅓ cup	blanched almonds, roughly ground in blender	75 ml
¼ tsp	lemon extract	1 ml
	grated rind of 1 lemon	

1. Preheat oven to 425°F (220°C).
2. Line baking sheets with parchment paper or oil lightly.
3. In a bowl beat butter and sugar until light and fluffy. Add egg whites and beat for a few seconds.
4. Fold in flour, then fold in ground almonds, lemon extract, and lemon rind.
5. Drop batter by teaspoonfuls at least 4 inches (10 cm) apart on prepared baking sheets. With the back of a spoon spread into 3 inch (7 cm) circles.
6. Bake in oven for 3 to 4 minutes, or until lightly browned around edges.
7. With a long spatula remove cookies immediately and drape them over a rolling pin to form a curved shape. If cookies harden before you can

remove them all from the cookie sheet, return them to the oven for a few seconds, and they will soften again. Store in an airtight container.

Makes 2 dozen.

PANFORTE DI SIENA

This little Italian treat is like a chewy, nutty candy with loads of peel and other goodies.

¾ cup	hazelnuts	175 ml
¾ cup	blanched almonds	175 ml
½ cup	all-purpose flour	125 ml
¼ cup	unsweetened cocoa	50 ml
1 tsp	ground cinnamon	5 ml
¼ tsp	ground allspice	1 ml
½ cup	finely cut candied orange peel	125 ml
½ cup	finely cut candied lemon peel	125 ml
½ cup	finely cut candied citron	125 ml
½ cup	honey	125 ml
½ cup	granulated sugar	125 ml
	confectioner's or icing sugar	

1. On a jelly roll pan, spread hazelnuts. Toast in a 350°F (180°C) oven for 10 to 15 minutes.
2. Remove to a tea towel and rub warm hazelnuts in the towel to remove their skins.
3. Reduce oven to 300°F (150°C).
4. In a bowl combine flour, cocoa, cinnamon, and allspice. Add hazelnuts, almonds, and candied peels. Toss well to coat evenly. Set aside.
5. Butter the bottom and sides of a 9 inch (23 cm) springform pan. Line the bottom with waxed paper and butter again.
6. In a heavy saucepan combine honey and sugar. Bring to a boil and cook until candy thermometer reaches 238°F (114°C) or until a small amount dropped in cold water forms a soft ball.
7. Remove immediately and pour over flour-nut mixture. Stir well. Mixture will be very stiff.
8. Spread in prepared springform pan and bake in oven for 30 to 35 minutes, until golden.
9. Cool cake on wire rack, then remove pan sides. Sprinkle with confectioner's sugar. To serve, cut into wedges.
   Keeps for several weeks in covered container.

Makes 24 servings.

LAZY CHEESE KNISHES

Knishes, for the un-knishiated, are little turnovers stuffed with cream cheese and imagination.

I serve them warm for teas, or as an added treat at a light luncheon, and my many overnight guests are gently teased into wide-awakeness with coffee and knishes at breakfast.

Make batches and freeze. They reheat perfectly.

DOUGH:

1 cup	all-purpose flour	250 ml
½ cup	cold sweet butter	125 ml
1 cup	creamed cottage cheese	250 ml

1. In a bowl combine flour and butter, cutting in with a pastry blender.
2. Cut in cottage cheese; mix well.
3. With hands, shape dough into a ball. Wrap in waxed paper or aluminum foil, and chill well for 1 to 2 days.

FILLING:

1	package (8 oz/250 g) cream cheese, softened	1
1	egg yolk	1
3 tbs	granulated sugar	45 ml
½ tsp	ground cinnamon	2 ml
¼ tsp	salt	1 ml

1. Preheat oven to 375°F (190°C).
2. In a bowl combine cream cheese, egg yolk, sugar, cinnamon, and salt; mix well.
3. On a lightly floured surface, roll out dough and cut into 4 inch (10 cm) rounds. Place 1 tsp (5 ml) filling on each round.
4. Fold dough over, seal edges with a fork. Prick top of pastry with a fork.
5. Place on 2 greased cookie sheets and bake in oven for 20 to 25 minutes, or until golden brown. Serve warm.

Makes 24 knishes.

BUTTER TARTS

These are syrupy, super-delicious, and guaranteed to ruin your teeth and your figure.

PASTRY:

2 cups	all-purpose flour	500 ml
1 tsp	baking powder	5 ml
1 tsp	salt	5 ml
½ cup	sweet butter, at room temperature	125 ml
½ cup	shortening, at room temperature	125 ml
¼ cup	confectioner's or icing sugar	50 ml
1	egg, slightly beaten	1
1 tsp	vanilla	5 ml

1. In a bowl combine flour, baking powder, and salt.
2. In a mixer bowl cream together butter and shortening; blend in sugar and beat in egg and vanilla.
3. Gradually mix in dry ingredients, 2 tbs (25 ml) at a time, mixing well after each addition until a dough forms.
4. Wrap and chill dough about 30 minutes, until firm enough to roll.
5. On a floured board or between sheets of waxed paper roll dough to ⅛ inch (3 mm) thick. With a floured cutter, cut into rounds to fit 18 tart pans. Press into pans.

FILLING:

½ cup	raisins	125 ml
	hot water	
½ cup	corn syrup	125 ml
¼ cup	firmly packed brown sugar	50 ml
¼ cup	soft sweet butter	50 ml
pinch	salt	pinch
1	egg, slightly beaten	1
½ tsp	vanilla	2 ml

1. Preheat oven to 375°F (190°C).
2. In a small bowl cover raisins with hot water; let stand 5 minutes.
3. In another bowl combine corn syrup, brown sugar, butter, and salt. Drain raisins and add to butter mixture. Stir until sugar is dissolved and butter melted. Stir in egg and vanilla.
4. Divide mixture among tart shells, filling them ¾ full and making sure the raisins are evenly distributed.
5. Bake in oven for 15 minutes, until pastry is golden and filling lightly browned and bubbling.
6. Let cool in pans for 10 minutes, then remove to cake rack to continue to cool.

Makes 18 tarts.

PIES AND CAKES

MOM AND APPLE PIE

No matter how perfect a mother you have, it doesn't necessarily follow that she bequeathed you the perfect apple pie recipe. However, I am assuming you do have an acceptable one by now, and I will give you only the exotica of pie recipes, along with a Lemon Tang Pastry which I find goes with every kind of pie.

The secret of making pastry is cold! cold! cold! If you are going to make pastry, put even your rolling pin in the freezer for a while to make sure you get off to the right start and keep that delicate mixture of flour and shortening working for you.

LEMON TANG PASTRY
(NO FAIL)

5 cups	all-purpose flour	1.25 l
2 tsp	granulated sugar	10 ml
2 tsp	salt	10 ml
½ tsp	baking soda	2 ml
1 lb	cold lard	500 g
1	egg	1
1 tbs	lemon juice	15 ml
	cold water	

1. In a large bowl combine flour, sugar, salt, and baking soda. Mix well. With pastry blender or 2 knives cut in lard until mixture is crumbly and resembles small peas.

2. In a measuring cup combine egg and lemon juice; beat well. Add water to egg mixture to measure 1 cup (250 ml).
3. Pour over flour mixture, stir until a ball of dough starts to form.
4. Turn out onto floured board, divide into 6 portions, shape into balls, and wrap in plastic wrap. Press down to smooth and push out any air bubbles.
5. Use immediately or wrap and store for later use.
6. Can be refrigerated for 2 to 3 weeks or frozen up to 6 months.

Makes pastry for 3 double-crust 9 inch (23 cm) pies (one ball to a crust).

APPLE CRUMBLE PIE

Spartan or Northern Spy apples and Granny Smiths are best for this.

Lemon Tang Pastry (recipe p. 285)
for single crust 9 inch (23 cm) pie

6 cups	thinly sliced, peeled apples	1.5 l
¾ cup	finely packed brown sugar	175 ml
1 tsp	ground cinnamon	5 ml
¼ tsp	salt	1 ml

CRUMBLE TOPPING:

½ cup	rolled oats	125 ml
½ cup	all-purpose flour	125 ml
¼ cup	100% bran cereal	50 ml
½ cup	firmly packed brown sugar	125 ml
½ cup	cold sweet butter	125 ml
¼ cup	sunflower seeds or chopped almonds	50 ml
	cold heavy or whipping cream, optional	

1. Roll out pastry and fit into 9 inch (23 cm) pie plate. Trim overhang about ¾ inch (2 cm) from edge; fold under, press into a high edge, and flute.
2. In a large bowl, toss together apple slices. Combine brown sugar, cinnamon, and salt. Stir into apples.
3. Preheat oven to 425°F (220°C).
4. Meanwhile, prepare topping: In bowl combine rolled oats, flour, bran cereal, and brown sugar. With a pastry blender cut in butter until mixture is crumbly; stir in sunflower seeds or almonds.
5. Spoon apple mixture into pie shell, spreading slices around the edge and mounding them slightly in the center. Sprinkle evenly with crumble topping.

6. Bake in oven for 15 minutes; reduce heat to 375°F (190°C) and continue baking for 30 to 35 minutes, or until apples are tender and crust is golden. Let cool on rack.
Serve hot or at room temperature drizzled with unwhipped whipping cream, if desired.

Makes 6 to 9 servings.

SPRING FRESH STRAWBERRY RHUBARB PIE

There is nothing more wonderful at the height of the spring harvest than a fresh fruit pie served with a scoop of vanilla ice cream.
I serve my pies warm. But when I have people staying over for the weekend, I frequently catch them polishing off the remains of a pie with their breakfast coffee.

2 cups	rhubarb, cut in ½ inch (1 cm) pieces	500 ml
2 cups	sliced strawberries	500 ml
¼ cup	all-purpose flour	50 ml
1½ cups	granulated sugar	375 ml
	Lemon Tang Pastry (recipe p. 285) for double-crust 9 inch (23 cm) pie	
1 tbs	sweet butter	15 ml
1 tsp	light cream	5 ml
	granulated sugar	
	vanilla ice cream, optional	

1. In a large bowl combine rhubarb, strawberries, flour, and sugar. Let stand 15 minutes.
2. Preheat oven to 425°F (220°C).
3. On a floured surface, roll out 2 balls of pastry. Line a 9 inch (23 cm) pie plate with ½ the pastry; trim to edge of pie plate.
4. Place fruit in pie plate; dot with butter. Cover fruit with remaining pastry; seal and flute edges. Cut a few slits in top to let steam escape. Brush top of pie with cream and sprinkle generously with sugar.
5. Bake in oven for 15 minutes, reduce temperature to 350°F (180°C), and bake 35 to 40 minutes longer, until fruit is tender and crust lightly browned. Cool on rack. Serve with vanilla ice cream, if desired.

Makes 8 servings.

RHUBARB CRISP

Wonderfully tart and pink, the way you think spring should taste.

4 cups	cut-up rhubarb (½ inch/1 cm pieces)	1 l
¾ cup	granulated sugar	175 ml
¼ cup	all-purpose flour	50 ml
½ tsp	ground cinnamon	2 ml

TOPPING:

1 cup	whole wheat flour	250 ml
¾ cup	brown sugar	175 ml
½ cup	rolled oats	125 ml
½ cup	sweet butter, melted	125 ml

1. In an 8 inch (20 cm) square baking dish, combine rhubarb, sugar, flour, and cinnamon; mix well.
2. Preheat oven to 375°F (190°C).
3. To make topping: In a small bowl combine flour, brown sugar, oats, and butter; mix well. Sprinkle over rhubarb mixture.
4. Bake in oven for 35 minutes, or until top is golden brown and crisp.

Makes 9 servings.

LEMON CLOUDS IN MERINGUE BASKETS

This is a desert to satisfy both my lemon guests and my chocolate guests. I shave a curl of bittersweet chocolate onto each of the bite-size lemon meringues.

4	eggs, separated	4
¼ tsp	cream of tartar	1 ml
1½ cups	granulated sugar	375 ml
¼ cup	lemon juice	50 ml
1 tbs	grated lemon rind	15 ml
1 cup	heavy or whipping cream	250 ml
	shaved bittersweet chocolate	

1. Preheat oven to 275°F (140°C).
2. In a mixer bowl beat egg whites until foamy. Add cream of tartar and beat until moist stiff peaks from. Gradually beat in 1 cup (250 ml) sugar until a glossy stiff meringue forms.
3. Using a large spoon or spatula and ⅔ of the meringue, spread 4 inch (10 cm) circles of meringue on parchment-paper-lined cookie sheets. Pipe or spoon remaining meringue around edges of circles to form a basket.
4. Bake in oven for 50 to 60 minutes, or until quite dry. Cool completely.

5. In top of double boiler, beat egg yolks slightly, beat in remaining sugar, lemon juice, and rind. Place over simmering water and cook for about 6 minutes, until very thick. Remove from heat and cool.
6. Whip cream. Fold half of cream into lemon mixture. Spoon mixture into baskets. Cover with remaining whipped cream.
7. Garnish with shaved chocolate.

Makes 6 to 8 servings.

SOUTHERN PECAN PIE

This pie is wickedly gooey, sweet, and pecany.

Lemon Tang Pastry (Recipe p. 285)
for single crust 9 inch (23 cm) pie

2	eggs, well beaten	2
1 cup	granulated sugar	250 ml
1 cup	light corn syrup	250 ml
¼ cup	sweet butter, melted	50 ml
¼ tsp	salt	1 ml
1 cup	coarsely chopped pecans	250 ml
12	pecan halves	12
	vanilla ice cream, optional	

1. Roll out pastry and fit into 9 inch (23 cm) pie plate.
2. Preheat oven to 400°F (200°C).
3. In a large bowl combine eggs, sugar, syrup, butter, and salt; stir in chopped pecans. Pour into pastry-lined pie plate and decorate with pecan halves.
4. Bake in oven for 15 minutes. Reduce heat to 350°F (180°C) and bake 25 minutes longer, until crust is lightly browned and filling set.
5. Allow pie to cool for several hours. Serve at room temperature with vanilla ice cream, if desired.

Makes 6 servings.

OREO ICE CREAM PIE

This is a dessert to make for fun and variations. While I suggest coffee ice cream topped with whipped cream and slivered almonds, my younger daughter, Kelly, prefers chocolate ice cream topped with hot peppermint sauce. It's like a do-it-yourself sundae.

2 cups	Oreo cookie crumbs (about 15 cookies)	500 ml
⅓ cup	soft sweet butter	75 ml

FUDGE SAUCE:

3	squares (each 1 oz/28 g) unsweetened chocolate	3
½ cup	water	125 ml
¾ cup	granulated sugar	175 ml
¼ tsp	salt	1 ml
¼ cup	sweet butter	50 ml
1 tsp	vanilla	5 ml
4 cups	coffee ice cream	1 l
1 cup	whipped cream	250 ml
2 tbs	toasted slivered almonds	25 ml

1. In a large bowl combine cookie crumbs and butter; mix well. Press crumb mixture evenly onto the bottom and sides of a 9 inch (23 cm) glass pie plate. Chill.
2. To make fudge sauce: In a small heavy saucepan combine chocolate with water. Cook over low heat, stirring occasionally, about 5 minutes, until chocolate is melted.
3. Stir in sugar and salt; cook, stirring, 5 minutes, until sugar is dissolved and mixture is thickened.
4. Remove from heat; stir in butter and vanilla. Let cool.
5. Fill cookie shell with scoops of ice cream, mounding in the center. Chill 10 minutes.
6. Spread ½ cup (125 ml) fudge sauce over top of pie. Store in freezer until ready to serve.

Garnish with dollops of whipped cream around the edge and sprinkle with almonds. Serve with reserved fudge sauce, if desired.

Makes 8 servings.

DREAM CAKES

I get a dreamy sense of fulfillment when I set out the ingredients to make a cake.

It's because cakes bring a sense of occasion: the birthday cake, the wedding cake, the Christmas cake, the anniversary cake, the graduation cake, the bar mitzvah cake, and so on and so on.

MY FAVORITE COFFEE CAKE

This one reheats beautifully, so you can tuck it in the oven when you put the coffee on and serve it hot for your breakfast guests.

½ cup	sweet butter	125 ml
1 cup	granulated sugar	250 ml
2	eggs	2
2 cups	all-purpose flour	500 ml
1 tsp	baking powder	5 ml
1 tsp	baking soda	5 ml
½ tsp	salt	2 ml
1 cup	sour cream	250 ml
1 tsp	vanilla	5 ml

FILLING:

½ cup	firmly packed brown sugar	125 ml
1 cup	finely chopped pecans	250 ml
1 tsp	ground cinnamon	5 ml

1. Preheat oven to 350°F (180°C).
2. In a large mixing bowl cream together butter and sugar 3 minutes, until light and fluffy. Add eggs, one at a time, beating well after each addition.
3. In a bowl sift together flour, baking powder, baking soda, and salt. Add to creamed mixture alternately with sour cream, beating well. Beat in vanilla.
4. In a bowl, combine brown sugar, pecans, and cinnamon.
5. Grease and flour a 9 inch (23 cm) square pan. Spread half the batter in pan.
6. Sprinkle with half the filling mixture. Add remaining batter, smooth top. Sprinkle with remaining filling.
7. Bake in oven for 45 to 50 minutes, or until tester comes out clean.

Makes 9 servings.

PECAN BUTTERSCOTCH COFFEE CAKE

This is the cake for a fabulous sweet table after an evening at the theater.

The fluffy pecan filling, tucked in by the butterscotch glaze, makes this a wonderfully attractive cake to show and serve.

This recipe is for two cakes. If you don't use both of them, freeze one for another occasion.

⅓ cup	undiluted evaporated milk	75 ml
¼ cup	granulated sugar	50 ml
¼ cup	sweet butter	50 ml
½ tsp	salt	2 ml
⅓ cup	lukewarm water	75 ml
1 tsp	granulated sugar	5 ml
1	envelope active dry yeast	1
1	egg, slightly beaten	1
1 tsp	grated orange rind	5 ml
½ tsp	ground cinnamon	2 ml
¼ tsp	ground nutmeg	1 ml
1⅓ cups	all-purpose flour	325 ml

1. In a saucepan combine milk, ¼ cup (50 ml) sugar, butter, and salt; cook 2 to 3 minutes over medium heat, until butter melts. Remove from heat, stir, then cool to lukewarm.
2. In a medium-size bowl combine water and sugar. Sprinkle yeast over water, let stand 10 minutes, then stir well.
3. Add milk mixture to yeast, then add egg, orange rind, cinnamon, and nutmeg.
4. Beat in flour to make a dough which is soft but not sticky. Turn out onto lightly floured surface and knead 10 minutes, until smooth and elastic. Place in a greased bowl, lightly butter top of dough, cover, and let rise in a warm place 1¼ hours, or until doubled in bulk.
5. Divide dough in half. Pat each half into a buttered 8 inch (20 cm) round layer cake pan. Cover and let rise 45 minutes, until doubled in bulk.
6. Meanwhile, preheat oven to 375°F (190°C). Bake for 15 minutes, or until golden brown.

PECAN BUTTERSCOTCH FROSTING:

¼ cup	soft sweet butter	50 ml
¼ cup	confectioner's or icing sugar	50 ml
2 tbs	Caramel Syrup (see pg. 293)	25 ml
pinch	salt	pinch
2–3 drops	vanilla	2–3
2 cups	sifted confectioner's or icing sugar	500 ml
1–2 tsp	milk	5–10 ml
1 cup	coarsely chopped, toasted pecans	250 ml

1. In a bowl combine butter and ¼ cup (50 ml) unsifted sugar; beat 3 minutes until light and fluffy.
2. Add Caramel Syrup, salt, and vanilla; mix well.
3. Stir in sifted sugar alternately with enough warm milk to make a frosting of spreading consistency. Fold in pecans.

CARAMEL SYRUP:

1 cup	granulated sugar	250 ml
1 cup	boiling water	250 ml

1. In a heavy saucepan over low heat stir sugar about 5 minutes, until melted and slightly browned.
2. Carefully add water, stirring, about 5 minutes, until caramel melts and syrup thickens slightly. In a screw-top jar, store any remaining syrup in refrigerator up to 3 months.
3. To assemble: Remove coffee cakes from oven. While still warm spread with Pecan Butterscotch Frosting. Can be frozen at this point. Freezes for up to 8 weeks. May be reheated for serving.

Makes 2 coffee cakes.

FRENCH ORANGE BUTTER CAKE

This is a big cake for a teatime party that probably doesn't have much more than this and a bit of pâté with assorted breads for starters.
The orange sauce is poured over while the cake is still hot and porous and able to absorb most of the goodness.

2 cups	sweet butter	500 ml
1 cup	granulated sugar	250 ml
2 tbs	grated orange rind	25 ml
½ tsp	vanilla	2 ml
5	eggs	5
3 cups	cake and pastry flour	750 ml
1 tbs	baking powder	15 ml
¼ tsp	salt	1 ml
¾ cup	milk	175 ml

SAUCE:

⅔ cup	granulated sugar	150 ml
⅓ cup	orange juice	75 ml
¼ cup	sweet butter	50 ml

1. Preheat oven to 350°F (180°C).
2. In a large bowl cream together butter and sugar. Stir in orange rind and vanilla. Add eggs, one at a time, beating well after each addition.
3. In a small bowl sift together flour, baking powder, and salt. Stir flour mixture into batter alternately with milk; mix well.
4. Pour into a buttered and floured 10 inch (25 cm) tube pan. Bake in oven for 1 hour, or until golden brown.
5. While cake is in oven, make Sauce: In a small saucepan heat together sugar, orange juice, and butter.
6. Remove cake from oven. Pour sauce over cake while still hot. Cool cake on wire rack before moving from pan.

Makes 10 to 12 servings.

WALNUT CHIFFON CAKE WITH RUM BUTTER SAUCE

This is a true lady-of-the-house-type cake—all swirls and whirls and a pretty dotted Swiss look contributed by the nuts and the whipped cream and rum sauce.

6	eggs, separated	6
¼ tsp	cream of tartar	1 ml
1 cup	granulated sugar	250 ml
1 tsp	vanilla	5 ml
½ cup	cake and pastry flour	125 ml
1 cup	finely chopped pecans	250 ml
2 cups	heavy or whipping cream	500 ml

RUM BUTTER SAUCE:

½ cup .	dark brown sugar	125 ml
½ cup	whipped cream	125 ml
1½ tsp	sweet butter	7 ml
1 tbs	dark rum	15 ml
½ tsp	vanilla	2 ml

1. Preheat oven to 325°F (160°C).
2. In a large bowl, beat egg whites and cream of tartar about 2 minutes, until almost stiff.
3. Add ½ cup (125 ml) sugar, a little at a time, beating 3 minutes longer, until mixture is stiff and glossy.
4. In a bowl beat yolks and remaining ½ cup (125 ml) sugar 3 minutes, until light in color and forming ribbons. Add vanilla.

5. Fold yolks into whites; then fold in flour and nuts. Spoon into 10 inch (25 cm) tube pan; bake in oven 40 to 50 minutes, or until tester comes out clean. Remove from oven, invert tube pan, and let hang over plate. Cool. Cut horizontally in half to make 2 layers.
6. In a mixer bowl, whip cream. Refrigerate until ready to use.
7. To make Sauce: In a saucepan combine sugar, cream, and butter. Bring to a boil, reduce heat, continue cooking 15 minutes, until sugar dissolves. Stir in rum and vanilla. Cool to lukewarm.
8. Arrange one cake layer on a cake plate. Spread with whipped cream; place other layer on top and cover top and sides of cake with remaining whipped cream. Drizzle sauce over top and sides of cake. Refrigerate 30 minutes before serving.

Makes 12 servings.

LIGHT CARROT CAKE

An enduringly moist cake. You can even freeze it and it will remain moist. If you like carrot cake, this one is just right.

1 cup	granulated sugar	250 ml
1 cup	vegetable oil	250 ml
3	eggs	3
1½ cups	all-purpose flour	375 ml
1½ tsp	ground cinnamon	7 ml
1 tsp	baking powder	5 ml
1 tsp	baking soda	5 ml
½ tsp	salt	2 ml
2 cups	grated carrots	500 ml
1 cup	finely chopped pecans	250 ml

FROSTING:

1	pkg (8 oz/250 g) cream cheese softened	1
2 cups	confectioner's or icing sugar	500 ml
¼ cup	sweet butter	50 ml
2 tsp	vanilla	10 ml

1. Preheat oven to 300°F (150°C).
2. Grease and flour two 9 inch (23 cm) round cake pans.
3. In a large mixing bowl combine sugar and oil; mix well. Add eggs one at a time, beating well after each addition.
4. Sift together flour, cinnamon, baking powder, baking soda, and salt.
5. Add dry ingredients to wet, beat together 4 minutes, mixing well. Fold in carrots and nuts.

6. Divide batter in half and pour into cake pans. Bake in oven for 40 minutes.
7. Remove from oven and turn out onto cake racks. Cool.
8. To make Frosting: In a bowl beat together cream cheese, sugar, butter, and vanilla until smooth.
9. Put one cake layer on a round cake plate. Frost layer; place other layer on top, and frost top and sides of cake. Freeze frosted cake for up to 8 weeks.

Makes 12 servings.

GINGERBREAD CAKE

The classic. Slice thin and serve with Apple Compote. What more can I say?

2 cups	all-purpose flour	500 ml
2 tsp	baking soda	10 ml
1½ tsp	ground ginger	7 ml
1 tsp	ground cloves	5 ml
1 tsp	ground cinnamon	5 ml
½ tsp	freshly ground black pepper	2 ml
1 cup	sweet butter	250 ml
1 cup	firmly packed brown sugar	250 ml
3	eggs	3
1 cup	dark molasses	250 ml
1 cup	hot strong coffee	250 ml
	Apple Compote or vanilla ice cream	

1. Preheat oven to 375°F (190°C).
2. Butter and flour a 9 inch (23 cm) square pan.
3. Combine flour, soda, ginger, cloves, cinnamon, and pepper. Sift together and set aside.
4. In a large bowl cream butter and sugar; beat 2 minutes until light and fluffy.
5. Add eggs one at a time, beating well after each addition. Add molasses; beat 2 minutes longer until smooth.
6. Add sifted dry ingredients alternately with coffee in 3 additions to creamed mixture; mix well. (Mixture will be thin.)
7. Pour into prepared pan. Bake for 35 to 40 minutes, or until tester comes clean. Serve warm with Apple Compote or vanilla ice cream.

Makes 8 servings.

APPLE COMPOTE

5	apples, peeled and cut into ½ inch (1 cm) wide wedges	5
¾ cup	granulated sugar	175 ml
½ cup	water	125 ml
	juice and rind of 1 lemon	
2 tbs	apple jelly	25 ml
2 tbs	sherry	25 ml

1. In a large skillet combine apple wedges, sugar, lemon juice, and rind. Bring mixture to a boil, reduce heat, and simmer 15 minutes, until fruit is tender.
2. With a slotted spoon, remove apples from syrup, stir in jelly and sherry, bring mixture to a boil, continue cooking about 5 minutes, until thick. Spoon apples and syrup over Gingerbread Cake.

Makes 4 servings.

QUEEN ELIZABETH CAKE

This is also known as Lazy Date Cake, and I have no idea where either name comes from. All I know is that this has been a favorite of mine since I was very young.

The dates give the cake a natural sweetness and moisture, and the hot icing drizzled over the hot cake adds something special to the flavor.

1 cup	coarsely chopped dates	250 ml
1 cup	boiling water	250 ml
½ cup	sweet butter	125 ml
1 cup	granulated sugar	250 ml
1	egg	1
1½ cups	all-purpose flour	375 ml
1 tsp	baking powder	5 ml
1 tsp	baking soda	5 ml
1 tsp	vanilla	5 ml

ICING:

½ cup	finely chopped walnuts	125 ml
⅓ cup	firmly packed brown sugar	75 ml
¼ cup	sweet butter	50 ml
2 tbs	milk or cream	25 ml

1. Preheat oven to 350°F (180°C).
2. Butter and flour an 8 inch (20 cm) square pan.
3. In a small bowl combine dates and water. Set aside to cool.
4. In a large bowl combine butter and sugar; beat 5 minutes, until light and fluffy. Add egg, mixing well.
5. Sift together flour, baking powder, and baking soda. Add to sugar mixture. Stir in vanilla and dates.
6. Pour into prepared pan and bake in oven for 35 to 40 minutes, until brown and tester comes out clean.
7. While cake is baking, combine walnuts, brown sugar, butter, and milk in a saucepan. Bring to a boil and cook 2 minutes.
8. Pour over cake as soon as it is removed from the oven. Cool in pan on rack. Cut in squares to serve.

Makes 8 servings.

CHERRY POUND CAKE

This can be a staple in your cake repertoire all year round, or you can reserve it just for Christmas. I tend to make it only at that time of year, and for a quirk of good humor, I use half red and half green cherries.

1 cup	sweet butter	250 ml
1 cup	granulated sugar	250 ml
3	eggs	3
2 tsp	vanilla	10 ml
2½ cups	all-purpose flour	625 ml
2 tsp	baking powder	10 ml
1 tsp	ground cardamom	5 ml
½ tsp	ground mace	2 ml
½ tsp	salt	2 ml
½ cup	milk	125 ml
1 tbs	all-purpose flour	15 ml
1 cup	red and/or green glacé cherries	250 ml

1. Preheat oven to 325°F (160°C).
2. Grease a 5 × 9 inch (13 × 23 cm) loaf pan.
3. In a mixing bowl, cream together butter and sugar, until light and fluffy. Beat in eggs 1 at a time. Add vanilla.
4. Combine 2½ cups (625 ml) flour, baking powder, cardamom, mace, and salt. Add flour mixture to creamed mixture alternately with milk.
5. Sprinkle remaining flour over cherries. Toss to coat and fold into batter.
6. Spoon batter into loaf pan and bake in oven for 1½ hours, until tester inserted in center comes out clean.

Makes 1 loaf, 16 to 18 slices.

ARGENTINE NUT MERINGUE CAKE

A wonderful choice for special occasions—birthdays, anniversaries, weddings.
Depending on the number of people you are expecting, you can make two and
cut one into small pieces for folks to take home in special little boxes.

12	egg whites	12
½ tsp	cream of tartar	2 ml
1 lb	confectioner's or icing sugar	500 g
2 lbs	pecans, finely chopped	1 kg

1. Preheat oven to 300°F (150°C).
2. Grease and line with waxed paper three 15 × 10 inch (37 × 25 cm) jelly roll pans.
3. In a large bowl beat together egg whites and cream of tartar 2 minutes, until almost stiff.
4. Add sugar, a little at a time, beating 10 minutes, until mixture is stiff and glossy.
5. Reserve ¾ cup (175 ml) nuts, fold in remaining chopped nuts.
6. Divide cake batter evenly into prepared pans; bake in oven for 30 to 35 minutes, or until tester comes out clean. Immediately turn cake out onto clean tea towels and remove waxed paper. Allow cakes to cool.

ICING:

2 cups	sweet butter	500 ml
¾ lb	confectioner's or icing sugar	375 g
2 tbs	cocoa	25 ml
12	egg yolks	12
½ lb	semisweet chocolate, melted and cooled	250 g
2	egg whites, stiffly beaten	2

1. In a large mixing bowl cream together butter, sugar, and cocoa, about 5 minutes.
2. Add egg yolks; continue beating 3 minutes longer, until icing is light and fluffy.
3. Add chocolate; continue beating 1 minute, until chocolate is well blended. Fold in stiffly beaten egg whites.
4. Arrange cake layers on a large square serving plate, spreading ¼ of the icing on each layer.
5. Ice top and sides of cake with remaining icing. Garnish with reserved nuts.
6. Store in refrigerator 2 to 3 days before serving to allow to mellow.
   Note: This cake freezes well.

Makes 30 servings.

CHOCOLATE CHEESECAKE

A little cream cheese, a little sugar, a touch of chocolate, what's to fear? Maybe that is the rationale your guests will use to justify their second helpings.

CRUMB CRUST:

1	package (8 oz/250 g) chocolate wafers	1
⅓ cup	melted sweet butter	75 ml
2 tbs	granulated sugar	25 ml

FILLING:

3	eggs	3
1 cup	granulated sugar	250 ml
3	packages (8 oz/250 g) cream cheese, softened	3
2	packages (6 oz/164 g) semisweet chocolate pieces, melted	2
2 tsp	vanilla	10 ml

1. In a blender or food processor or with rolling pin, crush chocolate wafers into fine crumbs.
2. In a bowl combine wafer crumbs, butter, and sugar; mix well. Press evenly over bottom and sides (½ inch/1 cm from top) of 9 inch (23 cm) springform pan.
3. Preheat oven to 325°F (160°C).
4. In a large mixer bowl beat eggs and sugar about 5 minutes, until light and fluffy.
5. Beat in cream cheese until mixture is smooth. Add melted chocolate and vanilla; beat 3 minutes, until smooth.
6. Turn into crumb crust and bake 1 hour, until cheesecake is firm. Cool on wire rack and refrigerate overnight.

Makes 16 servings.

RIGO JANESI (CHOCOLATE CREAM SLICES)

This is the king of chocolate desserts. It is the kind chocolate lovers O.D. on. It is the dessert that turns my husband into a glassy-eyed chocolate freak intent upon devouring the whole thing himself. . . . And this is a big cake!

3 oz	unsweetened chocolate	84 g
½ cup	sweet butter	125 ml
½ cup	granulated sugar	125 ml
4	eggs, separated	4
pinch	salt	pinch
pinch	cream of tartar	pinch
½ cup	all-purpose flour	125 ml

1. Preheat oven to 350°F (180°C).
2. Lightly grease and line an 11 × 17 inch (27.5 × 48 cm) jelly roll pan with waxed paper.
3. In a heavy saucepan or double boiler, over hot, *not boiling*, water, melt unsweetened chocolate; cool to lukewarm.
4. In a mixer bowl cream together butter and ¼ cup (50 ml) sugar; beat 5 minutes, until light and fluffy.
5. Add melted chocolate; mix well. Beat in yolks one at a time, mixing well after each addition.
6. In a bowl combine egg whites, salt, and cream of tartar. Beat 3 to 4 minutes, until whites cling to beater.
7. Add remaining ¼ cup (50 ml) sugar and continue beating 7 minutes, until stiff peaks form.
8. Fold ⅓ of whites into yolk mixture, then pour yolk mixture over rest of the whites. Add flour and gently fold egg and flour mixture until no white is visible.
9. Pour batter into prepared pan and spread evenly. Bake in oven 15 to 18 minutes, until tester comes out clean.
10. Immediately invert cake onto clean tea towel and remove waxed paper. Cool.

FILLING:

1½ cups	heavy whipping cream	375 ml
10 oz	semisweet chocolate, chopped	280 g
¼ cup	rum	50 ml
1 tsp	vanilla	5 ml

1. In a heavy saucepan combine cream and chocolate; cook over medium heat 5 to 6 minutes, until chocolate is melted and mixture is well blended.

2. Reduce heat, stirring constantly; simmer 2 to 3 minutes, until mixture thickens into a heavy cream.
3. Chill about 2 hours. Stir in rum and vanilla; beat 1 to 2 minutes, just until filling is smooth and creamy and soft peaks form. Do not overbeat. Refrigerate until needed.

GLAZE:

1 cup	granulated sugar	250 ml
⅓ cup	water	75 ml
7 oz	semisweet chocolate, broken into small pieces	196 g

1. In a saucepan over medium heat, combine sugar, water, and chocolate. Stir 3 to 4 minutes, until sugar dissolves and chocolate is melted. Blend well.
2. Cover and let cool, 20 minutes.

1. To assemble cake: Cut cake in half, each piece 8½ inches (21 cm) wide.
2. Over bottom layer spread filling 2 inch (5 cm) thick. Place other layer on top.
3. Refrigerate cake 1 hour. Remove and spread glaze on top. Chill.
4. Serve by cutting cake into 35 small pieces (5 rows across and 7 rows down).

Makes 35 servings.

DELUXE CHOCOLATE MERINGUE CAKE

Spectacular to look at and even more so to taste.

CHOCOLATE BUTTERCREAM:

4	squares (each 1 oz/28 g) unsweetened chocolate	4
1 cup	soft sweet butter	250 ml
1 cup	granulated sugar	250 ml
½ cup	water	125 ml
pinch	cream of tartar	pinch
6	egg yolks, well beaten	6

1. Draw three 8 inch (20 cm) circles on parchment or brown paper. Arrange on two cookie sheets.
2. In a small saucepan or in a double boiler over hot, *not boiling*, water, melt chocolate. Add butter; mix well. Cool to lukewarm.
3. In a saucepan combine sugar, water, and cream of tartar; bring to a boil, then cook over medium heat about 10 minutes, until mixture is at the soft ball stage.*
4. Remove from heat. Pour over egg yolks, beating quickly about 3 minutes, until well blended.
5. Fold chocolate mixture into egg mixture; blend well. Cover and cool 12 hours or overnight.

MERINGUE LAYERS:

6	egg whites	6
1½ cups	granulated sugar	375 ml
1 tsp	white vinegar	5 ml
1½ tsp	vanilla	7 ml
	strawberry or apricot jam	
	candied orange peel	

1. Preheat oven to 250°F (120°C).
2. In a large mixer bowl beat egg whites about 4 minutes, until stiff.
3. Gradually add sugar, vinegar, and vanilla. Continue beating mixture about 10 minutes, until satiny and glossy.
4. Scoop meringue into pastry bag fitted with a ½ inch (1 cm) plain tip. Starting from the outside, pipe a spiral design to fill each paper circle. With a knife, smooth top.
5. Bake in oven for 1 hour; turn oven off and leave meringues in for 30 minutes or overnight, until dry.
6. Spread 2 layers of meringue first with a thin layer of strawberry or apricot jam, then with a layer of chocolate buttercream.
7. Place one layer on a cake plate and top with second. Place remaining meringue layer on top. Spread top and sides of cake with a thin layer of buttercream.
8. Garnish with candied orange peel. Chill.
The entire cake may be wrapped and frozen to be thawed when needed.

Makes 12 servings.

*Soft ball stage is reached when a drop of the sugar syrup forms a soft ball when put into cold water.

RICH CHOCOLATE CAKE

This is the moist, delicious chocolate cake everyone dreams of.

3	squares (each 1 oz/28 g) unsweetened chocolate, chopped	3
1 cup	boiling water	250 ml
2½ cups	sifted cake and pastry flour	625 ml
2½ tsp	baking powder	12 ml
1 tsp	baking soda	5 ml
½ tsp	salt	2 ml
½ cup	sweet butter	125 ml
2½ cups	granulated sugar	625 ml
3	eggs, separated	3
1 tsp	vanilla	5 ml
1 cup	sour cream	250 ml

1. Preheat oven to 350°F (180°C).
2. Lightly butter and flour two 9 inch (23 cm) round layer cake pans.
3. In a small bowl combine chocolate and water, stirring until chocolate melts. Cool slightly.
4. Sift together flour, baking powder, baking soda, and salt.
5. In a large mixing bowl cream butter. Add 2 cups (500 ml) sugar; continue to cream until light and fluffy. Beat in egg yolks one at a time. Stir in cooled chocolate and vanilla.
6. Add sifted dry ingredients alternately with sour cream. Mix well after each addition.
7. In a bowl beat egg whites and remaining ½ cup (125 ml) sugar until stiff peaks form. Carefully fold in chocolate mixture.
8. Pour evenly into prepared pans. Bake in oven for 40 to 45 minutes, until tester inserted in center comes out clean. Cool in pan. Remove. Fill and frost with Chocolate Frosting.

Makes 12 servings.

CHOCOLATE FROSTING

2	squares (each 1 oz/28 g) unsweetened chocolate	2
2 tbs	sweet butter	25 ml
1	egg yolk	1
1½ cups	confectioner's or icing sugar	375 ml
1 tsp	vanilla	5 ml
¼ cup	milk	50 ml

1. In top of a double boiler over simmering water, melt chocolate and butter. Set aside to cool for 10 minutes.
2. Transfer to a large bowl, beat in egg yolk, and continue beating until mixture is thick. Add sugar, vanilla, and milk; stir until mixture is creamy.

Makes 1½ cups (375 ml).

GENOISE CAKE WITH CHOCOLATE BUTTERCREAM AND PRALINE

This is a true celebration cake. Add sparklers, candles, a horseshoe, whatever . . . and bring it to the table in all its multilayered glory.

The beauty of this recipe is that you can make the Genoise Cake and the Praline well beforehand and store them in the fridge until you are ready to ice the cake on the celebration day.

GENOISE:

6	eggs	6
1 cup	granulated sugar	250 ml
1 cup	all-purpose flour	250 ml
⅓ cup	clarified sweet butter	75 ml
1 tsp	vanilla	5 ml

1. Preheat oven to 350°F (180°C).
2. Grease and flour two 9 inch (23 cm) round cake pans.
3. In a mixing bowl combine eggs and sugar. Set in saucepan of hot, *not boiling*, water and heat mixture about 3 minutes, over low heat, stirring occasionally, until lukewarm.
4. Transfer to a mixer and beat at high speed 15 minutes, or until light in color and triple in volume.
5. Sift in flour, ⅓ at a time, folding in each part gently, but thoroughly.
6. In a small bowl combine butter and vanilla; fold into batter 1 tbs (15 ml) at a time.
7. Pour evenly into prepared round cake pans and bake in oven for 25 minutes, or until tester comes out clean.
8. Remove and let sit 5 minutes, then turn out onto cake racks and cool.

SYRUP:

¾ cup	water	175 ml
½ cup	granulated sugar	125 ml
3 tbs	Pernod	45 ml

1. In a saucepan combine water and sugar; bring mixture to a boil and cook 3 minutes.
2. Remove from heat and stir in Pernod.
3. Spoon syrup over cake layers. Chill layers.

PRALINE:

1 cup	unblanched almonds	250 ml
1 cup	granulated sugar	250 ml
¼ cup	water	50 ml
⅛ tsp	cream of tartar	0.5 ml

1. On a baking sheet spread almonds. Bake in 350°F (180°C) oven for 10 to 15 minutes, or until lightly colored. Cool. Arrange on a piece of buttered foil.
2. In a heavy saucepan combine sugar, water, and cream of tartar; cook over high heat for 3 minutes, until mixture is a light caramel color. Pour over nuts; let cool until hard.
3. Reserve 10 whole coated almonds. In a blender or food processor, drop nuts in a few at a time with machine running until a fine powder forms.

CHOCOLATE BUTTERCREAM:

¼ cup	sweet butter	50 ml
½ cup	confectioner's or icing sugar	125 ml
2	egg yolks	2
½ tsp	vanilla	2 ml
4 oz	semisweet chocolate, melted and cooled	112 g

1. In a bowl beat together butter and sugar about 5 minutes, until light and fluffy.
2. Beat in yolks, 1 at a time, beating well after each addition. Stir in vanilla and chocolate; mix well. Refrigerate until ready to use.

WHIPPED CREAM FILLING:

1 cup	heavy or whipping cream	250 ml
1 tbs	confectioner's or icing sugar	15 ml
½ cup	praline powder	125 ml
2 oz	semisweet chocolate, grated	50 g

1. In a bowl beat cream about 2 minutes, until soft peaks form.
2. Fold in sugar, praline powder, grated chocolate, and vanilla; mix well. Refrigerate until ready to use.

3. To assemble cake: Place 1 cake layer on a glass cake plate, spread with ½ the whipped cream mixture; top with second layer and spread with remaining whipped cream.
4. Spread sides of cake with Chocolate Buttercream.
5. Sprinkle top with ½ cup (125 ml) praline powder.
6. Garnish sides with reserved whole almonds.

Makes 12 servings.

SUPER ITALIAN SUPPER

SCAMPI ALLEGRO

BRUSHETTA

CAESAR SALAD

MALFATI

BISCUIT TORTONI

I suggest serving two red wines for this Italian supper: Italian Valpolicella or a Chianti followed by a Chianti Classica Reserva or a Barolo. Or a Spanish light Rioja followed by an estate red. Or a California Zinfandel followed by an estate Cabernet Sauvignon.

BISCUIT TORTONI

The perfect ice cream ending to an Italian meal. Quick, refreshing, and very pretty in its paper cups.

2 cups	heavy or whipping cream	500 ml
⅔ cup	sifted confectioner's or icing sugar	150 ml
¼ cup	rum or Cognac	50 ml
1	egg white, stiffly beaten	1
½ cup	chopped toasted almonds	125 ml

1. In a large mixing bowl whip the cream until it begins to thicken. Gradually beat in sugar until soft peaks form. Stir in rum or Cognac. Fold in stiffly beaten egg white.

2. Spoon into 8 to 10 medium-size custard cups lined with paper cups; sprinkle with almonds.
3. Place in freezer for 4 hours, or until firm.

Makes 8 to 10 servings.

FROZEN BIRTHDAY PARTY ROLL

If you're thirty-nine and holding, you'll get the double entendre in the name of this little pecan treat.

It's like a jelly roll, only the filling is a creamy caramel-pecan combination which, when frozen, tastes like ice cream.

1 cup	cake and pastry flour	250 ml
1½ tsp	baking powder	7 ml
¼ tsp	salt	1 ml
3	eggs	3
1 cup	granulated sugar	250 ml
⅓ cup	cold water	75 ml
1 tsp	vanilla	5 ml
	confectioner's or icing sugar	
½ cup	chopped pecans	125 ml
1 cup	heavy or whipping cream	250 ml
¼ cup	firmly packed brown sugar	50 ml

1. Preheat oven to 375°F (190°C).
2. Lightly grease and line a 10 × 15 inch (25 × 37 cm) jelly roll pan with waxed paper. Grease again.
3. Combine flour, baking powder, and salt. Set aside.
4. In a mixer bowl beat eggs about 5 minutes, until thick and yellow-colored.
5. Add granulated sugar gradually and continue to beat until light and fluffy. Add water and vanilla and mix well.
6. Fold dry ingredients into egg mixture until well mixed.
7. Spread batter in prepared pan. Bake in oven for 12 to 15 minutes, until top springs back when touched.
8. Loosen edges and immediately turn out of pan onto tea towel sprinkled generously with confectioner's sugar. Remove waxed paper and starting at one narrow end roll cake up in towel. Cool on wire rack.
9. In a small skillet lightly toast pecans.
10. In a mixer bowl combine cream and brown sugar and chill.
11. When cake has completely cooled, whip cream and brown sugar until stiff. Fold in pecans.
12. Unroll cake, fill with even layer of cream filling, and reroll.

13. Wrap in plastic wrap and freeze until firm. Remove from freezer ½ hour before serving.

CARAMEL SAUCE:

¼ cup	sweet butter	50 ml
1	egg yolk	1
⅓ cup	corn syrup	75 ml
⅔ cup	firmly packed brown sugar	150 ml
½ tsp	vanilla	2 ml

1. In top of double boiler over simmering water, melt butter. Stir in egg yolk, corn syrup, and brown sugar and cook, stirring, about 5 minutes, until smooth and a light caramel color.
2. Remove from heat and stir in vanilla. Serve warm over slices of pecan roll.

Makes 8 to 10 servings.

FINLAYSON'S CHOCOLATE FONDANT CAKE

This is the personally perfected recipe of a chocolate addict named Judith Finlayson, one of Toronto's top newspaper columnists and cooks.

½ lb	unsweetened chocolate	250 g
½ lb	finely granulated sugar	250 g
½ cup	strong coffee	125 ml
½ lb	sweet butter, cut into 6 pieces	250 g
4	eggs	4
1 tbs	all-purpose flour	15 ml
	whipped cream	

1. Line a 9 inch (23 cm) layer cake tin with aluminum foil. Hang foil over sides of pan. Butter foil.
2. In a blender or food processor grind chocolate and sugar until very fine.
3. In a heavy saucepan over low heat combine chocolate, sugar, and coffee; cook 3 to 4 minutes until chocolate has melted. Remove from heat, add butter a piece at a time, until butter is completely melted.
4. In a small bowl beat eggs 3 to 4 minutes, until lemon colored. Slowly add flour; mix well.
5. Fold egg mixture into chocolate and blend well.

6. Pour mixture into prepared pan; set pan in a water bath and cook 45 minutes over low heat on top of stove.
7. Meanwhile, preheat oven to 250°F (120°C).
8. Remove pan from water and bake in oven for 30 minutes, or until tester comes out clean. Cool.
9. Cover lightly with cloth and refrigerate 2 to 3 days before serving.
10. Unmold and serve with whipped cream.

Makes 12 servings.

THE CLASSIC CHOCOLATE TRUFFLE

I had to beg Simon Kattar, a caterer in Toronto, to give me the recipe for this rich, sinful, and delicious confection.

TRUFFLES MIXTURE:

¼ lb	milk chocolate	125 g
¼ lb	dark chocolate	125 g
½ tsp	grated orange rind	2 ml
pinch	salt	pinch
½ cup	heavy or whipping cream	125 ml

DIPPING CHOCOLATE:

⅓ lb	dark chocolate	170 g
1 tsp	vegetable oil	5 ml
	cocoa powder for coating	

1. In a blender or food processor grate milk chocolate and dark chocolate. Add orange rind and salt.
2. In a saucepan heat ½ cup (125 ml) cream. *Do not let boil.* Pour into processor. Process with an on/off motion until mixture is smooth and all chocolate has been melted.
3. Remove mixture from processor. Put in a container and freeze overnight.
4. With a teaspoon and your hands, shape truffles one at a time in the shape of a rough ball and place on a cookie sheet covered with waxed paper.
5. Place back in freezer 1 hour, until truffles are firm.
6. To make dipping chocolate: In the top of a double boiler over boiling water melt dark chocolate.
7. Add vegetable oil to the melted chocolate and blend in.

8. Remove truffles from freezer and dip each one into melted chocolate and put once again on a cookie sheet. Let stand 1 to 2 hours, until chocolate coating is firm.
9. Roll truffles in cocoa powder to coat.

Makes 24 truffles.

CREAMY RICH CHEESECAKE

Now, after all those pages of chocolate, here is the simple, plain, honest cheesecake on which you can spread almost anything for a topping.

CRUST:

1¼ cups	graham cracker crumbs	300 ml
⅓ cup	melted sweet butter	75 ml

FILLING:

3	packages (each 8 oz/250 g) cream cheese, softened	3
1 cup	granulated sugar	250 ml
5	eggs	5
1 tsp	vanilla	5 ml
1 cup	sour cream	250 ml
2 tbs	rum	25 ml
1 tbs	granulated sugar	15 ml

1. To make Crust: In a small bowl combine crumbs and butter; mix well. Press onto bottom and sides of a 9 inch (23 cm) springform pan. Refrigerate until needed.
2. To make Filling: Preheat oven to 325°F (160°C). In a mixing bowl beat cheese 2 to 3 minutes, until fluffy. Add sugar and beat 5 minutes longer, until smooth and creamy. Add eggs, 1 at a time, beating well after each addition. Add vanilla; beat 1 minute until well combined.
3. Pour filling into crust and bake for 1 hour, or until tester comes out clean. Remove from oven and let cool 5 minutes.
4. In a small bowl combine sour cream, rum, and sugar; mix well.
5. Spread over cheesecake. Return to oven and bake for 5 minutes longer. Remove and cool well.

Makes 12 servings.

THE SUNDAY ALL-DAY
PARTY

PÂTÉS AND LOAVES
AND BURGERS

THE PÂTÉ PARTY WITH BEER AND WINE

What could be more festive for a brunch?

What could be more effective after a theater outing or a concert than a table all set up with a selection of delicious pâtés?

My all-time favorite is Pâté with Burnt Onions and Crackling. There is something special about the contrast between the smooth chicken liver pâté and the crunchy burnt onions and crackling.

But close behind on my list are Baked Country Terrine, Shrimp Pâté with Dill, the Chicken Loaf, and the French Country Meat Loaf. And for those who may balk at so much richness, toss in the Diet Chopped Liver to reassure.

Give your whole party a festive, almost picnic patina by setting the pâtés, breads, rolls, pickles, condiments, and butters on a table covered with pine boughs or other fragrant evergreens. If you can find two large half barrels for the beer and the wine, fill them with ice and dot the inside with chrysanthemum blooms. As the ice melts the flowers will float and look like a country garden.

PÂTÉ MOUSSE AU CALVADOS

The apples, shallots, and Calvados give this pâté a taste that is tart but smoothed by the cream and the loving care you lavish on it. It spreads easily on crackers or on crisp apple slices.

1 lb	chicken livers	500 g
¾ cup	soft sweet butter	175 ml
½ lb	mushrooms, coarsely chopped	250 g
¼ cup	coarsely chopped shallots	50 ml
¼ cup	coarsely chopped apple	50 ml
½ cup	Calvados	125 ml
1 tsp	lemon juice	5 ml
1 tsp	salt	5 ml
¼ tsp	white pepper	1 ml
pinch	dry mustard	pinch
	crisp unpeeled apple slices	

1. Wash chicken livers, trim, and pat dry.
2. In a skillet heat ¼ cup (50 ml) butter. Add mushrooms, shallots, and apple and sauté for 5 minutes, until softened. Place in a food processor or blender.
3. In the same skillet heat ¼ cup (50 ml) butter. Add chicken livers and fry over high heat for 5 minutes.
4. Add Calvados; reduce heat and simmer, stirring, 3 minutes, until tender. Add to mushroom mixture.
5. Process 2 to 3 minutes, until very smooth. Cover and refrigerate for about 30 minutes, or until cooled and slightly firm.
6. Add remaining butter, lemon juice, salt, pepper, and mustard. Process or cream until well mixed and smooth.
7. Pack into small dishes or crocks. Cover and refrigerate about 2 hours, or until serving time. Serve with apple slices or crackers.

Makes about 2½ cups (625 ml).

PEPPERCORN PÂTÉ WITH MADEIRA

Chicken liver and Madeira is a wild and exciting combination.

⅓ cup	butter	75 ml
1	large Bermuda onion, chopped	1
2	cloves garlic, chopped	2
1 lb	chicken livers	500 g
1 tbs	chopped fresh tarragon, or 1 tsp (5 ml) dried	25 ml
1 tsp	salt	5 ml
½ tsp	freshly ground black pepper	2 ml
1 tsp	dried thyme leaves	5 ml
¼ tsp	cayenne pepper	1 ml
¼ tsp	ground cloves	1 ml
¼ tsp	ground allspice	1 ml
¼ cup	Madeira	50 ml
1 tsp	cracked black or green peppercorns	5 ml

1. In a skillet heat butter, add onion and garlic; sauté 10 minutes, until softened.
2. Add chicken livers and sauté 5 to 7 minutes, or until no longer pink. Sprinkle with tarragon, salt, pepper, thyme, cayenne pepper, cloves, and allspice.
3. Transfer chicken livers to blender or food processor; purée until smooth. Add Madeira and process to combine.
4. Pack pâté into 2 cup (500 ml) crock and top with cracked peppercorns. Refrigerate 1 day before serving.
5. Allow pâté to stand at room temperature 30 minutes before serving.

Makes 8 servings.

BAKED COUNTRY TERRINE

Here is a chicken liver pâté that combines chicken livers with pork.

1 lb	chicken livers	500 g
1	medium onion, peeled and quartered	1
1	clove garlic, finely chopped	1
1¼ lb	ground pork	625 g
2	eggs, slightly beaten	2
⅓ cup	all-purpose flour	75 ml
2 tsp	salt	10 ml
½ tsp	ground allspice	2 ml
½ tsp	cracked black, white, pink, or green peppercorns	2 ml
¾ cup	light cream	175 ml
½ cup	brandy	125 ml
2	bay leaves	2

ASPIC:

1	envelope unflavored gelatin	1
1 cup	rich beef stock	250 ml
2 tbs	brandy or sherry	25 ml

1. Preheat oven to 300°F (150°C).
2. Grease a 9 × 5 inch (23 × 12 cm) loaf pan or baking terrine.
3. In a processor or blender combine livers, onions, and garlic. Process until smooth. Transfer to a large bowl.
4. Stir in pork and eggs. Add flour, salt, allspice, and peppercorns. Mix well. Add cream and brandy, beating until smooth.
5. Spoon into loaf pan or baking terrine. Place 2 bay leaves on top. Cover with foil.
6. Place in roasting pan; add boiling water to a depth of 1½ inches (4 cm). Bake in oven for 1 hour 45 minutes, or until firm.
7. Remove from oven, discard bay leaves. Weight terrine by covering top with a small board or another pan. Top board with weights, such as 2 to 3 food cans. Chill in refrigerator overnight.
8. In morning prepare Aspic; Sprinkle gelatin over stock to soften. Place over low heat, stirring until gelatin is dissolved. Remove from heat. Add brandy or sherry. Cool until syrupy.
9. Unmold terrine. Clean loaf pan or baking terrine; place baked terrine back into pan. Spoon aspic over top. Chill about 2 hours, until firm. Unmold, then invert onto serving plate so that aspic is on top. Garnish and slice to serve.

Makes 12 servings.

PÂTÉ WITH BURNT ONIONS AND CRACKLING

Serve with the burnt onions and crispy crackling spread on top. For a large pâté party, make extra onions and serve them all around the pâté plate.

For a first course or as an hors d'oeuvre, serve with hot buttered toast quarters.

BURNT ONIONS AND CRACKLING:

1 cup	clusters of raw chicken fat,* finely chopped, from 2½ lb (1 kg) chicken	250 ml
4	large yellow onions, coarsely chopped	4
½ tsp	salt	2 ml

*Collect chicken fat clusters from raw chickens and store fat in a plastic bag in the freezer until ready to render.

PÂTÉ:

¼ cup	rendered chicken fat (see pg. 318)	50 ml
¼ cup	sweet butter	50 ml
2	medium yellow onions, coarsely chopped	2
1	bay leaf	1
¼ tsp	ground thyme	1 ml
1 lb	chicken livers	250 g
1½ tsp	salt	7 ml
¼ tsp	ground allspice	1 ml
¼ tsp	ground ginger	1 ml
¼ tsp	ground nutmeg	1 ml
¼ tsp	dry mustard	1 ml
pinch	cayenne pepper	pinch
2 tbs	Cognac	15 ml

1. In a large heavy skillet heat chicken fat and onions over low heat. Cook, stirring frequently, about 1 hour, until fat renders and turns into crackling and onions are crisp and burnt.
2. Strain rendered fat through sieve into a container for further use. Store in refrigerator.
3. Reserve crackling and burnt onions to serve with pâté; refrigerate.
4. To make Pâté: In a saucepan melt chicken fat and butter. Add onions, bay leaf, and thyme; sauté 5 minutes, until onion is softened.
5. Add chicken livers, cook, stirring, about 10 minutes, until lightly browned.
6. Add salt, allspice, ginger, nutmeg, mustard, and cayenne; cook 5 minutes more. Remove bay leaf.
7. Transfer to a food processor or blender; process while hot for 2 to 3 minutes, or until smooth. Add Cognac, process 10 seconds more.
8. Pack into a crock or dish; cover and chill in refrigerator for 2 hours, or until serving time.
9. To serve, top with a generous amount of Burnt Onions and Crackling.

Makes 18 to 20 appetizer servings.

QUICK PÂTÉ

The combination of chicken liver and cream cheese makes this one particularly smooth. Pack it in a crock and serve with quartered and buttered toast.

¼ cup	sweet butter	50 ml
2	medium onions, chopped	2
½ lb	chicken livers	250 g
½ cup	soft cream cheese	125 ml
2	hard-cooked eggs	2
½ tsp	salt	2 ml
½ tsp	ground nutmeg	2 ml
¼ tsp	white pepper	1 ml
1 tbs	Cognac or sherry	15 ml

1. In a medium skillet melt butter. Add onions and sauté about 5 minutes, until tender.
2. Add livers; sauté about 10 minutes, until brown. Cool slightly.
3. Transfer to a blender or food processor. Add cream cheese, eggs, salt, nutmeg, and white pepper. Process until smooth. Add Cognac or sherry; blend again.
4. Turn into crock or serving bowl. Refrigerate.

Makes 2 cups (500 ml).

BEA'S DIET CHOPPED LIVER

Makes a great quick lunch for friends. I usually serve it on shredded Romaine lettuce with a really mustardy deviled egg.

2 lb	chicken livers	1 kg
1 lb	beef liver	500 g
2 tbs	vegetable oil	25 ml
4	medium onions, chopped	4
3	hard-cooked eggs	3
½ tsp	salt	2 ml
¼ tsp	freshly ground black pepper	1 ml
	toast triangles	
	shredded lettuce	

1. Preheat oven to 375°F (190°C).
2. On a lightly greased baking sheet arrange chicken and beef livers. Bake in oven for 10 minutes, or until brown. Drain excess liquid from liver while baking.

3. In a large skillet heat oil; add onions and sauté until soft. Cool.
4. In a meat grinder or food processor combine liver, onions, eggs, salt, and pepper. Grind or chop with an on/off motion about 2 minutes, until roughly chopped.
5. Serve on toast topped with shredded lettuce.

Makes 2 cups (500 ml).

SHRIMP PÂTÉ WITH DILL

A beautiful cold pâté. Pack it into a crock and spread on thinly sliced whole wheat bread when you serve it.

2 lb	raw or frozen shrimp	1 kg
1	large onion, chopped	1
1	stalk celery, chopped	1
	bouquet garni of thyme, parsley, bay leaf, peppercorns	
1 tbs	white wine	15 ml
4 cups	water	1 l
¼ tsp	salt	1 ml
	juice of ½ lemon	
1 cup	sweet butter	250 ml
2 tbs	sherry or dry red wine	25 ml
1 tsp	chopped fresh dill	5 ml
½ tsp	hot pepper sauce	2 ml
½ tsp	ground nutmeg	2 ml
¼ tsp	white pepper	1 ml
12	slices toasted bread, crusts removed	12

1. In a medium saucepan combine onion, celery, bouquet garni, white wine, water, and salt to make a court bouillon. Bring to a boil and cook about 5 minutes.
2. Add shrimp, bring back to a boil; cook about 3 minutes until shrimp curl and are pink.
3. Remove shrimp from liquid, drain, dry, cool, and peel.
4. In a food processor or blender add shrimp a few at a time to chop coarsely. Gradually add lemon juice.
5. In a bowl cream butter, stir in chopped shrimp, sherry or wine, dill, hot pepper sauce, nutmeg, and pepper. Pack into a small bowl or crock.
6. Refrigerate 3 to 4 hours or until serving time.
7. Cut bread into triangles, spread with pâté and serve.

Makes 12 servings.

VEGETABLE PÂTÉ

Red, green, and white layers of carefully spiced vegetables make this an eyeful as well as a mouthful. I slice it and serve it hot with a Béchamel sauce or cold with Dijon Mayonnaise.

SPINACH LAYER:

4	bunches, fresh spinach (2 lb/1 kg)	4
4	eggs, lightly beaten	4
1 tsp	salt	5 ml
½ tsp	freshly ground black pepper	2 ml
½ tsp	ground nutmeg	2 ml

1. In a steamer over boiling water, steam spinach for 2 minutes. Cool slightly. Squeeze dry. Chop finely.
2. Add eggs, salt, pepper, and nutmeg; stir well. Set aside.

TOMATO LAYER:

2 lb	ripe tomatoes, about 6	1 kg
1 tsp	sweet butter	5 ml
1	small onion, finely chopped	1
2	cloves garlic, finely chopped	2
4	eggs, lightly beaten	4
1 tbs	chopped fresh basil, or 1 tsp (5 ml) dried	15 ml

1. In a pot of boiling water blanch tomatoes for 20 seconds. Chill in cold water. Peel off skin. Cut in quarters, remove seeds, and chop coarsely.
2. In a large skillet, heat butter, add onion, garlic, and tomatoes. Sauté about 45 minutes, until all moisture is gone. Let cool.
3. Stir in eggs and basil. Set aside.

LEEK LAYER:

6	large leeks, white part only	6
1 cup	heavy or whipping cream	250 ml
4	eggs, lightly beaten	4
½ tsp	ground thyme	2 ml
½ tsp	salt	2 ml

1. Wash leeks; chop finely. In a pot of boiling water blanch for 3 minutes. Drain well.

2. In a saucepan combine leeks and cream. Bring to a boil and cook over medium heat about 7 minutes, until cream has disappeared. Cool.
3. Stir in eggs, thyme, and salt.

TO ASSEMBLE:
1. Preheat oven to 375°F (190°C).
2. Butter an 8 cup (2 l) loaf pan.
3. Spread ½ spinach mixture over bottom of pan. Spread on tomato mixture.
4. Spread leek mixture on top of tomato mixture and finish with the remaining spinach mixture to make 4 layers. Cover with greased foil.
5. Set in a pan with 1 inch (2.5 cm) boiling water on bottom. Bake in oven for 1¾ to 2 hours, or until tester inserted near center comes out clean.
6. Remove from oven. Let stand for 10 minutes. Turn over to cool. Remove from pan.
   Serve warm or cold.

Makes 20 slices.

DIJON MAYONNAISE

½ cup	mayonnaise (recipe p. 227)	125 ml
2 tsp	sour cream	10 ml
1 tsp	Dijon mustard	5 ml
½ tsp	anchovy paste	2 ml
½ tsp	minced garlic	2 ml
½ tsp	lemon juice	2 ml
½ tsp	brandy	2 ml
½ tsp	salt	2 ml
¼ tsp	freshly ground black pepper	1 ml

1. In a small bowl combine mayonnaise, sour cream, mustard, anchovy paste, garlic, lemon juice, brandy, salt, and pepper; mix well.
2. Cover and refrigerate about 1 hour, or until ready to serve. Keeps in refrigerator up to 4 weeks.

Makes 1 cup (250 ml).

MEATLOAF PANS

There are all kinds of fancy pans sold for making loaves, but my advice is to make it in a rectangular baking pan rather than a loaf pan. Just shape it and let it bake. All you lose is a little fat, which you would have to skim off anyway, and lifting the loaf onto a serving plate is much easier when you can get a grip on it.

FRENCH COUNTRY MEATLOAF

I serve this loaf with Dijon mustard and a cold salad.

All meatloaves cry out for sauces and condiments, particularly when cold. Try some of the recipes in the Condiments and Pickle section, like Dilled Carrot Sticks or Pickled Beets.

This is a large loaf and wonderful served cold.

2 lb	lean ground beef	1 kg
1 lb	ground veal	500 g
1 lb	ground pork	500 g
1	large onion, coarsely chopped	1
1 cup	chopped fresh parsley	250 ml
8	green onions, finely chopped	8
¼ cup	chopped fresh basil leaves, or 1 tbs (15 ml) dried	50 ml
2 tsp	Dijon mustard with garlic and parsley*	10 ml
2 tsp	salt	10 ml
1 tsp	freshly ground black pepper	5 ml
½ tsp	hot pepper sauce	2 ml
3	eggs, well beaten	3
¾ cup	fresh breadcrumbs	175 ml
½ cup	light cream	125 ml
12	slices bacon	12

1. Preheat oven to 350°F (160°C).
2. In a large bowl combine beef, veal, pork, onion, parsley, green onions, basil, mustard, salt, pepper, and hot pepper sauce.
3. Combine eggs, breadcrumbs, and cream; stir into mixture.
4. Lay 6 bacon slices side by side in a 9 × 13 inch (23 × 33 cm) baking pan. Place meat mixture on top of bacon. With hands shape into a loaf. Lay remaining bacon slices on top of loaf. Bake in oven, basting frequently with pan juices, 1½ to 2 hours, until meat is no longer pink.
5. Cool for 30 minutes, until easy to handle.
6. Wrap in foil and place in a pan or dish. Weight loaf by covering with a small board or a pan. Top board with weights, such as 2 or 3 food cans. Refrigerate overnight.
7. Remove weights and foil. Slice and serve cold.

Makes 12 servings.

*Available at specialty food stores.

THREE CHEESE MEATLOAF

If you've never served meatloaf at a party, try this one. It will wow your guests.

It must be served hot from the oven, so that it comes to the table with all three cheeses bubbling.

I serve it with a Mashed Potato Souffle.

2 lb	lean ground beef	1 kg
1	large onion, finely chopped	1
½	green pepper, finely chopped	½
½ cup	fine dry breadcrumbs	125 ml
1 tsp	salt	5 ml
½ tsp	freshly ground black pepper	2 ml
½ tsp	paprika	2 ml
2	eggs, lightly beaten	2
1¼ cups	milk	300 ml
2 tsp	Italian seasoning mix*	10 ml
¾ cup	diced Mozzarella cheese	175 ml
¾ cup	diced Swiss cheese	175 ml
½ cup	freshly grated Parmesan cheese	125 ml

1. Preheat oven to 350°F (180°C).
2. In a large bowl combine beef, onion, green pepper, breadcrumbs, salt, pepper, and paprika.
3. Combine eggs and milk; stir into meat mixture. Blend in 1½ tsp (7 ml) Italian seasoning mix and the three cheeses.
4. In the center of a 9 × 13 inch (23 × 33 cm) baking pan, with hands mold meat mixture into a loaf shape, leaving about 2 inches (5 cm) on either side to make loaf easier to remove from pan. Sprinkle remaining ½ tsp (2 ml) Italian seasoning mix on top of loaf.
5. Bake in oven for 1 hour, until lightly browned. Transfer to a warm platter. Cut in slices to serve.

Makes 8 servings.

*Italian seasoning mix: mix ½ tsp (2 ml) each dried oregano, basil, savory, and rosemary leaves.

> *A traditional Japanese New Year's combination. Use birds of paradise, cut at different heights, with fresh pine bows. Clean, simple, and very elegant, especially in a modern black ceramic vase.*

GREEK LAMB LOAF

Greeks seem to have a natural affinity for lamb, and that may be the only connection with this recipe's name.

The mint, parsley, cinnamon, and allspice give this loaf a truly unique Mediterranean flavor.

1½ lb	ground lamb	750 g
½ cup	fine dry breadcrumbs	125 ml
2	medium onions, chopped	2
2 tbs	chopped fresh parsley	25 ml
1 tbs	chopped fresh mint	15 ml
½ tsp	salt	2 ml
¼ tsp	freshly ground black pepper	1 ml
¼ tsp	ground cinnamon	1 ml
¼ tsp	ground allspice	1 ml
2	eggs, lightly beaten	2

1. Preheat oven to 350°F (180°C).
2. In a large bowl combine lamb, breadcrumbs, onions, parsley, mint, salt, pepper, cinnamon, and allspice; add eggs and mix thoroughly.
3. With hands shape mixture into a 9 × 5 × 2 inch (23 × 12 × 5 cm) loaf. Place in center of a baking pan.
4. Bake in oven for 45 minutes, until firm and browned.
   Serve hot or cold.

Makes 6 servings.

LOAVES AND BURGERS

These are true meatloaves and yet can also double on the barbecue or grill or skillet as patties or burgers. They are great ideas for informal parties, especially in the summertime.

You don't have to serve the burgers on buns à la McDonald's. Some, like the veal burgers, come with their own sauce and are much better served with salad and/or side dishes and their own condiments. So let's follow up the Greek Lamb Loaf with another version of Lamb Burgers and Loaf.

LAMB BURGERS OR LAMB LOAF

The burgers have to marinate for four hours. The loaf goes straight to the oven.

2 lb	ground lamb	1 kg
½ cup	dry breadcrumbs	125 ml
1	large onion, finely chopped	1
1 tsp	chopped fresh coriander (cilantro), or ½ tsp (2 ml) dried	5 ml
1 tsp	ground cumin	5 ml
½ tsp	ground turmeric	2 ml
½ tsp	crushed chili pepper	2 ml
½ tsp	salt	2 ml
¼ tsp	freshly ground black pepper	1 ml
1	egg, lightly beaten	1
½ cup	yogurt	125 ml
1 tbs	lime juice	15 ml

MARINADE:

2 cups	yogurt	500 ml
2	cloves garlic, finely chopped	2
1½ tsp	white pepper	7 ml
1 tsp	chopped fresh mint	5 ml

1. In a bowl, combine lamb, breadcrumbs, onion, coriander, cumin, turmeric, chili pepper, salt, and pepper.
2. Combine egg, yogurt, and lime juice. Stir into lamb mixture; mix thoroughly.
3. Divide into 8 portions; with hands shape each portion into a burger. Place burgers in a glass baking dish.
4. For Marinade, combine yogurt, garlic, pepper, and mint. Pour half over burgers. Reserve remainder.
5. Cover and marinate burgers for 4 hours in refrigerator, turning once.
6. Remove burgers from marinade. Sauté, broil, or grill, turning once, about 10 minutes, until browned. Serve immediately with remaining marinade.

Makes 8 servings.

VARIATION: *Lamb Loaf*

1. Preheat oven to 350°F (180°C).
2. Prepare Lamb Burger mixture. With hands shape lamb mixture into loaf, 9 × 6 × 2 inch (23 × 15 × 5 cm). Place in center of baking pan. Bake in oven for 40 minutes, until firm and browned.
3. Serve loaf hot or cold with marinade as a sauce on the side, if desired.

Makes 1 loaf.

VEAL BURGERS OR VEAL LOAF

Think of these as junior hamburgers and treat them accordingly.

1 lb	ground veal	500 g
2	shallots, finely chopped	2
1	clove garlic, finely chopped	1
¼ cup	fine dry breadcrumbs	50 ml
2 tbs	chopped fresh parsley	25 ml
½ tsp	dried thyme leaves	2 ml
½ tsp	salt	2 ml
¼ tsp	freshly ground black pepper	1 ml
¼ tsp	ground nutmeg	1 ml
2 tbs	milk	25 ml
2 tbs	sweet butter	25 ml

1. In a large bowl combine veal, shallots, garlic, breadcrumbs, parsley, thyme, salt, pepper, and nutmeg. Add milk; mix thoroughly.
2. Divide evenly into 4 portions and with hands shape into burgers.
3. In a skillet heat butter, cook burgers, turning once, for 8 to 10 minutes, until lightly browned and slightly pink inside.

SAUCE FOR BURGERS:

¼ cup	white wine	50 ml
¼ cup	chicken stock	50 ml
1 tsp	Dijon mustard	5 ml
⅛ tsp	white pepper	0.5 ml
½ cup	heavy or whipping cream	125 ml
1 tbs	chopped fresh parsley	15 ml

1. Add wine to skillet, scraping down brown bits to deglaze skillet. Stir in chicken stock, mustard, and pepper.
2. Heat to simmering; add cream, stir, and simmer 4 to 5 minutes, until slightly thickened. Stir in parsley.
3. Spoon over burgers and serve.

Makes 4 patties.

VARIATION: *Veal Loaf*

1. Preheat oven to 350°F (180°C).
2. Shape veal mixture into 8 × 5 × 2 inch (20 × 12 × 5 cm) loaf.
3. Place in center of baking pan and bake in oven for 40 minutes, until firm and lightly browned.
4. Serve hot or cold.

Makes 1 loaf.

For an intimate, late night meal for two on the patio, tie long strands of raffia around ten to fifteen votive candles and suspend them at varying heights in the trees surrounding the dining table.

CHICKEN BURGERS OR CHICKEN LOAF

If you are barbecuing, paint these burgers with butter to keep them from sticking. Otherwise, the cream does the job of keeping the breast meat moist and delicious.

2 lb	boneless chicken breasts	1 kg
2	eggs	2
1½ cups	heavy or whipping cream	375 ml
½ cup	fine dry breadcrumbs	125 ml
½ cup	ground almonds, toasted	125 ml
1	large onion, finely chopped	1
¼ cup	finely chopped fresh parsley	50 ml
1 tbs	finely chopped fresh tarragon, or 1 tsp (5 ml) dried	15 ml
2 tsp	salt	10 ml
1 tsp	freshly ground black pepper	5 ml
½ tsp	ground nutmeg	2 ml
2 tbs	sweet butter	25 ml

1. In a food processor or meat grinder, grind chicken.
2. In a large bowl combine chicken, eggs, cream, breadcrumbs, almonds, onion, parsley, tarragon, salt, pepper, and nutmeg; mix thoroughly.
3. For ease in handling, refrigerate chicken mixture 30 minutes before making burgers. Divide mixture into 8 portions and shape into burgers.
4. In a skillet heat butter, add burgers, and cook, turning once, about 10 minutes, until firm and no longer pink.

Makes 8 patties.

VARIATION: *Chicken Loaf*

1. Preheat oven to 350°F (180°C).
2. Spread chicken mixture in a buttered 9 × 5 inch (23 × 12 cm) loaf pan. Place pan in larger pan and pour hot water into larger pan to a depth of 1 inch (2.5 cm).

3. Bake in oven for 35 minutes, until tester inserted in center comes out clean.
4. Serve hot, or cold with Summer Fruit Chili Sauce (recipe p. 368).

Makes 1 loaf.

SOPHISTICATED SALMON BURGER OR SALMON LOAF

I advise using a skillet when you make the burgers. Somehow the barbecue does not do justice to the combined flavor of fresh and smoked salmon.

2 cups	flaked, cooked, fresh salmon	500 ml
¼ lb	smoked salmon, coarsely chopped	125 g
¾ cup	mashed potatoes (2 medium)	175 ml
1	small onion, finely chopped	1
1 tbs	chopped fresh parsley	15 ml
1 tbs	fresh lemon juice	15 ml
1 tbs	chopped fresh dill, or 1 tsp (5 ml) dried	15 ml
¼ tsp	freshly ground black pepper	1 ml
1	egg, slightly beaten	1
¼ cup	light cream	50 ml
2 tbs	sweet butter	25 ml

1. In a large bowl combine fresh and smoked salmon, potatoes, onion, parsley, lemon juice, dill, and pepper.
2. Combine egg and cream; stir into salmon mixture; mix well.
3. Divide into 4 portions and with hands shape into burgers.
4. In a large skillet heat butter, add burgers; cook, turning once, for 8 to 10 minutes, until golden brown.

Makes 4 patties.

VARIATION: *Salmon Loaf*

1. Preheat oven to 350°F (180°C).
2. Substitute ½ cup (250 ml) fine breadcrumbs for the mashed potatoes. Make salmon mixture. With hands shape it into loaf, about 8 × 5 × 3 inches (20 × 12 × 7.5 cm). Place in center of a baking pan. Bake in oven for 30 minutes, until firm and golden brown. Serve hot or cold.

Makes 1 loaf.

MOVIE NIGHT

Come on Over—It's Movie Night

Throw an informal evening with your VCR and a new movie or two. You could bring back the double feature. Naturally you'll want to have dishes of treats from the "lobby." The ones suggested here are a little more sophisticated and tasty than just plain buttered popcorn.

BEVERLY HILLS SPICED POPCORN AND NUTS

This will "sell out" for your movie night. If you make extra, you can put it in a bottle, tie a ribbon around it, and give it to a hostess as a bread and butter gift.

½ cup	popping corn	125 ml
2 tbs	vegetable oil	25 ml
2 tbs	sweet butter	25 ml
½ cup	peanuts, salted or unsalted	125 ml
½ cup	pecans	125 ml
2 tsp	ground cumin	10 ml
1 tsp	garlic powder	10 ml
½ tsp	chili powder	2 ml
½ tsp	white pepper	2 ml
½ tsp	salt	2 ml

1. In a hot air popper or in a large pot with a tight-fitting lid, pop corn.
2. In a large saucepan heat oil and butter. Add peanuts, pecans, cumin, garlic powder, chili powder, white pepper, and salt. Sauté over medium

heat 1 to 2 minutes, until aromatic and lightly colored. *Be careful not to burn.*

3. Add popped corn and toss until well coated with seasonings.
   Store in a tightly covered container. Keeps 2 to 3 weeks.

Makes 8 cups (2 l).

SUGAR AND SPICE NUTS

The orange rind gives these nuts an extra zip, and the contrast with the spicy nuts is delightful.

1½ cups	pecan halves	325 ml
1 cup	unblanched whole almonds	250 ml
1 cup	walnut halves	250 ml
1 cup	whole filberts	250 ml
1	egg white	1
1½ tbs	water	20 ml
⅔ cup	granulated sugar	150 ml
1 tsp	salt	5 ml
1 tsp	ground cinnamon	5 ml
1 tsp	ground coriander	5 ml
1 tsp	ground ginger	5 ml
1 tsp	ground nutmeg	5 ml
1 tsp	ground cloves	5 ml
	grated rind of 1 orange	

1. Preheat oven to 275°F (150°C).
2. In a large bowl combine pecans, almonds, walnuts, and filberts.
3. In a mixer bowl beat egg white and water 2 minutes, until foamy. Add sugar, salt, cinnamon, coriander, ginger, nutmeg, cloves, and orange rind. Fold egg mixture into nuts.
4. Arrange on a large baking sheet and bake, turning occasionally, for 45 minutes, until brown and crisp. Cool.
   Store in a tightly covered container at room temperature for up to 3 weeks.

Makes 6 cups (1.5 l).

BOMBAY CURRIED WALNUTS

An exotic Eastern flavor that you'll never get at the local cinema.

¼ cup	sweet butter	50 ml
2 tbs	curry powder	25 ml
2 tbs	Worcestershire sauce	25 ml
2 tsp	salt	10 ml
4 cups	walnut halves	1 l

1. Preheat oven to 300°F (150°C).
2. In a skillet, over medium heat, combine butter, curry powder, Worcestershire sauce, and salt. Add nuts, stirring to cover with seasonings.
3. Transfer to a baking pan and bake in oven for 10 to 15 minutes, until nuts are golden brown. Cool.
   Store in airtight containers up to 3 weeks.

Makes 4 cups (1 l).

CURRY PUFFS

Little turnovers filled with delicious mounds of beef and spices.

2 tbs	sweet butter	25 ml
2	cloves garlic, finely chopped	2
1	thin slice fresh ginger root, finely chopped (about 1 tsp/5 ml)	1
1½ tbs	finely chopped onion	20 ml
1 tbs	curry powder	15 ml
¼ lb	ground beef	125 ml
1 tbs	lime juice	15 ml
½ tsp	salt	2 ml
	Lemon Tang Pastry (recipe p. 285) for double crust pie	

1. Preheat oven to 450°F (230°C).
2. In a skillet heat butter. Add garlic, ginger root, onion, and curry powder; sauté 3 minutes, until onion is softened.
3. Add beef; cook and stir constantly about 5 minutes, until browned. Stir in lime juice and salt; mix well. Remove from heat and cool 15 to 20 minutes.
4. Roll out pastry to ¼ inch (5 mm) thickness and cut into 2 inch (5 cm) rounds.
5. Place 1 tsp (5 ml) meat mixture on 1 round, cover with another round, and press edges with a fork to hold them together.

6. Place on baking sheets and bake in oven for 15 minutes, or until golden brown.

Makes 4 dozen puffs.

BITE-SIZE EMPANADAS

These are slightly sweet, super savory, somewhat hot little meat turnovers. They freeze perfectly, ready to be popped into the oven for snacking purposes.

2 cups	all-purpose flour	500 ml
⅓ cup	granulated sugar	75 ml
1½ tsp	ground cinnamon	7 ml
¼ tsp	salt	1 ml
¾ cup	sweet butter	175 ml
1	egg yolk	1
2½ tbs	milk	30 ml
2 tbs	Madeira	25 ml
1	egg, lightly beaten	1
	additional granulated sugar and ground cinnamon for sprinkling	

FILLING:

½ tsp	sweet butter	2 ml
1½ tbs	finely chopped onion	20 ml
½ lb	medium ground beef	250 g
⅓ cup	finely chopped peeled pears	75 ml
¼ cup	finely chopped peeled peaches	50 ml
¼ cup	finely chopped green pepper	50 ml
¼ cup	finely chopped, peeled, and seeded tomatoes	50 ml
1 tbs	Madeira or sherry	15 ml
1 tsp	chopped chives	5 ml
1 tsp	salt	5 ml
1 tsp	chili powder	5 ml
1	egg, lightly beaten	1
1 tsp	granulated sugar	5 ml
½ tsp	ground cinnamon	2 ml

1. To make Empanadas: In a large bowl combine flour, sugar, cinnamon, and salt. With a pastry blender or 2 knives, cut in butter until mixture is crumbly and resembles small peas.
2. Blend together egg yolk, milk, and Madeira. Pour into flour mixture and mix with a fork until dough is formed.

3. Chill 1 hour.
4. To make Filling: In a skillet heat butter, add onion, and sauté 1 minute. Add beef and cook, stirring, 2 minutes, or until brown. Transfer to a bowl. Add pears, peaches, green pepper, tomatoes, Madeira or sherry, chives, salt, and chili powder; mix well.
5. Preheat oven to 400°F (200°C).
6. Roll out dough to ¼ inch (5 mm) thickness. Cut into 4 inch (10 cm) rounds.
7. Place 1 tsp (5 ml) meat filling on each round. Fold round in half and seal edges by pressing with a fork. Prick several times. Brush with beaten egg and sprinkle with sugar and cinnamon. Place on a baking pan or cookie sheet. Bake in oven for 20 minutes, or until brown. Serve hot.

Makes 3 dozen.

DATE AND CHEESE BITES

The tang of sweetness from the date combined with the zip from the grated Cheddar seems always to please.
   This one also looks great and takes only a few moments to mix and roll.

½ cup	sweet butter	125 ml
2 cups	shredded Cheddar cheese	500 ml
2 cups	all-purpose flour	500 ml
½ tsp	salt	2 ml
¼ tsp	cayenne pepper	1 ml
¼–½ cup	milk	50–125 ml
20	small pitted dates, cut in half	20

1. Preheat oven to 375°F (190°C).
2. In a medium saucepan melt butter. Stir in cheese and remove pan from heat. Continue stirring to melt cheese partially.
3. Combine flour, salt, and cayenne. Stir into butter-cheese mixture; mix well. Add only enough milk to make dough pliable.
4. Take about 1 tbs (15 ml) of dough, place in palm of hand, and flatten. Push a date half into center of dough and press dough around it to form a ball.
5. Place on ungreased baking sheet and bake in oven for 10 to 15 minutes, or until lightly brown.

Makes 40 small balls.

BRUSHETTA

These should be served on a plate to catch the drippings of oil, garlic, and tomato.
A divine nibbler.

6	slices crusty Italian bread, ½ inch (1 cm) thick	6
¼ cup	extra virgin olive oil	50 ml
3	cloves garlic, minced	3
2	large fresh tomatoes, peeled, seeded, and finely chopped	2
1 tbs	chopped fresh basil	15 ml

1. Under a broiler or in a toaster, toast bread on both sides, until golden.
2. Mix together olive oil and garlic; brush on one side of toast.
3. Cover with tomato and sprinkle with fresh basil.

Makes 6 servings.

SKINNY DIPS (DEEP-FRIED POTATO SKINS) WITH A CHOICE OF CHEESE 'N' CHILI AND BACON ONION DIPS

The best part of the potato: crisp, crunchy, deep-fried skins. The scooped-out pulp is great for potato salad.
Serve with martinis or cold beer.

SKINNY DIPS (DEEP-FRIED POTATO SKINS)

4	baking potatoes	4
	oil for deep frying	

1. Bake potatoes in a 400°F (200°C) oven for 1 hour. Let cool.
2. Cut potatoes in half lengthwise, then crosswise. Cut each quarter into 3 fingers.
3. Scoop out most of the pulp, leaving ¼ inch (5 mm) of potato inside of the skin. Reserve pulp for another use.
4. In a deep fryer, heat oil to 375°F (190°C). Fry potato skins in hot oil for 60 to 90 seconds, or until crisp. Remove and drain on paper towel.
5. Serve with Bacon Onion Dip or Cheese 'n' Chili Dip.

Makes 8 to 10 servings.

BACON ONION DIP

1 cup	sour cream	250 ml
2	slices crisp-cooked bacon, crumbled	2
¼ cup	shredded aged Cheddar cheese	50 ml
1 tsp	chopped chives	5 ml
1	small onion, finely chopped	1
1 tsp	sweet butter	5 ml
½ tsp	dried chicken stock mix	2 ml

1. In a small bowl combine sour cream, crumbled bacon, cheese, chives, onion, butter, and chicken stock mix; mix well. Refrigerate 30 minutes, or until serving time.

Makes 1¼ cups (300 ml).

CHEESE 'N' CHILI DIP

1 tbs	vegetable oil	15 ml
½ cup	finely chopped onions	125 ml
1	clove garlic, finely chopped	1
2	dried chilies, veins and seeds removed	2
2	tomatoes, peeled and finely chopped	2
2 cups	shredded Cheddar cheese	500 ml
1	pkg (4 oz/125 g) cream cheese	1

1. In a saucepan, heat oil. Add onions and garlic; sauté 3 to 4 minutes until softened.
2. Add chilies and tomatoes, crushing tomatoes with a fork. Bring to a boil, reduce heat and simmer 6 minutes until slightly thickened.
3. Stir in cheeses, cook only until melted; *do not boil.*
4. Transfer to a food processor or blender; process until smooth.
5. Serve hot over potato skins or chilled in a crockery pot.

Makes 2 cups (500 ml).

FINGER GNOCCHI

These little bundles are the perfect size to pop into your mouth.

¼ cup	sweet butter	50 ml
1½ lbs	fresh spinach, cooked, squeezed, and chopped	750 g
¾ cup	ricotta cheese	175 ml
2	eggs, lightly beaten	2
¼ cup	all-purpose flour	50 ml
¾ cup	freshly grated Parmesan cheese	175 ml
½ tsp	salt	2 ml
½ tsp	freshly ground black pepper	2 ml
pinch	ground nutmeg	pinch
¼ cup	melted sweet butter	50 ml

1. In a large skillet melt butter. Add cooked spinach and sauté, stirring constantly, for 2 to 3 minutes, or until any extra moisture boils away and spinach begins to stick slightly to pan.
2. Stir in ricotta cheese and cook, stirring, for 3 to 4 minutes to mix thoroughly.
3. Transfer to a large mixing bowl. Stir in eggs, flour, ¼ cup (50 ml) Parmesan, salt, pepper, and nutmeg. Refrigerate for 30 minutes to 1 hour, until gnocchi mixture is firm.
4. Preheat oven to 400°F (200°C).
5. Shape gnocchi mixture into small balls about ½ inch (1 cm) in diameter. Drop into salted boiling water and cook, uncovered, for 5 to 8 minutes, turning once, until they puff slightly. Remove and drain on paper towel.
6. Pour 2 tbs (25 ml) melted butter on the bottom of an 8 × 12 inch (20 × 30 cm) shallow baking dish. Place gnocchi in dish. Dribble remaining butter over gnocchi. Sprinkle with remaining ½ cup (125 ml) Parmesan. Bake in oven for 5 minutes, or until cheese melts.
7. For a dinner party, serve with Salsa di Pomodoro.

Makes 4 to 6 servings.

SALSA DI POMODORO (TOMATO SAUCE)

2 tbs	olive oil	25 ml
½ cup	finely chopped onion	125 ml
1	can (19 oz/540 ml) Italian tomatoes, chopped coarsely but not drained	1
1	can (5½ oz/156 ml) tomato paste	1
1 tbs	chopped fresh basil, or 1 tsp (5 ml) dried	15 ml
3	cloves garlic, finely chopped	3
1 tsp	sugar	5 ml
1 tsp	salt	5 ml
½ tsp	freshly ground black pepper	2 ml

1. In à large saucepan heat oil over medium heat. Add onions and sauté 5 minutes, until soft.
2. Stir in tomatoes, tomato paste, basil, garlic, sugar, salt, and pepper. Bring to a boil, reduce heat, and simmer, stirring occasionally, for 40 minutes, until thick. Cool.
3. Transfer to a blender or food processor and purée until smooth, or press through a sieve.
4. Store in a covered container in refrigerator for 3 to 4 weeks. Heat to serve.

Makes 1½ cups (375 ml).

MARINATED MUSHROOMS

Spear these with the little cocktail picks that have colored paper ruffles on the finger end. They give the dish the frolicsome appearance it deserves.

⅔ cup	olive oil	150 ml
½ cup	water	125 ml
	juice of 2 lemons	
1	bay leaf	1
2	garlic cloves, bruised with flat of knife	2
6	peppercorns	6
½ tsp	oregano	2 ml
½ tsp	salt	2 ml
1 lb	small whole fresh mushrooms	500 g

1. In a saucepan combine oil, water, lemon juice, bay leaf, garlic, peppercorns, oregano, and salt. Bring to a boil, reduce heat, cover, and simmer for 15 minutes to blend flavors.
2. Strain marinade through a sieve and return to saucepan. Heat to simmering.
3. Add mushrooms and simmer, turning them over from time to time, for 5 minutes, then remove from heat. Let mushrooms cool in the marinade.
4. Serve at room temperature or refrigerate and serve chilled.

Makes 2 cups (500 ml).

SCRAMBLED EGGS WITH CHICKEN AND ALMONDS

Declare an intermission and whip up something substantial for your movie owls.
Use two large electric frying pans and serve directly from them. I add bowls
of sliced or quartered tomatoes and coarsely chopped onions.
Add a little glamour with trays of hot buttered tortillas.

1 tbs	sweet butter	15 ml
1	medium onion, chopped	1
½ cup	chopped cooked white and/or dark chicken	125 ml
½ cup	sliced blanched almonds	125 ml
½ cup	light cream	125 ml
¼ cup	chicken stock	50 ml
¼ cup	dry white wine	50 ml
½ tsp	chili powder	2 ml
¼ tsp	salt	1 ml
⅛ tsp	freshly ground black pepper	0.5 ml
4	eggs, well beaten	4
2 tbs	chopped fresh parsley	25 ml

1. In a medium skillet heat butter. Add onion; sauté 5 minutes, until softened.
2. Add chicken and almonds; mix well. Stir in cream, stock, wine, chili powder, salt, and pepper. Bring to a boil, reduce heat, and simmer 10 minutes, or until liquid is reduced to about ½ cup (125 ml).
3. Stir in eggs and scramble all ingredients until eggs are set but still moist. Sprinkle with parsley and serve.

Makes 2 servings.

EGGS IN CASSEROLE

If you'd rather prepare your movie-party eggs ahead of time, try this one. It can be made ready the night or day before and placed in the refrigerator to pop in the oven when the movie starts.

6	slices French bread, crusts removed	6
2 tbs	sweet butter, melted	25 ml
16	medium mushrooms, thinly sliced (1½ cups/375 ml)	16
1 cup	grated Cheddar cheese	250 ml
1 cup	grated Colby cheese	250 ml
6	slices bacon, cooked and crumbled	6
4	green onions, chopped	4
4	eggs	4
2 cups	milk	500 ml
2 tsp	Dijon mustard	10 ml
½ tsp	salt	2 ml
¼ tsp	freshly ground black pepper	1 ml
¼ tsp	paprika	1 ml
⅛ tsp	cayenne pepper	0.5 ml

1. Cut bread into cubes to measure 2 cups (500 ml). In bottom of 8-inch (20 cm) square baking dish arrange bread cubes. Drizzle butter over cubes.
2. Scatter mushroom slices, cheeses, bacon, and green onions over bread cubes.
3. In a bowl beat eggs, milk, mustard, salt, pepper, paprika, and cayenne until frothy. Pour over mixture in pan, cover, and refrigerate overnight.
4. Preheat oven to 325°F (160°C). Bake for 1 hour, until just firm and lightly browned.

Makes 6 servings.

THE PANTRY

The Kitchen Cupboard:
Jams, Pickles,
Relishes, Sauces

These are my joys, and the products on which I have built my business.

Making your own jams and condiments gives you a cupboard full of special tastes and treats that can add a brilliant note to any meal, from breakfast to after-theater snacks.

The most important thing to remember in home canning is to make sure everything used in the process is sterilized: jars, lids, tongs, ladle, funnel, and the pitcher used for pouring from pot to jars. There are two dependable methods to use, the oven and the boiling water method:

Oven Method: Wash all equipment in hot, soapy water; rinse well.
Set washed items on the oven rack and heat 15 minutes at 220°F (100°C). Remove from oven as needed.

Boiling Water Method: Wash all jars, lids, and handling equipment in warm, soapy water and rinse well.
Invert jars in 1¾ to 2 inches (4 to 5 cm) of water and make sure lids are covered.
Bring water to a boil and let boil for 15 minutes. Remove jars and lids from hot water as needed.

Take special care with lids. If you use self-sealing lids, sterilize them according to the manufacturer's instructions. If you use commercial jars, boil the lids for 5 minutes. Failure to take these easy precautions can turn what was meant to be a noble effort into a disaster a few weeks down the road.

JAMS AND MARMALADES

Something sweet to spread on toast or fill a pie or use as a glaze or topping.

Black Currant Jam

This will give you an afternoon filled with the rich scent of cassis as the black currants bubble and boil. Get them at the peak of their season, mid-July to mid-August.

4 cups	black currants, stems and flowers removed	1 l
2 cups	boiling water	500 ml
6 cups	granulated sugar	1.5 l
2 tsp	sweet butter	10 ml

1. Preheat oven to 300°F (150°C).
2. In a large saucepan combine currants and water. Bring to a boil and boil exactly 8 minutes.
3. In a large pan warm sugar in oven for about 10 minutes, add to currants, mix well.
4. Bring to a boil again, stirring occasionally. Boil hard for 4 minutes.
5. Remove from heat and add butter.
6. Pour into sterilized jars and seal tightly with lids.
7. Label and store in a cool, dry, dark place.

Makes three 4 oz (125 ml) jars.

OLD-FASHIONED STRAWBERRY JAM

This is a favorite recipe. The berries remain whole and the jelly surrounding them is alive with the taste of late spring strawberries. That is a rule of mine: Eat the first berries of the season fresh; use the last berries of the season for canning.

4 cups	medium-sized strawberries, washed and hulled	1 l
3 cups	granulated sugar	750 ml
¼ cup	fresh lemon juice	50 ml

1. In a large saucepan or preserving kettle combine strawberries and sugar; mix well. Let stand for 2 hours.
2. Bring to a boil and cook, uncovered, for 5 minutes. Stir in lemon juice.
3. Bring to a boil again and cook, uncovered, for 5 minutes, stirring frequently, until thick and jam stage is reached.
4. Remove from heat, stir, and skim off foam. Continue stirring and skimming for 5 minutes.
5. Pour into hot sterilized jars and seal. Label and store in a cool, dry, dark place.
   Note: Quick-freeze berries when they are still in season to make this jam later in the year.

Makes eight 6 oz (175 ml) jars.

To Test Jam Stage:
Chill a metal spoon, then dip it into the hot fruit mixture. Raise the spoon up above the saucepan away from the heat. Allow the mixture to cool slightly in the spoon, then tilt it and allow the chilled mixture to drip over the side of the spoon and back into the saucepan. If two drops flow together to form one sheet that falls off the spoon, you have reached the jam stage.

SEEDLESS RASPBERRY JAM

This is the thin red line you see in flans and French custard pies.

6 cups	fresh raspberries	1.5 l
3 cups	granulated sugar	750 ml

1. In a saucepan over medium heat, crush berries. Simmer, crushing occasionally, for 10 minutes.

2. Drain through a sieve, pressing out pulp and juice. Repeat this process once again, until seeds are removed.
3. In a saucepan combine each cup of the juice pulp mixture with 1 cup sugar. Bring to a boil; continue boiling and stirring about 8 minutes, until jam stage is reached.
4. Pour into sterilized jars. Seal with sterilized lids. Label and store in a cool, dry, dark place.

Makes three 8 oz (250 ml) jars.

PEACH CONSERVE

This has been a favorite of Sable & Rosenfeld customers for years. The bits of maraschino cherries complement the gold of the peaches. It is a festive jam to give to friends as gifts.

2	small oranges	2
8	ripe peaches	8
	juice of ½ lemon	
2½ cups	granulated sugar	375 ml
¼ cup	slivered blanched almonds	50 ml
10	maraschino cherries, finely chopped	10

1. With a sharp knife cut unpeeled oranges into thin slices, ¼ inch (5 mm) thick. Place in bowl, measure depth, and pour double the amount of water over slices. Let stand overnight at room temperature.
2. Pour oranges and water into a large saucepan. Bring to a boil and cook about 20 minutes, or until almost dry.
3. Blanch, peel, and coarsely chop peaches. Sprinkle lemon juice over peaches, add them to saucepan, bring to a boil; stir in sugar. Cook, stirring occasionally, for about 1½ hours, or until mixture sheets from a spoon.*
4. Stir in almonds and cherries. Allow to boil 1 minute.
5. Ladle into sterilized jars. Seal with self-sealing lids. Label and store in a cool, dry, dark place.

Makes 3 cups (750 ml).

*See p. 349.

GINGER PEAR CONSERVE

If you like ginger, here it is. A pot of jam on your breakfast room table is a hospitable thing. A pot of jam for each of your guests as they leave is even more so. Be sure to get good-looking labels for your jars, and date and sign each one.

4 lb	firm pears (about 16)	2 kg
	juice and peel of 2 lemons	
5 cups	granulated sugar	1 kg
2 oz	candied or preserved ginger, finely chopped	60 g

1. Peel, quarter, core, and coarsely chop pears. In a large bowl, combine pears and lemon juice; mix well.
2. Cut lemon peel into long thin strips. Scrape off white pith. Add sugar, ginger, and lemon peel to pears; mix well. Let stand overnight, stirring occasionally.
3. Next day, pour into large saucepan. Bring to a boil, reduce heat, and cook slowly, stirring frequently, for 1½ hours, or until mixture is thick and clear and sheets from a spoon.*
4. Ladle into sterilized jars and seal tightly with lids. Label and store in a cool, dry, dark place.

Makes four 8 oz (250 ml) jars.

RHUBARB-ORANGE MARMALADE

Remember the bitter mouth-puckering taste of homemade marmalade when you were a kid? Well, here it is again.

	rind and juice of 3 oranges	
4 cups	chopped rhubarb	1 l
1 cup	water	250 ml
½ cup	chopped raisins	125 ml
3 cups	sugar	750 ml

1. Cut rind into thin strips about ¾ inch (2 cm) long. In a heavy saucepan, combine rind, orange juice, rhubarb, water, and raisins. Bring to a boil; cook about 10 minutes, or until fruit is tender.
2. Stir in sugar; cook over medium heat, stirring occasionally, about 2 hours, until mixture is thick.
3. Ladle into sterilized jars and seal with sterilized lids. Label and store in a cool, dry, dark place.

Makes six 8 oz (250 ml) jars.

*See p. 349.

GINGER PEAR MARMALADE

Pears are available all year through now, so you can always pick some up and do a few jars.

Remember, preserves thicken as they cool. Don't be afraid to take your mixture off the stove even if it seems a bit runny.

2	lemons	2
2	oranges	2
1 cup	water	250 ml
17	medium pears	17
4 cups	granulated sugar	1 l
⅓ cup	chopped crystallized ginger	75 ml

1. Peel, then squeeze juice from lemons and oranges; set aside. Cut peels into thin slivers and scrape off white pith.
2. In a small saucepan simmer peels with water for 20 minutes, or until soft. Drain, reserving ½ cup (125 ml) of the water.
3. Peel and chop pears. In a large pot combine pears, lemon, and orange juice, orange peel, and reserved water. Bring to a boil, reduce heat, and simmer 15 minutes, until fruit is tender. Stir in sugar and ginger.
4. Cook, stirring occasionally, for 1 hour, or until thick.
5. Pour into sterilized jars and seal tightly with lids. Label and store in a cool, dry, dark place.

Makes seven 8 oz (250 ml) jars.

CONDIMENTS

Apple butter, mint sauce, chutneys. These are the very special taste makers that will surprise and fascinate your guests. They can make a curry magic or a hamburger sophisticated.

Inevitably you'll find favorites here to serve to your guests with joy.

APPLE BUTTER

Apple butter is usually thought of in connection with farm kitchens and week-ends in the country. But wherever you serve it, this apple butter will leave your guests starry-eyed.

Try spooning it over hot baked sweet potatoes, or mounding it on freshly baked gingerbread.

15	large MacIntosh apples	15
½ cup	water	125 ml
4 cups	firmly packed dark brown sugar	1 l
½ cup	white vinegar	125 ml
½ cup	dark corn syrup	125 ml
1 tbs	ground cinnamon	15 ml

1. Cut apples into quarters; remove cores, but do not peel.
2. In a large saucepan, combine apples and water. Bring to a boil, reduce heat, cover, and cook, stirring occasionally, about 15 minutes, until apples are tender.
3. Put through a Mouli or press through a sieve to strain out skin. Makes about 8 cups (2 l) applesauce.

4. Place applesauce in a large saucepan. Stir in brown sugar, vinegar, corn syrup, and cinnamon. Bring to a boil, reduce heat, and simmer, stirring frequently, about 3 hours, until thickened.
5. Ladle into hot sterilized jars and seal tightly with lids. Label and store in a cool, dry, dark place.

Makes three 8 oz (250 ml) jars.

MINT JELLY

Try this not only with roast lamb but with roast turkey.

2 cups	packed whole fresh mint leaves, stems removed	500 ml
4	fresh summer savory or rosemary leaves, stems removed	4
1 cup	water	250 ml
¾ cup	fresh orange juice	175 ml
3 cups	granulated sugar	750 ml
	green food coloring	
¾ cup	liquid pectin	175 ml
9	small fresh mint leaves	9

1. In a food processor, or by hand, chop mint to yield 1 cup (250 ml).
2. In a large saucepan combine mint, savory or rosemary leaves, water, and orange juice. Bring to a boil, remove from heat, and let stand 10 minutes.
3. Strain and return mint infusion to saucepan. Stir in sugar and food coloring to desired tint; bring to a boil.
4. Stir in the pectin; return to full rolling boil and boil hard for 1 minute.
5. Remove from heat, skim off foam, then stir for 2 minutes.
6. Strain into sterilized jars, dropping 3 fresh mint leaves on the top of each jar.
7. Seal with sterilized lids. Label and store in a cool, dry, dark place.
8. Once opened, store any unused portion in the refrigerator.

Makes three 8 oz (250 ml) jars.

QUICK MINT SAUCE

I prepare this while I am waiting for the Butterfly Lamb to come off the barbecue. I serve it in hollowed-out zucchini cups or on a radicchio leaf.

½ cup	Raspberry Vinegar (recipe p. 149)	125 ml
¼ cup	water	50 ml
2 tbs	powdered sugar	25 ml
½ cup	apple or currant jelly	125 ml
½ cup	fresh chopped mint	125 ml

1. In a saucepan combine vinegar, water, and sugar. Bring to a boil, stirring. Cook about 15 minutes to reduce by one third.
2. Stir in jelly and heat thoroughly. Remove from heat and stir in mint. Serve at room temperature.

Makes about 1¼ cups (300 ml).

FRESH MINT CHUTNEY

This is a quick chutney to serve along with Chicken Saag or Lamb Curry or any other Indian-type dish. It's bright green with just a dash of heat.

1 cup	mint leaves, washed and stemmed	250 ml
¼ cup	Chinese rice vinegar	125 ml
1	medium onion, chopped	1
½	jalapeño pepper, seeded, stemmed, and chopped	1
	salt, to taste	

1. In container of food processor combine mint leaves, vinegar, onion, pepper, and salt. Process with on/off motion 1 to 2 minutes, until finely chopped and mixed. Season with salt to taste.
2. Transfer to covered container. Chill well for about 30 minutes before using. Store in refrigerator.

Makes about 1 cup (250 ml).

PEACH CHUTNEY

I serve this with my curries, loaves and pâtés.

16	peaches, peeled and coarsely chopped	16
¾ cup	raisins, finely chopped	175 ml
⅓ cup	finely chopped fresh ginger root	75 ml
¼ cup	finely chopped onion	50 ml
1	clove garlic, finely chopped	1
4 cups	firmly packed brown sugar	1 l
2 cups	white vinegar	500 ml
2 tsp	mustard seed	10 ml
2 tsp	ground allspice	10 ml
1 tsp	salt	5 ml
½ tsp	chili powder	2 ml

1. In a large saucepan or preserving kettle combine peaches, raisins, ginger root, onion, and garlic. Stir in brown sugar, vinegar, mustard seed, allspice, salt, and chili powder.
2. Bring to a boil; boil, stirring frequently, for 1 hour, or until thick and a rich brown color.
3. Ladle into hot sterilized jars and seal tightly with lids. Label and store in a cool, dry, dark place.

Makes three 8 oz (250 ml) jars.

HOT PEPPER JELLY

Delicious as a duck, chicken, or ham glaze, or spread over black bread and cream cheese.

2	green sweet peppers	2
10	chili peppers	10
6 cups	granulated sugar	1.5 l
1½ cups	cider vinegar	375 ml
1	bottle (6 oz/175 ml) liquid pectin	1

1. Wash green and chili peppers; remove stems, seeds, and veins. (Use gloves when handling chili peppers.) Cut into pieces.
2. In a food processor or blender combine peppers; process until puréed.
3. In a large saucepan combine puréed peppers, sugar, and vinegar. Bring to a boil and cook for 15 minutes.
4. Strain through a cheesecloth-lined sieve into a clean saucepan. Stir in pectin. Bring to a boil again and boil 1 minute. With a metal spoon skim off foam.
5. Pour into sterilized jars and seal tightly with lids. Label and store in a cool, dry, dark place.

Makes five 8 oz (250 ml) jars.

GLAZED GRILLED FRUIT (OR VEGETABLES)

You'll notice that the three fruits and the one vegetable suggested are of the quick-cooking nature.

I have been told of glazing everything from apples to zucchini. As far as I am concerned, with these four in your repertoire, you are more than adequately prepared.

8	peaches, nectarines, or large apricots	8
¼ cup	melted sweet butter	50 ml
2 tbs	honey	25 ml
2 tbs	lemon juice	25 ml
1 tbs	brandy	15 ml
	Hot Pepper Jelly (recipe p. 356)	
	Fruit Chili Sauce (recipe p. 368)	

1. Wash fruit, do not peel. Cut in half and remove pits.
2. To make glaze: In a bowl combine butter, honey, lemon juice, and brandy.
3. Place fruit halves, cut side down, on oiled barbecue rack about 6 inches (15 cm) above medium hot coals. Brush with glaze. Grill 3 minutes.
4. Turn, brush glaze on cut side. Grill 3 minutes longer, until lightly browned and glazed.
5. Transfer to a heated plate, cut side up. Spoon jelly or chili sauce into cavity.

Makes 8 servings.

VARIATION: *Glazed Red Onion*
1. Cut 4 red onions crosswise into ½ inch (1 cm) thick slices. Place on an oiled barbecue rack about 6 inch (15 cm) above medium hot coals.
2. Brush with above glaze. Grill 4 minutes.
3. Turn and brush glaze on other side. Grill 4 minutes longer, until lightly browned and glazed. Transfer to a heated plate.

Makes 8 servings.

SAFFRON BANANAS

The bland bananas, sour cream and/or yogurt, and golden saffron are just what a hot curry demands.

½ tsp	saffron threads, or ⅛ tsp (0.5 ml) saffron powder	2 ml
2 cups	sour cream or yogurt or mixture of both	500 ml
2	bananas, sliced	2

1. In a bowl combine saffron and sour cream. Add bananas, stirring to cover with cream.
2. Refrigerate 2 hours before serving.

Makes 4 servings.

SPICED CHERRIES

Cherry Ripe, Cherry Ripe, Ripe I cry. . . . That old London street chant is on my mind when the Bing cherries appear in the market. I like to use them mounded around my Chinese Chicken or with any roast, hot or cold.

4 cups	granulated sugar	1 l
1¼ cups	cider vinegar	300 ml
2 tsp	ground cinnamon	10 ml
1 tsp	ground allspice	5 ml
1 tsp	ground cloves	5 ml
1 tsp	ground nutmeg	5 ml
12 cups	Bing cherries, pitted	3 l

1. In a heavy saucepan over medium heat, combine sugar, vinegar, cinnamon, allspice, cloves, and nutmeg. Heat, stirring, about 5 minutes, until sugar dissolves.
2. In a large bowl or crock combine cherries and syrup. Let stand in refrigerator for 3 days, stirring frequently.
3. Pour cherries into sterilized jars. Seal with sterilized lids. Label and store in a cool, dry, dark place.
4. Once opened, store any unused portion in the refrigerator.

Makes three 16 oz (500 ml) jars.

WHOLE PLUMS IN PORT

The wonderful thing about canning is that you can devote a week to it in the spring for the berries, a week to it in the summer for the pickles, and a week to it in the fall for all the latecomers. Three weeks' work is not much for a pantry full of fabulous tastes in beautiful colors.

Plums in Port come with the fall, and they take only minutes of your time to prepare. You can serve them with a curry as a condiment or by themselves as a dessert.

8 cups	small blue plums	2 l
½	lemon, cut into thin slices, seeds removed	½
2 cups	granulated sugar	500 ml
1⅓ cups	water	325 ml
1⅓ cups	port or sherry	325 ml

1. Prick each plum 10 to 12 times, then place into sterilized jars. Place 2 lemon slices in each jar.
2. In a saucepan combine sugar and water. Bring to a boil, reduce heat, and simmer 2 to 3 minutes, until sugar dissolves.
3. Cool slightly, about 10 minutes, then stir in port.
4. Pour into jars and fill, leaving ½ inch (1 cm) headspace. Fit lids on jars; process in boiling water bath for 20 minutes.
5. Remove carefully and let stand overnight to seal. Label and store in a cool, dry, dark place.

Makes four 16 oz (500 ml) jars.

ETHEL'S CURRY RELISH

This recipe was wrung from a friend who is one of the most inventive cooks I know, and it is a real winner.

¼ cup	olive oil	50 ml
¼ cup	vegetable oil	50 ml
2 tbs	sweet butter	25 ml
2	medium onions, chopped	2
1	large carrot, sliced	1
2	stocks celery, coarsely chopped	2
1	green apple, unpeeled, cored and thinly sliced	1
¼ cup	curry powder	50 ml
¼ cup	all-purpose flour	50 ml
2½ cups	chicken stock	625 ml
2 tbs	apple jelly	25 ml
1 tbs	honey	15 ml
1 tbs	fresh lemon juice	15 ml
1 tsp	tomato paste	5 ml
1 tsp	shredded coconut	5 ml
3	cardamom seeds, crushed	3
1	large clove garlic, finely chopped	1
1	cinnamon stick, 2 inches (5 cm) long	1
1	piece ginger root, 1 inch (2.5 cm) long	1
½ tsp	salt	2 ml
½ tsp	freshly ground black pepper	2 ml

1. In a large skillet heat oils and butter. Add onions, carrot, celery, and green apple; sauté for 5 minutes, until vegetables are soft.
2. Stir in curry powder and cook 5 minutes.
3. Stir in flour; cook 5 minutes longer. Stir in stock, jelly, honey, lemon juice, tomato paste, coconut, cardamon, garlic, cinnamon, ginger root, salt, and pepper.
4. Bring to a boil, reduce heat, and simmer, stirring occasionally, for 1 hour.
5. Store in covered container in the refrigerator, up to 4 weeks.
6. If a sauce texture is preferred, place mixture in a food processor or blender and purée until smooth.

Makes 2½ cups (625 ml).

BEET RELISH

If I'm getting set to slice beets and wind up with red hands, I usually decide to double this recipe.

I love to serve it with pork tenderloin roasts, pâtés, and roast beef.

1 cup	chopped cooked beets	250 ml
3 tbs	prepared horseradish	45 ml
2 tbs	lemon juice	25 ml
2 tsp	powdered sugar	10 ml
½ tsp	salt	2 ml

1. In a large bowl combine beets, horseradish, lemon juice, sugar, and salt; mix well.
2. Store in a covered container in refrigerator for up to 1 month.

Makes 2 cups (500 ml).

PICKLED BEETS

After you serve the beets, keep the pickled beet juice and pop hard boiled eggs in it overnight. Sliced on a green salad, they look divine.

2 lb	beets	1 kg
1½ cups	cider vinegar	375 ml
1 cup	granulated sugar	250 ml
2 tbs	dry mustard	25 ml
½ tsp	salt	2 ml
2	medium onions, thinly sliced	2
2 tsp	celery seed	10 ml
20	peppercorns	20

1. In a large saucepan, in boiling water to cover, cook beets about 25 minutes, or until tender. Drain, reserving 1 cup of the cooking water. Cool slightly. Slip skins off beets; slice and set aside.
2. In a small saucepan combine vinegar and reserved cooking water; bring to a boil.
3. Combine sugar, mustard, and salt. Stir into vinegar and bring to a boil again.
4. In sterilized canning jars arrange beets and onions in layers. Add a little celery seed and 4 to 6 peppercorns to each jar. Cover with hot vinegar mixture.
5. Seal with sterilized lids; cool and store in refrigerator for up to 2 months.
6. Let stand for a few days before serving.

Makes six 8 oz (250 ml) jars.

CORN RELISH

Serve this with French Country Meatloaf or grilled burgers of all persuasions. You'll find the chunks of fresh tomatoes and peppers add zip to its already lively taste.

10 cups	peeled, finely chopped red tomatoes	2.5 l
4 cups	peeled, finely chopped cucumbers	1 l
4 cups	finely chopped onions	1 l
1½ cups	finely chopped green pepper	375 ml
8 cups	corn, cut from the cob	2 l
½ cup	coarse salt	125 ml
7 cups	cider vinegar	1.75 l
6 cups	granulated sugar	1.5 l
½ cup	all-purpose flour	125 ml
½ cup	dry mustard	125 ml
2 tsp	celery seed	10 ml
2 tsp	turmeric	10 ml

1. In a large saucepan or Dutch oven combine tomatoes, cucumbers, onions, green pepper, and corn. Sprinkle with salt and let stand 1 hour. Drain well.
2. In a saucepan combine 6 cups (1.5 l) vinegar and sugar. Bring to a boil.
3. In a small bowl combine flour, mustard, celery seed, turmeric, and 1 cup (250 ml) vinegar; stir into a paste. Mix with a little of the hot vinegar, then stir into the hot mixture. Pour over the vegetables. Bring mixture to a boil, reduce heat, simmer, stirring occasionally, about 1 hour, until thick.
4. Pour into sterilized jars and seal with sterilized lids. Label and store in cool, dry, dark place.
5. Once opened, store any unused portion in the refrigerator.

Makes eight 16 oz (500 ml) jars.

LADY ROSS RELISH

Who Lady Ross was I haven't the slightest idea. But she sure knew her pickles. This is the definitive relish made with cucumbers, apples, and celery.

6	medium cucumbers, peeled and finely chopped	6
6	medium onions, finely chopped	6
2	large apples, cored and finely chopped	2
1	red sweet pepper, seeded and finely chopped	1
1	small head celery, finely chopped	1
¼ cup	pickling salt	50 ml
4 cups	white vinegar	1 l
4 cups	granulated sugar	1 l
2 tbs	mustard seed	25 ml
2 tbs	dry mustard	25 ml
1½ tsp	turmeric	7 ml
½ cup	all-purpose flour	125 ml
2 tbs	water	25 ml

1. In a large bowl combine cucumbers, onions, apples, pepper, and celery. Sprinkle with salt, stir, and let stand overnight. Drain well.
2. In a large saucepan combine vinegar, sugar, and mustard seed. Bring to a boil.
3. Combine dry mustard, turmeric, flour, and water; mix to form a paste and stir into vinegar mixture. Cook about 1 minute until slightly thickened.
4. Add drained vegetables. Bring to a boil and stir well.
5. Ladle into hot sterilized jars and seal tightly with lids. Label and store in a cool, dry, dark place.

Makes seven 8 oz (250 ml) jars.

MARINATED VEGETABLES

These are marvelous diet nibbles.

½	small cauliflower, broken into small florets	½
2	carrots, cut in strips	2
2	stalks celery, cut in 1 inch (2.5 cm) pieces	2
1	green pepper, cut in ¼ inch (5 mm) strips	1
1 cup	pitted green olives	250 ml
½ cup	chopped canned pimento	125 ml
¾ cup	red wine vinegar	175 ml
½ cup	olive oil	125 ml
¼ cup	water	50 ml
2 tbs	granulated sugar	25 ml
1 tsp	salt	5 ml
½ tsp	ground oregano	2 ml
½ tsp	freshly ground black pepper	2 ml

1. In a large saucepan combine cauliflower, carrots, celery, green pepper, olives, and pimento. Stir in vinegar, olive oil, water, sugar, salt, oregano, and pepper.
2. Bring to a boil, stirring constantly, reduce heat, cover, and simmer for 5 minutes, until vegetables are just crisp. Cool.
3. Refrigerate 24 hours. Drain well before serving.

Makes 4 to 6 servings.

CRUNCHY DILLED CARROT STICKS

Serve instead of pickles.

2 lb	carrots, scraped and cut into 4 inch (10 cm) sticks	1 kg
½ cup	chopped fresh dill	125 ml
2	cloves garlic, peeled and halved	2
2 cups	white vinegar	500 ml
2 cups	water	500 ml
¼ cup	granulated sugar	50 ml
2 tbs	salt	25 ml
½ tsp	cayenne pepper	2 ml

1. In a saucepan of boiling water cook carrots, covered, for 5 minutes, until just tender crisp.

2. Drain and rinse under cold water until chilled. Pack into hot sterilized jars. Into each jar, place half a garlic clove and 1 tbs (15 ml) dill.
3. In a saucepan combine vinegar, water, sugar, salt, and cayenne. Bring to a boil.
4. Pour into jars, leaving ¼ inch (5 mm) headspace. Seal with sterilized lids.
5. Store in refrigerator 3 to 4 days before serving. Keeps for 2 to 3 weeks.

Makes six 8 oz (250 ml) jars.

HOT MUSTARD PICKLES

The vegetables come through wonderfully crunchy. Serve with meatloaves, pâtés, and cold sliced meats.

4 cups	thick slices of skinny cucumbers	1 l
2 cups	small cauliflower florets	500 ml
2 cups	peeled pickling onions	500 ml
1	green sweet pepper, seeded and cut in 1 inch (2.5 cm) chunks	1
1	red sweet pepper, seeded and cut in 1 inch (2.5 cm) chunks	
½ cup	pickling salt	125 ml
6 cups	boiling water	1.5 l
2 cups	granulated sugar	500 ml
½ cup	all-purpose flour	125 ml
¼ cup	dry mustard	50 ml
2 tsp	turmeric	10 ml
3 cups	white vinegar	750 ml

1. In a preserving kettle or saucepan combine cucumber, cauliflower, pickling onions, green and red pepper.
2. Combine salt and boiling water; stir until salt dissolves. Pour over vegetable mixture. Let stand, stirring occasionally, for 24 hours.
3. Slowly heat, stirring until just boiling and vegetables are thoroughly scalded; drain well.
4. In a large saucepan combine sugar, flour, mustard, turmeric, and vinegar. Whisk until flour and mustard are wet. Heat, stirring, about 5 minutes, until mixture boils and thickens. Stir into hot vegetables.
5. Ladle into hot sterilized jars. Seal tightly with lids. Label and store in a cool, dry, dark place.

Makes four 16 oz (500 ml) jars.

BREAD AND BUTTER PICKLES

These are somewhat sweeter than the hot mustard pickles. I personally think you will want to have a few jars of each for your condiment cupboard.

I find myself going for a jar of these whenever I serve tuna or chicken salad sandwiches.

3 quarts	small cucumbers, washed	3 l
1 lb	small yellow onions	500 g
1 cup	pickling salt	250 ml
4 quarts	ice water	4 l
5 cups	white vinegar	1.25 l
4 cups	granulated sugar	1 l
1 tbs	celery seed	15 ml
1 tbs	mustard seed	15 ml
1 tsp	turmeric	5 ml
½ tsp	white pepper	2 ml
2	red sweet peppers	2

1. Cut cucumbers and onions into ¼ inch (5 mm) slices.
2. In a crock or preserving kettle combine salt and water. Add cucumbers and onions; allow to soak overnight. Drain next morning but do not wash.
3. In a large saucepan combine vinegar, sugar, celery seed, mustard seed, turmeric, and pepper. Bring to a boil, stirring until sugar dissolves; boil for 10 minutes. Pour over cucumbers and onions.
4. Cut peppers lengthwise in quarters, remove seeds, and cut across into ¼ inch (6 mm) slices. Add to cucumber mixture; mix well.
5. Ladle into hot sterilized jars, leaving ½ inch (1 cm) headspace. Seal tightly with lids. Label and store in a cool, dry, dark place.

Makes six 8 oz (250 ml) jars.

ZUCCHINI PICKLE

The old reliable zucchini gives a sweet crunch. Serve this pickle with patés and loaves.

3 lb	zucchini, unpeeled, thinly sliced	1.5 kg
2	medium onions, coarsely chopped	2
¼ cup	salt	50 ml
2 cups	vinegar	500 ml
1½ cups	granulated sugar	375 ml
2 tsp	mustard seed	10 ml
1 tsp	celery seed	5 ml
1 tsp	turmeric	5 ml
1 tsp	dry mustard	5 ml

1. In a large bowl combine zucchini and onions; sprinkle with salt, cover with cold water, and let stand 2 hours. Drain, rinse with fresh water, and drain again.
2. In a large pot combine vinegar, sugar, mustard and celery seeds, turmeric, and dry mustard; bring to a boil and cook 2 minutes.
3. Add vegetables, remove from heat, and let stand for 2 hours.
4. Bring to a boil again; cook 5 minutes.
5. Pour into sterilized jars and seal. Label and store in a cool, dry, dark place.

Makes six 6 oz (175 ml) jars.

COLLEEN'S CHILI SAUCE

This is a sweet combination of late summer and early fall vegetables and fruits. Serve it with your favorite roasts and pâtés.

12	ripe tomatoes, peeled and coarsely chopped	12
3	apples, cored, peeled, and coarsely chopped	3
2	large onions, coarsely chopped	2
1	small head celery, finely chopped	1
1	small green pepper, finely chopped	1
1 lb	brown sugar (3 cups/750 ml firmly packed)	500 g
1 cup	white vinegar	250 ml
1 tbs	pickling salt	15 ml
¼ cup	pickling spice tied in cheesecloth	50 ml
⅛ tsp	cayenne pepper	0.5 ml

1. In a large preserving kettle or saucepan combine tomatoes, apples, onions, celery, and green pepper; mix well.
2. Add brown sugar, vinegar, pickling salt, pickling spice bag, and cayenne. Bring to a boil, reduce heat, and cook slowly for 1 to 1¼ hours, until thickened.
3. Ladle into hot sterilized jars. Seal with self-sealing lids. Label and store in a cool, dry, dark place.

Makes seven 16 oz (500 ml) jars.

SUMMER FRUIT CHILI SAUCE

To smell this chili sauce is to walk through an orchard and spice garden just before the last picking.

12	medium-large ripe tomatoes	12
6	fresh peaches	6
6	fresh Bartlett pears	6
3	large onions, coarsely chopped	3
1	small hot pepper, finely chopped	1
3½ cups	firmly packed brown sugar	875 ml
2 cups	cider vinegar	500 ml
1 tbs	salt	15 ml
2 tbs	pickling spice	25 ml

1. Plunge tomatoes and peaches into a pot of boiling water. Let sit for 10 seconds, then plunge into iced water. Slip skins off and discard. Chop coarsely. Drain excess liquid from tomatoes.
2. Peel and core the pears and cut in ½ inch (1 cm) cubes.
3. In a large pot or Dutch oven combine tomatoes, peaches, pears, onions, pepper, sugar, vinegar, and salt. Tie spices loosely in a piece of cheesecloth and add to pot. Bring to a boil, reduce heat, and simmer for 2 hours, or until thick.
4. Pour into sterilized jars and seal tightly with lids. Label and store in a cool, dry, dark place.

Makes eighteen 16 oz (500 ml) jars.

FRUIT SAUCE FOR MEAT

I'm sure this is how those great classic sauces from England got their start. A jar of this, a jar of that, whip them together, and see how it pleases His Lordship.

This is a delightfully strange combination of preserves, mustard, and horseradish. I serve it with cold, thinly sliced lamb or any leftover meat.

½ cup	apple jelly	125 ml
½ cup	pineapple preserves	125 ml
2 tbs	prepared horseradish	25 ml
1 tbs	dry mustard	15 ml

1. In a small bowl combine apple jelly, pineapple preserves, horseradish, and mustard; mix well.
2. Store in refrigerator in a container with tight-fitting lid. Keeps for 6 to 8 weeks.

Makes 1 cup (250 ml).

Index